Digital Rebellion

THE HISTORY OF COMMUNICATION

Robert W. McChesney
and John C. Nerone, editors

*A list of books in the series
appears at the end of this book.*

Digital Rebellion

The Birth of the Cyber Left

TODD WOLFSON

UNIVERSITY OF ILLINOIS PRESS

Urbana, Chicago, and Springfield

♾ This book is printed on acid-free paper.

Library of Congress Cataloging-in-Publication Data
Wolfson, Todd, 1972–
Digital rebellion : the birth of the cyber left / Todd Wolfson.
pages   cm. — (History of communication)
ISBN 978-0-252-03884-6 (hardback)
ISBN 978-0-252-08038-8 (paper)
ISBN 978-0-252-09680-8 (ebook)
1. Social movements—Technological innovations. 2. Political
participation—Technological innovations. 3. Internet—Political
aspects. 4. Mass media—Political aspects. 5. Radicalism. I. Title.
HM881.W65   2014
302.23'1—dc23   2014020605

For my parents,
Linda and Les Wolfson

Contents

Acknowledgments

The struggle for justice is hard, but it is made easier by thousands of every-day people, fighting to build a society based on the belief in dignity for all. This book is a small contribution to this long struggle. And while it bears my name and the burden of my shortcomings, I could not have put it together without the generous help and insight of many comrades, colleagues, and friends. I was blessed to think, grow, and learn with many minds.

Digital Rebellion emerged out of my dissertation, and it would not have been possible without the support of faculty and colleagues at the University of Pennsylvania. Chief among them is Peggy Reeves Sanday, my advisor, who endured my intellectual whimsies and political commitments with patience. Her integrity and belief in an engaged academic project as well as her dedication to intellectual rigor set a compass for my career. Along with Peggy, I would like to acknowledge the rest of my dissertation committee for their generous support, including Kathy Hall, Michael Delli Carpini, and John Jackson—each of whom played vital roles in this undertaking.

Along with my advisors, an army of colleagues at Penn pushed my thinking, sharpened my understanding, and forced me to reckon with my rather large blind spots. In this regard, I must offer a special thanks to Peter Funke. Every idea I had and every page I wrote came out of a long, ongoing conversation. In many ways he is a coauthor on this work, and hope I can be half as useful to him as he has been to me. Accompanying Peter are the many colleagues at Penn that consistently compelled my thinking: Michael Janson, Robert Fairbanks, Raymond Gunn, Sergio Saenz, Saskia Fischer, Gregory Wolmart, Amy Bach, Lauren Silver, John Fitzgerald, Caitlin Anderson, Mark Bostic, Jeff Hornstein, and many others. I have also had the good fortune to receive the advice of many scholars along the way, including Ed Herman, Michael Hardt, Adolph Reed, Sam Gindin, Leo Panitch, Dorothy Kidd, John Downing, Christina Dunbar-Hester, Jack Bratich, George Collier, Stanley Aronowitz, Douglas Kellner, Harry Cleaver, and especially Nick Dyer-Witheford. I also want to thank the University of Illinois Press and particularly the support of Danny Nassett.

This work is seriously indebted to the Media Mobilizing Project and the many political projects and people that I have been blessed to be involved with over the last decade. This includes Shivaani Selvaraj, Mica Root, Phil Wider, Nijmie Dzurinko, Desi Burnette, Ron Blount, Alix Webb, Bryan Mercer, Rebekah Phillips, Kristin Campbell, Hannah Sassaman, Erika Almiron, Rachel Goffe, Megan Williamson, Fred Pinguel, Amalia Deloney, Martin Lautz, John Hough, Steve Chrevenka, Al Alston, Carmen Cuadrado, Amendu Evans, Audra Trayham, Peter Bloom, Lawrence Jones, Koby Murphy, Quon Blanche, Charles Clark, Willie Baptist, Liz Theoharris, Liz McElroy, Mohammad Shukur, Bill Zoda, Tekle Gebrehmdin, Patrick Anamah, Gary Broderick, Dina Yarmus, Ron Whitehoren, Patty Eakin, and many other people I have had the good fortune to build with in Philadelphia, across Pennsylvania, and beyond. I would also like to thank many people from the indymedia movement that took time out to grant me interviews or shared their thinking on indymedia and social-movement building, including Jay Sand, Jeff Perlstein, Amy Dalton, Joshua Breitbart, Susanna Thomas, Aaron Couch, DeeDee Halleck, Chris Burnett, Sascha Meinrath, Dan Merkle, Sheri Herndon, John Tarleton, Greg Ruggiero, Inja Coates, Alec Meltzer, Rich Gardener, Mike Rosenberg, Petri Dish, Josh Marcus, Michael Eisenmenger, C. W. Anderson, and Matthew Arnison. The work of indymedia has truly been an inspiration.

I would also like to thank my family, who made me stronger and more in touch with life through a mixture of torture, love, and play. In particular my parents, Linda and Les, my sister and brother, Shelly and Jonathan, and their partners Cary and Nelly, and my favorite nieces and nephews, Emery, Reece, Pierce, Nev, and Indy.

I owe a particularly large debt of gratitude to my son Sebastian, who in two short years has given me more joy than I could have ever imagined. I am sure the joy will increase, exponentially with the arrival of his brother or sister, who is about to join us, ready or not. Finally, this book would not have been possible without my partner in life, Alison Taylor. She has been my lifeline as I trudged through this process, from copy editing to helping me refine my analysis. Alison has taught me a great deal in the last decade, and both this book and I are immeasurably better for it.

History, Capitalism, and the Cyber Left

> In attempting to articulate their visionary ideals, and
> thereby negate the accepted view of reality, different
> American Lefts have displayed different intellectual
> temperaments. The Lyrical Left tended at first to rely upon
> the regenerating force of culture and the imaginative power
> of poetry as a means of manifesting "premature truths";
> the Old Left saw in the "science" of Marxism a method of
> historical understanding that would enable man to triumph
> over the "contradictions" of capitalism; and the New Left
> embraced an existential ethic of moral choice and human
> commitment as a way of overcoming
> the paradoxes of alienation.
>
> —John Patrick Diggins, *The Rise and Fall*
> *of the American Left*

In an instant, the immaterial aspects of the financial capitalist system melted away, as the tightly held logic of neoliberalism came crashing inward. The world watched with fear and awe as the collapse of the speculative markets quickly exposed the entire financial system, and foundational institutions—imbued with all of the power and majesty of global capital—crumbled before our eyes. The price of the hubris, however, went beyond the boardrooms of Lehman Brothers, and in a few short months the grim realities of the crisis took a vicious toll on working people. Families lost their houses to foreclosure, elderly couples lost their life savings to the rapacious market, and working people lost their jobs and livelihood to the aggressive greed of an unchecked financial system.

In the shadow of the growing economic disaster, which unjustly meted out punishment on the most precarious, political leaders stepped in with massive bailouts, engineered by the very people who created the crisis, in an effort to save banks deemed "too big to fail." And in time, as our collective memory waned, these same political leaders fixed their gaze on the meager support system of the poor and working class, demanding austerity budgets and calling for shared sacrifice. The sacrifice, however, was not shared, as the market rebounded for the few, while the growing legion of poor and working people were left to shoulder the burden of the twenty-first century's first global economic and human crisis.

While the financial collapse has heaped untold misery on the working class, this crisis, like those before it, has also presented real political opportunity. As people suffer and injustice reigns, trust in state power and financial markets has evaporated, and the ties that bind us to the current social and political configuration have loosened. With this social dislocation comes the possibility for uprising.

The Great Refusal, as Herbert Marcuse (1991) once called it, has begun to show itself, as organizers, activists, and everyday people across the world respond to the economic crisis and growing specter of poverty and inequality. In this "post-collapse" moment, we have witnessed new forms of organizing and protest that have rekindled the radical imagination. Beginning in 2009, communities from Cairo, Tunis, and Reykjavik to Santiago, Athens, and New York rose up, redrawing the political landscape and in some cases rebalancing the political scales. In some of these rebellions, dictators and their corrupt systems were swept asunder; in others, the struggle continues to this day; and in others still, a new narrative emerged that challenged the neoliberal logic that socializes risk while privatizing profit.

While the character of each of these struggles is distinct, some critical commonalities bind this cycle of resistance together as a diverse but singular moment of rebellion. Traits like the creative use of new media and social networks in resistance, the desire for meaningful democratic participation, the physical and virtual occupation of space, and the leadership of young people, who increasingly face dwindling job prospects and growing student debt. These patterned attributes help to form the silhouette of a new figure of resistance, a new sociopolitical formation.

Digital Rebellion is an attempt to map the underlying logic of this new figure of resistance as it has materialized across the world. I undertake this mapping exercise through a historical and ethnographic analysis of the Global Social Justice Movement from 1994 to 2006, with a particular focus on the indymedia movement. While indymedia and the Global Social Justice Movement precede the contemporary moment of struggle by less than a decade, in many ways the tactics and strategy of resistance in that period already seem quaint, as activists waged their fights using bullhorns, bulky

Web sites, monodimensional mobile phones, and black balaclavas instead of Guy Fawkes masks. However, much like objects in a rearview mirror, the Global Social Justice Movement is much closer than it appears. It is my contention that the logic of struggle that developed through that period offers the necessary tools to understand the mental terrain of occupiers and Cairo combatants today.

At this broad level, extending the cyclical theory of social movements,[1] in *Digital Rebellion* I argue that historical and sociocultural patterns connect different periods of political protest. Specifically, I argue that the patterns of struggle in a particular period are best understood as developing, in an ideal sense, through a multilateral dialogue between social-movement actors and both the past and present.

Examined from one perspective, social movements and social-movement actors are in conversation with the corporeal world in which they exist. Viewed through this materialist lens, we can see that a particular logic of resistance emerges in response to the social systems and social world of which it is a part. Thus, in the era of Fordist capitalism, revolutionary movements formed large centralized party-like formations that mirrored the economy of scale that was the dominant episteme of the time. Correspondingly, in the contemporary moment of informational capitalism, activists forge nimble, networked formations as a facsimile of the networked society they exist within. In this sense, movements both challenge and integrate, sometimes unconsciously, different elements of their social environs.

The logic of resistance in a particular moment, however, does not develop in a straightforward conversation between activists and their physical present. Instead, the logic and vision of resistance in a particular period[2] also develop in dialectic tension with history, and specifically the previous stages of resistance. Along these lines, the Old Left and New Left were in constant, though sometimes hidden, dialogue[3] about issues of structure, strategy, and composition, and as I argue throughout this book, contemporary social movements are also in dialogue with the history of resistance that has preceded it. This premise forms the theoretical underpinning of this book, which is that in order to appreciate the social-movement logic of a particular moment, one must understand this triangulated interaction between social-movement actors; the materialist present; and the long, unfolding history of resistance. Using this lens, we can then begin to trace the commonalities and differences between the Student Non-Violent Coordinating Committee and Students for a Democratic Society, on the one hand, and the Global Social Justice Movement or Occupy Wall Street, on the other hand.

Defining and Historicizing the Cyber Left

To get analytic purchase on the transformations in contemporary social movements, I introduce the term *Cyber Left*. Through this concept, I contend that we are on the cusp of a new stage in left-based social movements, enmeshed with the changing nature of new digital technologies and the globalizing economic order. I use the term *Cyber Left* to historicize this emergent mode of movement building, and I argue that the way activists have employed communication tools (from the Internet to cell phones) has shifted spatial and temporal configurations within movements, creating new possibilities for organizational structure, democratic governance, and media strategy.

With the growing fervor of technological utopianism coming on the heels of Occupy Wall Street and the Arab Spring, the use of the term *cyber* is admittedly complicated. To this end, I want to make clear that I do not use *cyber* to argue that social movements have moved online, nor do I suggest that social life has been transformed solely by the networking power of Facebook or Twitter, nor do I argue that this shift in the operations of social movements is necessarily positive. In fact, the most successful movements are still driven by face-to-face relationships, trust, analysis, a strong understanding of local concerns, leadership development, and on-the-ground organizing, as I discuss throughout this book. Instead, I use *cyber* as a descriptive term to define the novel set of processes and practices within twenty-first-century social resistance that are engendered by new technologies and in turn have enabled new possibilities for the scale, strategy, structure, and governance of social movements.

Along these lines, it would be a simplification to argue that the transformation in social movements is determined by one factor, whether that factor was the shift to a neoliberal, informational form of capitalism or the manifold technological advances that have dramatically sped up social life. To engage with the intersection of technology and digital activism, I take a critical and dialectical approach to technology.[4] As I discuss in detail in part II, this dialectical approach places technological practices and relations of domination and resistance into conversation with one another. In approaching technology in this manner, it becomes clear that technological tools are not neutral, as they are produced and reproduced with social intention by those with power. At the same time, technological practice is a site of contested struggle, and therefore, technological tools can be utilized to create social change.

While I use the term *cyber* to capture the new dynamics in contemporary movements, this is a study that is focused on chronicling the American *left*.[5] Historians of the American left generally speak of two central phases of social-movement history in the United States. The Old Left, from the early twentieth century to the end of World War II,[6] was influenced by Marxism and the Bolshevik Revolution[7] and principally focused on trade unionism, the development of political parties, and the central antagonism between the bourgeoisie and proletariat.[8] In the postwar period, the U.S. government waged a war on critical Old Left institutions like the Communist Party, and this, alongside the horrors of Stalinism, led to the eventual collapse of the Old Left. Out of the ashes of the Old Left, however, the civil rights movement emerged and acted as a critical bridge to the New Left.[9] In the 1960s, New Left institutions such as Students for a Democratic Society developed on the heels of the civil rights movement, while being shaped by Mao's peasant-based revolution in China. Challenging the dogma of the Old Left, New Left activists questioned the central role of class and the industrial proletariat, articulating a host of concerns from gender and racial equality to ending the Vietnam War and U.S. imperialism.[10] The New Left in turn led to the birth and growth of the nuclear-disarmament movement, the environmental movement,[11] the gay-rights movement,[12] and later stages of the feminist movement.[13]

Following these two broad stages of social movements, I contend through this research that we are seeing the outlines of a new phase, the Cyber Left, that has taken the shape of a globalized, digitized, radically democratic network formation. This new stage of resistance is grounded in the experiences and insights of the Zapatista Army of National Liberation (EZLN) in Mexico. In 1996, the EZLN made a widespread call to activists, revolutionaries, and media makers to forge "a collective network of resistance against neoliberalism" and "a network of *communication* among all our struggles." Out of this call and the vision and relationships it established came indymedia, People's Global Action, the World Social Forum process, and many other networks and institutions that mark the initial stage of this period of struggle.

Analysis based on periods or stages has limitations because it elides historical continuity and/or obscures dissonance within a specific movement in time. However, periodization is useful in establishing ascendant characteristics, especially as they are keyed to global economic restructurings, such as those that have characterized the world economy of the last forty years.[14] And there are more problems in not identifying such periods. Fredric Jameson (1991) argues that if we don't see patterns or periods in history, then we are forced to argue that the contemporary moment is an anarchic jumble of phenomena with no sociohistorical or economic link.

Accordingly, in *The Rise and Fall of the American Left* (1992), the historian John Patrick Diggins takes up the question of social-movement periodization in his analysis of the character and intellectual temperament of the U.S. left across the twentieth century. In framing this genealogical study of the left, Diggins argues that "a generation is not simply a people coexisting in the same time period. What identifies a group as belonging to a particular generation are both a shared perspective on common historical problems and a similar strategy of action, taken as a result of that perspective" (43–44). Diggins goes on to articulate that the collective outlook that forges the spirit of a particular generation, or stage in social-movement building, is the negation of "what is" in an attempt to create "what ought to be."[15] The essence of this concept is that each generation, or stage of the American left, imagines the contours of a more just society against the shape of the actually existing world. Consequently, each generation's social horizon, and the character of its movements for social change, is bound by the political imaginary[16] of the period. In addition to responding to the social, political, and economic environment, I contend through this work that each stage of the left is also reacting to previous generations and the historical legacy of movement building. In this sense, the Old Left put forward the science of Marxism as a challenge to the romantic socialism of previous periods[17] as well as the modern capitalist engines of Fordism and Taylorism. Likewise, the New Left put forward an existential, individualistic ethic as a challenge to the hierarchy of the Old Left and the conformity of the "Company Man," which marked the period. Building on this, as the twenty-first century unfolds and contemporary movements for change arise, they will be forged in reaction to the history of social movements and the corporeal world of which they are a part.

With this in mind, this book seeks to determine in what ways the Cyber Left is a reaction to previous periods of movement building, as well as the rise of informational capitalism and new information and communication technologies. Correspondingly, in what ways does the Cyber Left build on insights of the Old and New Left, and in what ways does it reject previous periods and strategies? This set of concerns forms the backdrop of this study, which aims to be a step in understanding the common problem and the shared strategy for action of contemporary movements for social change.

From Origins to Logic of Resistance

The proposition that social movements are historically rooted yet fundamentally transforming informs the structure of this book. *Digital Rebellion* is broken into two parts: "Origins" and "Logic of Resistance." Part I is comprised of three chapters focused on the history and birth of indymedia and the Cyber Left more broadly. The primary goal of "Origins" is to trace the historical conjuncture wherein the Cyber Left came to life and to detail the development of this new face of activism as it emerged in Mexico and spread across North and South America, Europe, and the rest of the globe.

In part II, I map the varied arguments scholars have made, both implicit and explicit, regarding the intersection of technology and social change. Following this, I argue for a critical and dialectical approach to technology and social movements. In the subsequent chapters, I bring this approach to life as I utilize a mixture of cyber-based or virtual ethnography as well as traditional ethnography to establish the cultural logic of the Cyber Left through the three mutually reinforcing features of twenty-first-century social movements: *structure,* or decentralized, transnational network formation; *governance,* or local, national, and global application of direct, participatory democracy; and *strategy,* or the utilization of new technologies and other strategies to bind a distinctive, diversified transnational social movement.

In the conclusion, I reexamine the Cyber Left against the backdrop of informational capitalism and history. Through this lens, I discuss indymedia as a precursor to Occupy Wall Street and many of the emergent social movements that have developed since the economic crisis of 2008.

Beyond mapping the logic of resistance in a particular moment of history, I contend that it is incumbent on scholars to begin to analyze the potentialities and pitfalls of that logic. My political and intellectual journey has colored my understanding of the logic of the Cyber Left—a fact that emerges throughout this text. In this book you will see both exuberance for the strategy of Cyber Left activists and their predecessors as well as a healthy skepticism. I wish to hold this tension, as it helps to capture what is most exciting about this age—the ideals of democracy, horizontality, and networks—with what is most problematic—again the ideals of democracy, horizontality, and networks.

In the initial stages of my research, the seemingly limitless possibilities at the intersection of networks, social media, and participatory democracy captivated me as I watched the unbounded growth of Cyber Left institutions like indymedia and the World Social Forum. However, as time went on, the potion wore off, and some, though not all, of the magic of this new age of activism became problematic. I began to see techno-utopian tendencies that favor the leadership of white, male, college-educated activists at the expense of building a movement connected to those most oppressed; I saw social-movement organizations that were detached from the local and from the struggles and concerns of everyday people; and I saw a movement that was not particularly interested in strategy, organizing, and building power. In fact, my disquiet around the logic of Cyber Left institutions led me to work with other organizers and activists to build a new organization, the Media Mobilizing Project. The aim of the Media Mobilizing Project was to extract what we saw as the silver linings of this new strategy of resistance, like the innovative use of media to build across many fronts of struggle, while discarding some of the problematic aspects, such as privileging process over outcome and openness and horizontality over intentionality.[18] Along these lines, this book is a situated yet clear-eyed appraisal of the strengths and weaknesses of digital activism and the logic of informational capitalism that underlies it—an appraisal that comes from my time as an ethnographer and an organizer.

While the principal goal of this book is to describe and analyze the logic that drives left-based social movements, this project began as a place-based urban ethnography of the Independent Media Center of Philadelphia. Over three years, I was deeply embedded in indymedia as a researcher and activist. During that period, I worked as a journalist, organizer, meeting facilitator, editor, and curator, first with Philly IMC and then with national and global collectives within the network. As an anthropologist, I also endeavor to ethnographically render indymedia, which I argue is exemplary of the broader logic of activism. To that aim, I begin with the story of Bradley Roland Will, one of the leaders and tragic, iconic symbols of indymedia and the Global Social Justice Movement as his life offers a window on to the logic and practice of the Cyber Left.

PART I

Origins

> Imperfect, insurgent, sleepless, and beautiful, we directly
> experienced the success of the first IMC in Seattle, and
> saw that the common dream of a "world in which many
> worlds fit" is possible—step by step, piece by piece, space
> by space, pdf by pdf, word by word, over the net, on pirate
> broadcast, in the streets, streamlining live, and most
> importantly: face to face. . . . [F]anned by the real showdown
> of the WTO and our capacity to bypass corporate media, the
> IMC brushfire spread.
>
> —Greg Ruggiero, indymedia organizer

Death at the Barricades

On October 29, 2006, the homepage of the New York City Independent Media Center (IMC) was transformed from a local news portal to a "virtual memorial," celebrating the life and sudden death of indymedia journalist and activist Brad Will. The Web site was overflowing with reports of Brad's murder and messages of mourning, outrage, and solidarity from his friends and comrades across the globe. Mingled with the sad news and passionate testaments was a montage of photos and videos that included images of Brad strumming his guitar, defending community gardens, and documenting political protests (with an HD video camera he picked up on eBay.) The illustrations captured Brad's gentle spirit, indomitable will, and passion for international activism. Sitting in front of my computer in Philadelphia, I explored the proliferating material and found a link that transported me to Brad's final video: *Infamia en Oaxaca/Infamy in Oaxaca*.[1] I waited with apprehension as the video uploaded and then watched as images of a street battle in Oaxaca City, which took place just two days prior, unfolded before my eyes.

The video opened at the Santa Lucia del Camino barricades outside Oaxaca City. In the midday sun, community members explained the roots of the conflict between the Institutional Revolutionary Party (PRI) governing the state and the Asemblea Popular de los Pueblos de Oaxaca (APPO), a grassroots coalition comprised of teachers, social workers, and citizens. A distressed yet resolute woman captured the intensity of the struggle, staring into Brad's camera and declaring, "We are townspeople here who are fighting for our rights . . . we don't want to live like this anymore, we don't want to live in a state of repression."

The confrontation between community members and the governing party flared up during the summer, when members of the teachers' union went on strike and seized the town center, *el zocalo,* demanding funding increases for schools and students and pay increases for teachers. The governor of the state, Ulises Ruiz Ortiz, responded by sending in state police to eject the teachers from the public square. The violent conflict, in which the teachers expelled the police from the center of the city, led to the founding of the APPO and a six-month standoff between the two groups.[2]

Brad landed in Oaxaca three months after the initial confrontation, to document the ongoing rebellion as part of the growing indymedia movement. Indymedia is a global, federated network of Independent Media Centers that work to create an open, accessible media infrastructure, "for the creation of radical, accurate, and passionate tellings of the truth."[3] Founded as a direct challenge to the corporate media, the aim of the first Independent Media Center was to report on the 1999 World Trade Organization meetings and counter-demonstrations in Seattle. In the decade since the now-famous Battle of Seattle, the indymedia movement has expanded rapidly and at the time of Brad's death consisted of thousands of activists, computer programmers, and independent journalists, as well as hundreds of interlinked Web sites, radio stations, newspapers, video collectives, and community-organizing arms throughout the world. As indymedia developed, it has become more than a conventional alternative media outlet, at times playing the role of think tank, organizing arm, activist laboratory, and mobilizing tool for the Global Social Justice Movement.[4]

The mood of indymedia is captured by the pervasive phrase, "Don't hate the media, be the media." The embodiment of this do-it-yourself (DIY) sensibility, Brad Will spent the final months of his thirty-six-year life filming social movements throughout the Americas. Seeking out political hot zones, Brad's camcorder became a conduit, relaying stories and images of people fighting for social change throughout the hemisphere—from indigenous communities rising up to stop multinational coal companies from seizing lands in north-western Venezuela, and urban squatters fighting eviction in central Brazil, to activists struggling against gentrification and displacement in the Lower East Side of Manhattan. Following this trajectory, the flashpoint in Oaxaca was a logical destination for Brad, and when he touched down in Mexico the conflict was quickly hurtling toward its violent zenith. The APPO, still in control of large parts of Oaxaca City, was demanding the resignation of Governor Ortiz. Meanwhile, Mexican President Vicente Fox threatened an imminent suppression of the "radical groups, out of control" in Oaxaca City.

As soon as Brad disembarked in Oaxaca City, he began filming the struggle. Over several days he captured the excitement and unease that saturated the chaotic streets. About a week before his death, Brad sent a report to the New York City Independent Media Center in which he fervently described what he was seeing in Mexico: "What can you say about this movement—this revolutionary moment—you know it is building, growing, shaping . . . it is clear that this is more than a strike, more than expulsion of a governor, more than a blockade, more than a coalition of fragments—it is a genuine people's revolt."[5]

The accompanying video that he shot during the crisis, *Infamy in Oaxaca,* is comprised of two distinct segments. The opening portion of the video consists of interviews with community members, recorded shortly after a skirmish with local paramilitary, in which a young man who was a member of the APPO was killed. Eight minutes into the video, however, there is a striking shift in tone. The camerawork becomes shaky, and the audio track changes from dialogue to the immediacy of sporadic gunfire. The accompanying images are unmistakable—cars ablaze, the frenzied energy of tangled masses, and the chilling mixture of fear and excitement in the eyes of people as they decried injustice. As I watched the second half of *Infamy,* it became clear that I was no longer watching interviews about a struggle in Oaxaca; instead I was in the front seat of a battle over the Santa Lucia del Camino barricades.

As if to mark this shift, the video captures the briefest glimpse of Brad's lanky shadow crossing a stark landscape, the silhouette of a camera hoisted atop his shoulder. The footage then becomes dark and blurry, as Brad ducked down and shimmied underneath a semi-trailer, dodging gunfire. "The one with the white shirt," he intones, using his camera to get positive identification of the assailants, members of an unidentified paramilitary force. In the same moment, the assailants see Brad underneath the trailer and shoot at him. The gunshots kick up dirt a few feet in front of the makeshift bunker, and Brad is on the move. Moments later, Brad joins a surging crowd attempting to hold off the paramilitary and keep control of the barricades, and by extension the town center.

Suddenly, seemingly driven toward its own tragic internal logic, the video is punctuated by a gunshot, the cry of pain, and a disorienting spin of images. The camera falls to the ground, but continues filming. At this point, it was difficult to make out what was happening, but it is evident that a body is being carried to safety, and while the camera was still recording, it is clear that Brad was no longer behind the lens. Sixteen minutes into the video, the screen fades to black. Unfortunately, Brad never made it to safety that day, dying an hour later from a gunshot wound to the chest, en route to a local Red Cross. Epitomizing the spirit of the indymedia movement of which he had become such an integral part,[6] Brad's camcorder captured his own death, leaving a trace of his final moments for the world to witness.[7]

Brad Will and the New Ethos of Struggle

The day after Brad's death, I received a call from Darcy,[8] a friend, "informant," and Oregon-based indymedia activist who told me about the tragic event. At the time of Brad's death, I had been studying the indymedia movement for over a year and had been both an active participant in the Philadelphia-based Independent Media Center (Philly IMC) as well as a member of the national and global editorial teams. Darcy asked me to spread the news of his passing and post a "breaking news" report on the Philly IMC Web site, which I did. Within days, the haunting video and story ricocheted across the indymedia movement's global digital-communications infrastructure, leaving the incandescent image of Brad filming at the Santa Lucia barricades in its wake.[9] In the months to follow, Brad became an icon of the indymedia movement. His picture appeared on the banner of local IMC Web sites, and his spirit was invoked in discussions about the strategic direction of the network.

The symbolic power of Brad's life was partly due to his magnetic personality, but it was more than just his charisma. Brad exemplified the essence of what it meant to be an indymedia activist and a member of the larger Cyber Left. Brad was white, college-educated, and he came from a relatively privileged background, growing up in a sleepy suburb outside of Chicago. But he devoted his life to the cause of freedom and justice, both his own and that of broader humanity. As Brad explained in an interview: "My major focus is . . . how like the creative voice can participate in the political struggle. . . .

I'm a poet and I'm an activist, . . . and those two things should not have to be mutually exclusive."[10]

It was through his camera that Brad expressed his art and his politics. As cinema-studies scholars often argue, the goal of a filmmaker is to lure the audience into associating with the viewpoint of the camera, thus taking on the identity of the omniscient eye. This was certainly the case with *Infamy in Oaxaca*. While I watched the struggle at the barricades in Oaxaca City, it felt like I was a target of paramilitary gunfire. This suspicion was correct, as it turned out that Brad was a marked man. Almost a year after his death, the *San Francisco Bay Guardian* reported that a local pirate radio station in the region was repeatedly broadcasting the chilling phrase, "Si ves un gringo con cámara, matanlo" (If you see a gringo with a camera, kill him) (Ross 2007).

This striking detail brings up a seemingly uncomplicated question: Of all the people in the crowd on that hot October day in Oaxaca—from local political figures to protestors with firearms—why was the person with the video camera the target? The question is not simply one concerning the facts on the ground during the Oaxaca uprising. Rather, it is a historical and political question that captures a set of shifting dynamics regarding the role of information and communications in a globalized and increasingly digitized world.

To speak to this question, at one level this book chronicles the practices of indymedia journalists like Brad, who have devoted their lives to documenting people struggling for social change. It is an investigation of organizers, activists, and community members who recognize the growing importance of tools like the video camera and an independent Web server as weapons to be utilized in social struggles over land, a living wage, and what is understood as "the good" or "the just." Building on the work of anthropologists focused on indigenous media,[11] or what George Marcus (1996) has called the activist imaginary, this frame opens a window on the ways communities use new media to "talk back," converging with the growing ethnographic studies of media production, reception, flow, and appropriation.

At a second level, however, the way indymedia activists utilized the Web to cultivate a community of supporters from across the globe to quickly act online and offline around Brad's death and the struggle in Oaxaca marked something deeper. As I watched the news of Brad's death move rapidly across a transnational communications network, mobilizing communities to hold protests and vigils around the world, it crystallized a growing conviction that the novel use of digital communication technologies by activists has shifted the fabric of sociality and, in turn, social movements. At this secondary level, this study is an account of the nature of social change, and the deep shift in the structures, strategies, and scale of contemporary social movements, like indymedia, as they are impacted by and in turn reappropriate new information and communication technologies. It is these deep structural shifts in an informational, capitalist society that set the conditions for indymedia's birth and growth.

The Battle of Seattle and the Birth of Democratic Media

While many factors led to the development of the first IMC, one of the key triggers was the ongoing state deregulation, and correspondent corporate consolidation, of the media sector.[12] As Ben Bagdikian (2004) details, the process of consolidation unfolded over the latter half of the twentieth century and continued unabated in the first decade of the twenty-first century, leading to a drastic reduction in the number of companies that own mass-media outlets. According to his oft-cited research, today there are five mega-companies that own the majority of the world's media outlets from television, radio, and newspapers to book publishing and film. As academic analysis on the process of consolidation begins to mount, there is growing consensus among scholars that the lack of diversity of ownership and opinion in mass media poses a fundamental challenge to democratic processes.[13] In one of the foundational analyses of mass-media bias, Edward S. Herman and Noam Chomsky (1987) argue that mass media must, by its very nature, construct a worldview that conforms to the needs of corporate advertising. This profit-driven equation has led to the valorization of some political perspectives and the marginalization of other perspectives, narrowing political dialogue, in a process Stuart Hall (1979) aptly described as "the great moving right show" (14).

Recognizing the marginalization of "progressive" perspectives and left-based social movements in the mass media, members of the U.S. and global left began to organize around the mass media in the late 1990s.[14] This has led to three complementary strategies. The first approach was the development of strong movements for structural reform of the media sector. Within this branch, which is alternatively called the Media Reform or Media Democracy movement, a growing number of organizations have fought to establish laws that increase the diversity of media ownership, challenge media and telecommunications consolidation, and forge new channels of communication such as low-power FM radio.[15] Alongside policy-based reform of the media sector, a separate overlapping contingent of groups focused on the unequal treatment and stereotypical representation of people of color, poor people, young people, women, and other oppressed groups in the mass media. Developing a framework around media justice groups within this paradigm have focused on fighting for equal access to and control over the means of communication, while recognizing the critical intersection between media justice and social justice. The founder of the Center for Media Justice, Malkia Cyril, captures this vision: "The biggest defining characteristic of media justice is that it's not about the media, it's about justice, justice comes first," Cyril continues, media "is a medium for change, it is not change itself."[16]

Finally, a third distinct constellation of actors recognized the manifold possibilities of participatory media in the age of the Internet and thus fought to build an alternative media infrastructure to challenge the mass media. While there are many organizations and institutions that characterize this outlook, the materialization of indymedia in Seattle was arguably the most critical moment in the development of an alternative media infrastructure.

The first Independent Media Center came to life on the contested streets of Seattle on November 30, 1999, during the World Trade Organization (WTO) Third Ministerial Conference. The goal of the conference, known as the "Millennium Round," was to unite over one hundred nations around trade-liberalization policies, leading to the reduction of national tariffs and taxes and ultimately the unhindered flow of goods and services among countries. Capturing a growing sentiment of unease around global trade, the Millennium Round was met with huge determined protests that were led by citizens concerned about the increasing power, and the inherently undemocratic nature, of supranational decision-making bodies, such as the North American Free Trade Agreement (NAFTA), the Multilateral Agreement on Investment (MAI), the Free Trade Area of the Americas (FTAA), and the WTO.

As activists prepared for mass demonstrations, there was widespread concern that protestors would either be vilified by the mass media or "blacked out" of WTO coverage altogether.[17] One of the founders of indymedia, Jeff Perlstein, captured this prevailing sentiment as he detailed the rationale for establishing the first IMC: "We couldn't just let CNN and CBS be the ones to tell these stories, and so that meant we needed to develop our own alternatives, and our own alternative network."[18] Based on this vision, the first IMC was born.

An innovative but uncertain media project, the mission of the Seattle Independent Media Center was to offer multiple media-based platforms (Internet, print, radio, video) for independent journalists, activists, and the general public to report on the WTO meetings and the ensuing counter-demonstrations that engulfed the city. As the Battle of Seattle developed into one of the most dramatic uprisings in recent U.S. history, the IMC platform for producing and distributing local independent media captured the imagination of activists, journalists, and citizens throughout the country and the world.

In Seattle, the mark of indymedia journalism was a profusion of first-person, proximal, experience-based reporting, which communications scholar Dorothy Kidd (2004) labeled "direct witness." With the speed, perspective, and sheer number of amateur journalists, the Seattle IMC acted as a clearinghouse of information for interested parties. Indymedia news was offered to the public with no oversight, no advertisement, and no middleman. This unrestricted immediacy of reporting and distribution of information has become one of the hallmarks of indymedia protest coverage and is the founding ideology upon which the network was forged. Through the practice of providing grassroots coverage of the protests, an innovative journalistic ethos and new breed of hybrid urban "citizen journalists" cum activists emerged. Armed with pads, pencils, camcorders, cell phones, and bright-green makeshift press passes,[19] indymedia reporters gathered their stories, and through the newly developed IMC Web site, they shared those stories with the world. The energetic inauguration of the indymedia movement presaged a new era of social media, grassroots citizen journalism, and digitized, networked resistance.

The aftermath of the Battle of Seattle saw IMCs quickly germinating throughout the industrialized nations, first in Washington, D.C., and London, then Philadelphia and Los Angeles, followed by Prague (IMF/World Bank), Davos (World Economic Forum), Genoa (G8), and Cancun (WTO). The early IMCs were first launched in conjunction with the protest circuit of the burgeoning Global Social Justice Movement. However, the idea of citizen newsrooms caught the attention of journalists, community groups, activists, and a broader populace and eventually reached a tipping point. Centers emerged throughout the globe, forming a loosely federated noncorporate media and communications structure. From 2000 to 2004, in the height of the movement's development, a new Independent Media Center was developed every seven days.

The Cultural Logic of the Cyber Left

Due to its accelerated growth and experimental nature, indymedia has inspired an abundance of academic scholarship. In trying to make sense of this new formation, which is part news outlet, part social movement, initial studies unearthed the ideological roots of the novel communication network.[20]

In the second wave of research, some scholars delineated the prefigurative politics and decentralized network structure that grounds the many layers of indymedia governance and content production.[21] Correspondingly, others focused on indymedia as exemplar of a Habermasian counter–public sphere,[22] a grassroots challenge to media consolidation,[23] a battle over the communications commons,[24] and an extension of the Global Social Justice movement.[25] The extensive body of research on indymedia has offered salient insights into the convergence of new information and communication technologies, globalization, and networked activism.

In my research, I apply a broader lens, focusing on indymedia as the exemplification of a new stage in social movements, the Cyber Left. In making the argument that there is a fundamental shift in the structure, strategy, governance, and logic of contemporary social movements, I join scholars[26] who have begun to describe and analyze the fundamental shift in contemporary social movements.[27]

Witness to parallel trends in my research, I describe the core characteristics of indymedia from networked activism and the transnational application of radical democracy to the multiscalar organizational structure. I maintain that there are three characteristics or dynamics of indymedia that set it, and the Cyber Left generally, apart from early movements for social change:

1. Strategy: utilization of new technologies and other strategies to bind a distinctive, diversified transnational social movement;
2. Structure: decentralized, multiscalar (local, national, global) network formation;
3. Governance: local, national, and global application of direct, participatory democracy.

Taken alone, none of the aspects are entirely new; however, woven together they constitute a new social formation and logic of struggle that is at once local and global, online and offline, and decentralized and democratic.

To briefly touch on each of these in turn: The strategy of indymedia and Cyber Left movements is to create platforms and processes where different fragmented struggles can be networked together, not in an effort to become one singular struggle but to become stronger together as a complex of struggles. This is exemplified by the Zapatistas, a Mayan/peasant army from Chiapas, the poorest region of Mexico. In conjunction with their military operations, the Zapatistas used mass media and other tools to call all poor and working people in Mexico into a coalition against the Mexican government and neoliberal capitalism. The catchphrase that was developed to describe the Zapatista strategy—"One NO to neoliberal capitalism, many YESES"—eventually became the rallying cry of the Global Social Justice Movement. This slogan underscores the new strategy of resistance of the Cyber Left, which has two fundamental principles captured by the No/Yes equation: (1) The many autonomous movements of the left share a common resistance ("one NO") to the terms and conditions of neoliberal capitalism; (2) despite a history of movement building that prioritized the working class, there is no central actor or political protagonist in twenty-first-century struggle—instead, indigenous movements, environmental movements, and labor movements are all vital ("many YESES"). Thus, while the strategic aim of the Cyber Left is to bring points of struggle together to build a bigger movement that can challenge the power of capitalism, there is an underlying belief in singularity. Said differently, Cyber Left actors and institutions presume that there are multiple irreducible fronts of struggle that must exist independently and cannot be subsumed under one banner, framework, or organizational structure. Indymedia takes up this strategy, utilizing the local, national, and global communications infrastructure to link people and struggles across space and theme, becoming a platform for this diversity of struggle.

Second, indymedia and other Cyber Left institutions tend to be structured as global, decentralized networks. In the specific case of indymedia, this means that the network is composed of a collection of local Independent Media Centers, usually based in urban settings across the world. The local IMCs are part of one loosely shared network, but they have almost complete autonomy. While local IMCs are the foundation of the indymedia network, there are also nation-state-based IMCs, regional IMCs, and one global IMC. This multilevel structure enables the network to scale up from the local to the global, challenging power structures at multiple scales. Each of the IMCs operates independently, in theory, while agreeing to a basic set of shared rules, which are called the Principles of Unity. This structure is in contradistinction to the past, where social-movement organizations were structured as political parties (Communist Party, Black Panther Party), unions (IWW, Teamsters, UNITE HERE), or organizations (Students for a Democratic Society, Student Non-Violent Coordinating Committee). Past structures tended to have a clear hierarchy and centralized configuration, whereas indymedia has little hierarchy within the network, and the organizational structure is not predetermined nor centralized.

Third, the internal governance of indymedia is a form of direct, participatory democracy, at the local, national, and global scale. As a governing doctrine, this means that each member of indymedia has a right to equal participation in any decision affecting the organization. Accordingly, indymedia has no formally expressed hierarchy, there are no elections, and there is no president or executive director of the network. Everyone is considered a leader. This form of governance builds on the tradition of *prefigurative politics*, and it emerged out of the praxis of the New Left. In her seminal study of the New Left, Winni Breines (1989) defined prefigurative politics as the practice of creating or sustaining "relationships and political forms that 'prefigured' and embodied the desired society" (6). In other words, you create within the organization the structures, practices, and relationships you strive to create in the world. Along these lines, indymedia activists have a collective vision of an egalitarian society without power and hierarchy, and therefore within the network, they aim to create what are known as horizontal or flat decision-making structures without hierarchy. Finally, while this practice is not new to the Cyber Left, the ability to practice this form of democracy at a global scale, bringing together activists from Seoul to São Paulo through wiki pages, chatrooms, and listservs, is novel and has facilitated the development of deeply democratic social movements at a global scale.

If we use a fine-grained lens and look solely at the singular attributes of the Cyber Left, it is difficult to make out a coherent logic of contemporary movement actors and institutions. Taken together, however, the three core dynamics of the Cyber Left—strategy, structure, and governance—form a discernable pattern of action, captured by the desire to build a new world order without hierarchy or entrenched forms of power. Before elaborating on this governing worldview of the Cyber Left, I want to place it in a broader historical context, revisiting the premise that there is a distinctive logic in each period of left-based social movements. John Patrick Diggins (1992) contends that "in attempting to articulate their visionary ideals, and thereby negate the accepted view of reality, different American Lefts have displayed different intellectual temperaments" (41). His argument that different generations have distinctive political dispositions offers a framework for understanding how the singular dynamics of the Cyber Left come together to create a political praxis of contemporary social-movement organizations and actors. As a way to focus on this broader political praxis, I use the concept of the Cyber Left's *cultural logic of resistance*. Along these lines, I argue that the Cyber Left cultural logic of resistance is defined by a desire to build a movement, and ideally a world, without hierarchy. Theorists have described this as a preference for flat or horizontal structures. This logic of horizontality is clearly present in the strategy, structure, and governance of the Cyber

Left, as each of these aspects of contemporary movements is marked by an aspiration to create open, flat, non-hierarchical arrangements.

The concept of a "cultural logic" comes from Fredric Jameson's *Postmodernism, or the Cultural Logic of Late Capitalism* (1991). Jameson argues that the shift toward a global, multinational form of capitalism, and the material outcomes of this shift, have led to a dominant logic of art, culture, and self that prioritizes fragmentation, individuation, flexibility, and decentralization: in short, the postmodern. Thus, while many theorists see the shift from the modern to the postmodern as a new cultural episteme, driven by breakthroughs in art and philosophy, Jameson argues that the new postmodern logic is driven by the shifting nature of social life under late capitalism. Following this, Jeffrey Juris (2008) adapted the concept in his study of contemporary social movements and activists. Juris explains, "I employ the term 'cultural logic of networking' as a way to conceive the broad guiding principles, shaped by the logic of informational capitalism that are internalized by activists and generate concrete networking practices" (11). For Jameson and Juris, culture and ways of perceiving and understanding the world, or particular historical logics, are linked to underlying material processes. Building on this work, this book focuses on describing and analyzing the dominant processes and practices of contemporary social movements, recognizing that they are more than a random bundle of characteristics, but instead form the outline of a new logic tied to global capitalism, the logic of the Cyber Left.

Party Like It's 1999: Toward a Critique of the Cyber Left

A last contribution of this study is that it aims to go beyond description of the characteristics of contemporary social movements and the Cyber Left to analyze this contemporary social formation. As Juris argues, the cultural logic of networking taken up by contemporary activists comes as a result of an internalized logic of informational capitalism. While I agree with Juris that there is a relationship between the decentralized, flexible logic of informational capitalism and the praxis of activists, this statement and its repercussions demand attention and elaboration. If Cyber Left organizations and actors aim to challenge capitalism, while at the same time being shaped by an internalized, ostensibly involuntary logic of capitalism, this requires that social-movement scholars critically examine this logic.

Unfortunately, the majority of scholars that undertake research on contemporary social movements uncritically celebrate this prevailing logic of horizontality as a deeply democratic form of movement building.[28] Of course, these romantic visions of painless social change and deeply egalitarian movements and societies are intoxicating, but as scholars we must interrogate the strategy of contemporary social movements to understand the problems or limitations. As Lenin once argued in surveying the German left, "It is obvious that the 'Lefts' in Germany have mistaken *their desire,* their politico-ideological attitude, for objective reality. That is a most dangerous mistake for revolutionaries to make" (1975, 570). I cite Lenin here because he cautions against confusing desire for fact, and thus foregrounds the obligation of scholars and activists to critically analyze not only political presumptions but also the effectiveness of contemporary movements. This book builds on the growing work of social-movement scholars by creating a rubric for understanding the contemporary logic of resistance, while also focusing on the limitations and pitfalls of this logic. Ultimately, I argue that the cultural logic of horizontality offers important breakthroughs in social-movement organizing, while playing into and arguably re-creating the fragmentation and social isolation it aims to dismantle. This is exemplified by the period after the Battle of Seattle, which marked the crest of a wave for the Global Social Justice Movement.

Building on the unexpected yet successful challenge to the WTO, a growing tide of activists and movement leaders were committed to challenging what they saw as the undemocratic, inhumane world developing underneath the "invisible hand" of global capitalism. In the months after Seattle, in protests across the United States and Europe, energy grew, and it became clear that the industrialized nations were witnessing a sharp uptick in the cycle of protest, which is best understood as "a phase of heightened conflict across the social system: with a rapid diffusion of collective action from more mobilized to less mobilized sectors" (Tarrow 1998, 142). More than ten years later, however, this exuberance has waned. The Global Social Justice Movement has faltered, with many of its central institutions, from People's Global Action and Reclaim the Streets to indymedia and the World Social Forum, in decline and, more importantly, many of the movements' demands unmet. If we are to assess the contemporary logic and general efficacy of the Cyber Left, it is necessary to reckon with this failing. I argue that the decline of the Global Social Justice Movement and this period of protest is directly tied to the Cyber Left's logic of resistance and has four main interrelated causes, which I enumerate and discuss below:

1. Lack of leadership from those most oppressed,
2. A deterministic understanding and use of technology,

3. An inability to make proactive decisions and build long-term powerful social-movement organizations,
4. Lack of a shared strategy and political-education program to build
   clear and committed leaders.

While there is growing literature on new transnational social movements, the literature has an uneasy relationship to questions of class and capitalism. Movement theorists and activists discuss and often critique capitalism; however, the material outcomes and correspondent social relations, or class relations, that emerge with a capitalist mode of production are largely left untouched. Correspondingly, the concept of who is worst off in society and why, and the different roles social forces play in social change, is not a central part of the analysis or strategy of Cyber Left institutions. This lack of grounded socioeconomic analysis becomes particularly poignant when we discuss the rise of the Global Social Justice Movement and the logic of resistance, which is built around practices that demand access to and knowledge of new technologies, as well as the ability to travel, speak in multiple languages, and/or endure long, unpaid meetings. These practices tend to favor individuals with a high degree of social and cultural capital. The outcome, as my research on the indymedia movement in the United States corroborates, is that white, male, middle-class activists largely lead the Cyber Left. Moreover, Cyber Left institutions in the United States are consistently unsuccessful in building leadership and representation from the poor and working class, people of color, and women. This question of composition and who leads ultimately becomes the determining factor in the goals, aims, and role of the Cyber Left.

Along these lines, in an attempt to distinguish between the different social classes or forces within left-based social movements, Peter Marcuse (2009) offers a distinction between those people deprived of immediate needs and those people discontented by the social relations of a society dominated by the logic of capital accumulation:

> The demand comes from those directly in want, directly oppressed, those for whom even their most immediate needs are not fulfilled: the homeless, the hungry, the imprisoned, the persecuted on gender, religious, racial grounds. It is an involuntary demand, those whose work injures their health, those whose income is below subsistence. The cry comes from the aspiration of those superficially integrated into the system and sharing in its material benefits, but constrained in their opportunities for creative activity, oppressed in their social relationships, guilty perhaps for an undeserved prosperity, unfulfilled in their lives' hopes. . . . For both, their one-dimensionality eats away at their humanity, and from the same source, but it does it in different ways. (190)

While the distinction between deprived and discontented is not ideal, and there is a great deal of overlap between these two groups, the dichotomy Marcuse draws is useful in offering a window onto the composition and goals of the Cyber Left. Marcuse makes two interconnected points. The first is that those most materially oppressed by capitalism (the deprived) and those alienated by the terms and conditions of capitalist society (the discontented) have different dispositions and relationships to capitalist society. The deprived aim to get their immediate needs fulfilled and challenge capitalism on the basis of material inequality and oppression. The discontented, however, have their material needs met, as they are integrated into the system, and therefore their challenge to capitalist society occurs on ideological grounds around issues of freedom, power, and the fulfillment of self—issues that revolve around the logic of horizontality discussed above. Because members of the deprived and discontented build movements that challenge capitalism from a different societal positioning, they bring forth different interests, strategies, and goals. I argue throughout this book that Cyber Left institutions, which are driven almost exclusively by the discontented middle class, develop organizations and a political vision that is largely disconnected from the vast poor and working class of the United States, and therefore they are not able to build common struggle. This leads to isolated networks of resistance that cannot claim to represent the mass of humanity because of their composition, ideology, and aim.

Connected to the question of class and composition of movements, a second problem for the Cyber Left is the role of technology in social change. Throughout my research, the consistent concern for members of indymedia is that technology, and new-media tools specifically, have become more important than social relationships, organizing, or movement building. In this sense, members of indymedia place a premium on building Web sites and creating innovative software coding, but they are less focused on building strong, integrated local Independent Media Centers. While this tendency has facilitated the development of groundbreaking new media platforms, such as open-publishing Web sites and social-networking tools, it has taken the focus away from building movements on the ground that are connected through social relationships, trust, and traditional organizing models. This underlying tendency toward technological solutions results in a form of technological determinism that emerges, again, because of the societal positioning and interests of those that make up the Cyber Left: the discontented. Instead of harnessing technology as a critical element in the material struggles of everyday life, members of the Cyber Left tend to lift technology out of social context, and the technology itself becomes the instrument of change.

A third problem of the Cyber Left is organizational. Cyber Left activists do not ask, what do we want to achieve, and therefore what is the most appropriate organizational form? Instead, they begin with creating an idealized organizational infrastructure, with the belief that through building the "correct" social structures within movements, society will change. Along these lines, Cyber Left institutions are networked, decentralized, and, as per the logic of horizontality, attempt to have flat, egalitarian decision-making structures, which mirror, or prefigure, the society Cyber Left actors aim to build. The result is that most Cyber Left institutions have weak organizational structures with little collective decision-making power because they have dismissed, a priori, centralized power and structures of accountability and leadership of any kind. The weak network structure compels organizations to prioritize local autonomous collectives over shared infrastructure and collective sovereignty, consequently not allowing for network-wide, proactive decision making within institutions. Ultimately, the flat, decentralized organizational structure leads to weak networks, an inability to make proactive decisions, and ultimately unsustainable social-movement institutions. The limitations of these organizations are illustrated by the fact that the central Cyber Left institutions have collapsed in ten short years and, moreover, by the fact that some activists celebrate these collapses as necessary to avoid entrenched bureaucracy.

A final overlapping problem within Cyber Left institutions is a lack of political education and leadership development. This deficiency is an outgrowth of the embrace of "leaderless" movements, and the outcome is that movements and movement institutions do not develop programs to help build the capacity, skills, and understanding of activists and organizers in the movement. This becomes a problem for the long-term sustainability of movements because, as scholar Marshall Ganz (2009) and movement organizer Willie Baptist (2009) both detail, the foundation of strong, lasting social movements is a leadership-development program that builds the skills of organizers and activists. Moreover, without leadership-development programs, movements and movement institutions tend to favor individuals with higher levels of social and cultural capital.

1

The EZLN and Indymedia

"One No, Many Yeses"

We will make a network of communication among all our
struggles and resistances. An intercontinental network
of alternative communication against neoliberalism, an
intercontinental network of alternative communication for
humanity. This intercontinental network of alternative communication will search to weave the channels so that words
may travel all the paths that resist. This intercontinental
network of alternative communication will be the medium by
which distinct resistances communicate with one another.

—Closing words of the Zapatista Army of National
Liberation (EZLN) at the Intercontinental
Encounter of La Realidad, 1996

Crucial Connections: NAFTA
and Indigenous Resistance

While the indymedia movement materialized on the streets of Seattle amid
clouds of tear gas and columns of brightly dressed protestors, the seeds were
sown three thousand miles to the south in the verdant rainforests of Chiapas,
Mexico, in 1994. As the political and economic elite of the United States,
Canada, and Mexico inaugurated the North American Free Trade Agreement, an army of masked guerillas from the Zapatista Army of National
Liberation (EZLN)[1] declared the birth of a new Mexican revolution. The
ensuing encounter between the indigenous army and the Mexican state, and
in particular the EZLN's flexible adaptation to modern warfare, has rewritten
the common story of twentieth-century revolution, leading to new strategies
and dynamics of social struggle. In this chapter, I look at the roots of the

Zapatista uprising in Chiapas to illustrate how it laid the foundation for the indymedia movement and other Cyber Left institutions.

In conjunction with the EZLN's bold and desperate declaration of war, their army swept through southern Mexico, seizing the capital of Chiapas, as well as local seats of government and some five hundred ranches throughout much of the state. The timing of the revolt was deliberate, because as a Zapatista communiqué declared, NAFTA was a "death sentence" for the indigenous communities of Chiapas. In concert with the attack, the Zapatistas began an enduring flirtation with the media, releasing a series of "Declarations of the Lacandon Jungle," while broadcasting their message from the captured Ocosingo radio station XOECH (Collier 1999). While communication operations were key to the uprising, the initial mission was military: at the outset, the EZLN threatened to "advance to the capital of the country" and "fight until the basic demands of the people have been met by developing a government of the country that is free and democratic" (Marcos 2001, 14–15). The EZLN strategy was to fight the "War of the Flea,"[2] which combines centralized strategic control with decentralized tactical operations, allowing for a flexible, mobile guerilla war modeled on Mao Zedong's successful military operations in China.

On the way to Mexico City and the seat of state power, the Zapatistas faced the harsh realities of combat with the well-funded, powerful Mexican army. The initial conflict between the Mexican army and the Zapatistas lasted ten days and cost hundreds of lives while displacing thousands of indigenous people throughout the southernmost state of Mexico. Overmatched by the weapons of the Mexican military, the EZLN shifted military tactics, broke into smaller units, and carried out a swift retreat into the mountains of southeastern Chiapas.[3] The Mexican army pursued the EZLN, with the intent of wiping out the indigenous uprising.

In this moment of crisis, EZLN leadership was forced to adapt their military strategy yet again, employing old- and new-media tools in an effort to make their case and mobilize the Mexican and global communities. News of the massive bloodshed in Chiapas and the first EZLN communiqué quickly reached a growing network of Non-Governmental Organizations (NGOs), NAFTA opponents, and human-rights activists. With the increased visibility of the struggle, this preexisting network began to support the cause of the Zapatistas and organized to stop the conflict. The activation of NGO leaders and human-rights activists, as well as a quickly shifting popular sentiment in favor of the EZLN (Cleaver 1998b) led to a negotiated ceasefire between the two sides on January 12, 1994. The ceasefire in turn led to the San Andreas Accords, a peace agreement between the EZLN and the Mexican government, reached in February 1996.

With the armistice between the government and the EZLN came the second and more enduring phase of the war, the "war of the word." As the Mexican foreign minister Jose Angel Gurria observed, "Chiapas . . . is a place where there has not been a shot fired in the last fifteen months. . . . The shots lasted ten days, and ever since the war has been a war of ink, of written word, a war on the Internet" (qtd. in Ronfeldt and Arquilla 1998, 69–70). In parallel fashion, after the initial conflict, the EZLN spokesperson Subcomandante Marcos portrayed the entire uprising as a matter of communication: "We rose up, not to kill or be killed, but so that they would listen to us" (Marcos 2001, 427). Similarly, a characteristically lyrical EZLN communiqué noted, "in order for them to see us, we covered our faces" (Marcos 2001, 115).

The mediated nature of the conflict in Chiapas, and in particular the multivalent, innovative approach of the EZLN, led the Mayan movement to gain a great deal of notoriety and scrutiny. In the years to follow, scholars and commentators endeavored to pin down the EZLN and this unfamiliar style of resistance. Consider some of the colorful descriptions that emerged: The EZLN is the first "postmodern revolutionary movement" (Burbach 2001, 116), the world's "first informational guerrilla movement" (Castells 1996, 79), the first "successful netwar" (Ronfeldt and Arquilla 1998, 1), the "hinge between the old guerilla model and the new model of biopolitical network structures" (Hardt and Negri 2004, 85), and the exemplification of a "new electronic fabric of struggle" (Cleaver 1998b, 81). While each characterization captures a different aspect of the Zapatista army, they all identify a distinct informational, fin-de-siècle quality within this indigenous revolutionary formation.

Giving voice to this sentiment of novelty, the renowned novelist and Mexican public intellectual Carlos Fuentes (1994) observed, "Many people with cloudy minds in Mexico responded to what happened in Chiapas by saying: 'Here we go again, these rebels are part of the old Sandinista-Castroite-Marxist-Leninist legacy. Is that what we want for Mexico?' The rebels proved exactly the contrary: Rather than the last rebellion of that type, this was the first post-communist rebellion in Latin America" (56). While Fuentes and others raise important points about the innovative strategy of the EZLN, the rich history of the movement suggests that a rush to emphasize originality is only partly right. The origins of the EZLN were in fact far more interesting, involving a sort of ethnographic encounter between Marxists and indigenous people, which led to a flexible, shifting model of resistance. Thus, while the focus on the innovation has uncovered important contributions the EZLN has made to contemporary social movements, from the use of communications networks and the development of autonomous zones to an authentic democratic process, the work has largely missed the flexible, dialectical nature of EZLN strategy and therefore failed to recognize the myriad problems of transporting the political praxis of the Zapatistas outside of Chiapas.

To complicate this romanticized embrace of EZLN influence, I focus on the conditions within Mexico that led to the EZLN's political praxis. I argue that the revolutionary strategy of the EZLN was shaped through the social and economic conditions of the region as well as a series of confrontations between Marxist revolutionaries, Mayans, and eventually the Mexican state. To this end, I look at the political economy of Chiapas, which set the stage for the conflict, as well as the layered practices of Mayan society and the rich history of revolution in Latin America, which were all central features in the development of the EZLN. Following this, I look at the material and ideological connections between the EZLN and leaders of indymedia, which led to the formation of the independent communications network in 1999. I then break down the distinct dynamics of the Zapatista theory of social change, Zapatismo, from the application of direct democracy and the focus on networked organizational structures to the use of media and communications in struggle. My central contention in this chapter is that Zapatismo, as a political strategy, emerged dialectically, through a series of confrontations, and was and is a fluid response to material conditions of struggle in Mexico. Flexibility characterizes Zapatismo as much as any of the specific components of their political praxis.

Chiapas: The Roots of the Revolution

Chiapas is a stunning place, marked by the splendors of a prosperous, fertile land with vast economic and cultural wealth. It is also marked by the extreme contradictions of the Mexican economy, which extracts capital and resources from the region while leaving the people and communities in a state of gross underdevelopment.[4]

Sitting on 3.8 percent of the land surface and containing less than 5 percent of the population (approximately 3.5 million people), the economic resources of Chiapas are dramatic in comparison with the other states of Mexico. Chiapas produces over 50 percent of the country's hydroelectric power, and it is the second largest producer of petroleum, with sizeable reserves of gas and oil. It is the largest exporter of coffee, the third largest producer of corn, the fifth biggest cattle producer, and among the top three producers in tobacco, bananas, soy, cacao, and lumber (Burbach 1996; Collier 1999). Chiapas is adjacent to and sits on a massive untapped oil reserve, and the diversity of the biological species in the Lacandon jungle is potentially a vital resource for biotechnology and correspondingly a massive source of future wealth.[5]

This remarkable wealth is only outpaced by the state's abject poverty, particularly in the indigenous Mayan communities. As the anthropologist George Collier (1999) explains, "Chiapas is almost an internal colony for the rest of Mexico. . . . Chiapas is aptly described as 'a rich land, a poor people'" (16). Chiapas has the worst indices of poverty and marginalization of all of Mexico's thirty-one states. Approximately three quarters of Chiapas residents are malnourished, half live on earthen floors, and 19 percent of the working population receives no income, while another 40 percent receives less then Mexico's minimum wage, which was approximately three dollars a day at the time of the Zapatista revolt. The infant mortality rate, at 54.7 per thousand, is the highest in the country, and approximately 30 percent of children do not go to school (Burbach 1996, 39).

These statistics are reinforced by Collier's research on agrarian changes in highland Chiapas. During three decades of research, he "saw a gap grow ever wider between the wealthy that were able to infuse their farming with cash derived from wage work . . . and the poor, who are finding it increasingly impossible to be able to afford to farm even their own land" (Collier 1999, 9). The Zapatistas describe the situation as the "two Mexicos"—the wealthy, culturally diverse, and colorful "first-world" Mexico that the government trumpets, and the extreme economically impoverished "third-world" Mexico, which defines the concrete existence of a large part of the population (Katzenberger 1995).

This intense variation in conditions, as well as a rich history of political organizing, played a central role in mobilizing the Mayans of southeastern Mexico and propelling them onto the path of revolt. More immediately, the spark was the political and economic restructuring that came in the form of new trade-liberalization and privatization policies, which President Carlos Salinas carried out through the 1980s and 1990s. This process was punctuated by a policy of land reform in 1992 and NAFTA in 1994.

Neoliberal Restructuring and the Response of the Dispossessed

In 1992, President Salinas modified Article 27 of the Mexican Constitution, ending the country's long-standing commitment to communal land holdings. One of the fruits of the 1917 revolution, Article 27 established a system of communally held lands across Mexico. The system included a process whereby landless farmers could petition the government to appropriate land for communal use. This communally held land, called *ejidos,* was often passed down through generations and could not be sold. The ejido structure was critical in guaranteeing that landless peasants could make a living. The land reform of 1992 in effect stated that there was no more land to distribute to the landless, while privatizing the already existing communally held land, ending the ejido system altogether.[6] Critics of the land reform argued that the modification of Article 27 was "the death knell of the peasantry" (Collier 1999, 88), threatening the survival of small subsistence farmers and entire indigenous communities (Holloway and Peláez 1998, 6; Hayden 2002). Many commentators argue that there is a direct causal link between the eradication of communal land holdings and the dramatic growth in the size and strength of the EZLN (Holloway and Peláez 1998; Collier 1999).

Two years later, following on the heels of the agrarian reform of 1992, the Mexican government, along with the United States and Canada, ratified the North American Free Trade Agreement. The intent of NAFTA was to promote free trade across the continent. For the largely indigenous farming communities of Mexico, however, NAFTA opened the Mexican market to mass-produced, subsidized, genetically modified corn from the U.S. farming industry. The Zapatistas foresaw the eventual outcome of NAFTA. Due to the trade imbalance between the countries, created by billions of dollars in yearly subsidies for U.S. corn, Mexican farmers would not be able to compete with American agribusiness, and ultimately millions of people who made their living off the land would suffer drastic reductions in income and living standards. This would lead to massive internal displacement, driving farmers into urban areas for work and ultimately leading to massive urban impoverishment. The scholarship on NAFTA and the larger neoliberal restructuring of Mexico supports this outlook, as between 1980 and 2002, internal migration within Mexico grew a staggering 352 percent (Meré 2007).

The Zapatistas recognized the impending results of the economic restructuring, which compounded an already dire situation for indigenous people in Chiapas. For this reason, members of the EZLN decided to rise up before they were pushed off their land or died of starvation. As the circumstances suggest, the revolt in Chiapas emerged first and foremost because of the structural conditions in the country. The deep poverty and inequality in Mexico and the lack of genuine political structures to address these conditions was the main cause of the Zapatista uprising, as members of the EZLN attest. Consider the testimony of Captain Irma of the EZLN, a twenty-two-year-old Ch'ol from the Chiapas highlands: "I fight because we have nothing, neither lands, schools nor hospitals. The land isn't sufficient for the crops.

We need training to work at other jobs, since if we're not trained well, what are we going to live from without land? . . . The government can say that it's kept all its promises, that it has helped, but those are only words" (qtd. in Katzenberger 1995, 37–38). Lieutenant Elena, an eighteen-year-old Tzeltal member of the medical corps of the EZLN, states: "People in my family have died for lack of medicine. It was poverty, which made me join the Zapatista Army. We used to harvest coffee, but they won't pay us what it's worth, and then if we want to transport our harvest, we have no road, and it's very hard to carry the load. My younger brother died not long ago—we can't get the ill past the military checkpoints" (qtd. in Katzenberger 1995, 38). While the structural conditions in Chiapas led to the conflict, the plight of the EZLN resonated across the globe. The life-and-death circumstances of the Mayans epitomized the dire conditions oppressed people throughout the world were facing under trade-liberalization policies that had emerged since the 1980s (Harvey 1991 and 2005; Davis 2005; Robinson 2004).

In *Globalization and Its Discontents* (2002), Joseph Stiglitz, onetime chief economist and senior vice president for development economics at the World Bank, discussed the worsening conditions of poor and working people in Mexico and across the world in the 1990s: "Despite repeated promises of poverty reduction made over the last decade of the twentieth century, the actual number of people living in poverty has actually increased by almost 100 million. This occurred at the same time that the total world income actually increased by an average of 2.5 percent annually" (5). Stiglitz's assertion is supported by research that shows that for the last twenty years of the twentieth century, income inequality has been increasing. According to a United Nations World Development Report on global poverty published in 2000, 2.8 billion, or almost 45 percent of the world population, survives on two dollars per day, while 1.2 billion, or 20 percent, lives on one dollar per day or less. The same report stated: "The statistics are shaming: more than 13 million children have died through diarrhoeal disease in the past decade. Each year over half a million women, one for every minute of the day, die in pregnancy and childbirth. More than 800 million suffer from malnutrition." In addition, the report asserted the following: "For many countries the 1990s were a decade of despair. Some 54 countries are poorer now than in 1990. In 21, a larger proportion is going hungry. In 14, more children are dying before the age of five. In 12, primary school enrollments are shrinking. In 34, life expectancy has fallen. Such reversals in survival were previously rare" (qtd. in Elliott 2001).

Global economic indicators show that a greater number of people in developed and developing countries—a quarter of the world's population, by

Mike Davis's research (2005)—are slipping into the position of a global sub-proletariat not worthy of economic exploitation but rather left to fight and die within the informal economy and growing shadow state. These grave conditions, in Chiapas and across the world, have forged a growing and increasingly desperate class of deprived people. Because of specific economic circumstances and a history of organizing in southern Mexico, the Mayan peasants recognized their shared conditions and collective interest and were one of the first movements in this period to rise up, declaring war in order to see, as they put it, "another world, an honest world, a world decidedly more fair than the one we live in now" (Marcos 2001).

While the material conditions of Chiapas were a necessary precursor for the uprising, two confrontations help to clarify Zapatismo. The first of these came in the convergence between urban Marxist revolutionaries and the Mayans of southern Mexico, which ultimately resulted in the formation of the EZLN. The second was the confrontation between the Zapatista army and the Mexican military and the intermediary role of an empowered, networked, digitized civil society. Out of these clashes a new model of struggle was born, one that prefigured the Cyber Left and was able to incorporate Marxist and Mayan roots, and put the superior Mexican state on the defensive through the use of media-driven practices not possible in earlier stages in history, tapping communications infrastructures never before utilized.

The Emergence of the EZLN:
Marxist and Mayan Roots

By many accounts, the EZLN was born when a group of six urban Marxist revolutionaries, including the now famous spokesperson Subcomandante Marcos, fled the urban revolutionary projects of Mexico and El Salvador and retreated to the mountains of Chiapas, setting up the Emiliano Zapata Guerilla Nucleus in late 1983. The group chose southeastern Mexico as a base of operations because it was the poorest state in Mexico, and because it was an area where there was a vibrant history of guerilla activity as well as a network of liberation theologians and peasant organizations that paved the way for a militant movement (Marcos 2003).

Influenced by classic models of revolution, the Marxist revolutionaries cut their teeth as members of the National Liberation Front (FLN)[7] of Mexico and the Farabundo Martí National Liberation (FMLN) of El Salvador.[8] As these movements came under siege in the 1980s, the group journeyed to Chiapas. They traveled to southernmost Mexico armed with theories and doctrines of peasant and proletarian-based revolution developed across the century by figures like Lenin, Mao Zedong, and Che Guevara. Using the Cuban Revolution as a model, the aim was to create an army of guerilla fighters that would materialize from the jungle and capture the Mexican state (Lorenzano 1998).

As the members of the Emiliano Zapata Guerilla Nucleus began to organize in Chiapas, they quickly faced the unexpected realities of social struggle in Chiapas and were forced to loosen their grip on revolutionary dogma. Marcos explains this shift in thinking:

> We came to the forest like a classic revolutionary elite in search of a subject—the proletariat in the classic Marxist-Leninist sense. But the initial approach was not adequate to deal with the reality of the indigenous communities. They have a different substratum, a complex history of uprisings and resistances. So we modified our approach "interactively." There is a "before" and "after" of the Zapatista movement in relation to 1994. The EZLN was not born from approaches deriving exclusively from the indigenous communities. It was created out of a mixture, a Molotov cocktail, out of a culture shock, which then went on to produce a new discourse, a mestizo movement that is critical and emancipatory. (Mantalbán 2002, 476).

For ten years after the establishment of the Emiliano Zapata Guerilla Nucleus, the Marxists and Mayans began to build trust, which was the foundation of the EZLN. This "mestizo" movement that emerged was specifically a synthesis of traditional Mayan culture and Marxist praxis. The urban revolutionaries brought an understanding of global capitalism and a vibrant history of revolution across the twentieth century. Meanwhile, the Mayans brought a base of dispossessed people with a vested interest in change as well as a sense of community and tradition. Consequently, the Mayans began to instruct the Marxists on dialogue, patience, and community, infusing democratic processes into the hierarchical party/military structures of past revolutions.

The confrontation between the "traditional" and "modern" produced a potent combination, and the EZLN began to develop a road map for long-term social change in Mexico and beyond. Again I turn to Marcos to account for this new formation: "We did not propose it. The only thing that we proposed to do was change the world; everything else has been improvisation. Our square conception of the world and of revolution was badly dented in confrontation with the indigenous realities of Chiapas. Out of those blows, something new (which does not necessarily mean 'good') emerged, that which today is known as 'neo-Zapatismo'" (qtd. in Lorenzano 1998, 126). The resulting Zapatista army, then, was not a classic foco-based guerilla vanguard, nor was it a "traditional" indigenous uprising, nor even "post-communist" or "postmodern." It was a community/class in revolt against global capitalism and the Mexican state, placing the locus of the rebellion in the oppressed people of Chiapas. This shift transformed revolutionary struggle in Latin America, moving away from a tight-knit group of guerillas to a community in revolt, opening the possibility of mass resistance. This convergence led to many of the core attributes of later Cyber Left movements, from the notion of participatory democracy to the focus on neoliberalism and the flexible strategy of movement building. The Zapatistas' new vision of the role of communications in struggle, however, came in the next conflict with the Mexican state.

From Mao to Marcos

The Marxist/Mayan synthesis that cultivated the EZLN led directly to the 1994 conflict with the Mexican state. The first Zapatista communiqué was entitled, "War! First Declaration from the Lacandon Jungle." In this appeal to Mexico and the world, the Zapatistas made their case for the uprising in Chiapas:

> We have nothing to lose, absolutely nothing, no decent roof over our heads, no land, no work, poor health, no food, no education, no right to freely and democratically choose our leaders, no independence from foreign interests, and no justice for ourselves or our children. But today we say ENOUGH is ENOUGH! We are the descendants of those who truly built this nation, we are the millions of dispossessed, and we call upon our brothers to join our crusade, the only option to avoid dying of starvation. (Qtd. in Marcos 2003, 643)

A later communiqué added, "We were invisible to you for 500 years, 500 years of looting by the beast, 500 years of two Mexicos—one Mexico which produces wealth, another which appropriates that wealth."[9]

The original objective of the uprising was to rally the country to the side of the EZLN and capture the state through armed uprising. The aim was to take power. However, in the early stages of the insurrection, the Zapatistas realized that the superior force of the Mexican army overmatched them. Additionally, they had not successfully called the poor of the country into an armed uprising. This left the EZLN in a vulnerable situation, as the Mexican army had the military power to violently repress the Zapatista army.

In this moment of crisis, the Zapatistas and their sympathizers turned to new media and the support of transnational activist networks to "get the word out," utilizing listservs and networks to rally support for their situation. As Ronfeldt and Arquilla (1998) explain regarding the early stages of the conflict: "During the few days that the EZLN held ground, it upstaged the government. Through star-quality spokesman 'Subcomandante Marcos' in particular . . . it insisted its roots were indigenous and its demands national in scope. . . . It appealed to nationwide support for its agenda" (2).

In an effort to elaborate on the differing posture and tactics between the Mexican state and the EZLN, Ronfeldt and Arquilla continue: "EZLN's media-savvy behavior and the Mexican government's heavy handed response quickly aroused a multitude of foreign activists associated with human rights, indigenous rights, and other types of nongovernmental organizations" (1998, 3). In the first days of the conflict, the EZLN called a press conference, urging the Red Cross and other international observers to come to Mexico. Playing on the iridescent quality that has made the Zapatistas successful, the EZLN leadership quickly declared that they were not a Marxist revolution bent on taking power but an indigenous movement concerned with human rights and democracy. Conversely, during the same period, the Mexican army was accused of human-rights abuses throughout Chiapas, and the PRI-led government exacerbated the problem by stopping journalists from entering Chiapas in an effort to control the flow of information.

Thus, while the EZLN was courting "civil society" through the mass media, the Mexican government came across as heavy-handed, leading to what one observer called a "CNN effect," where the views and positions of the EZLN received a great deal of favorable attention in the mass media (qtd. in Ronfeldt and Arquilla 1998, 51). The differing postures and tactics between the Mexican state and the EZLN "quickly aroused a multitude of foreign activists associated with human rights, indigenous rights and other types of nongovernmental organizations" (3).

The NGO Network Model Develops

As the situation in Chiapas deteriorated, a network of activists from NGOs across Mexico, the United States, and Canada descended on Mexico City and San Cristóbal de las Casas, opposing the conflict and building links with leaders of the EZLN. The confluence of activists and NGO leaders developed a pro-democracy movement in the shadow of the conflict, holding peace caravans through Chiapas and organizing rallies throughout Mexico and at Mexican Consulates in the United States and Canada. Over time, this group of NGO leaders and activists began to organize themselves, holding press conferences while developing a list of demands, which hued closely to the demands of the EZLN, with the additional call for an immediate ceasefire and a condemnation of violence. Emerging as an important third party in the conflict between the EZLN and the state (Ronfeldt and Arquilla 1998), the activists and NGO leaders saw themselves as cultivating a new model of activism based on harnessing intricate computer-mediated networks, connecting people, and inspiring action on- and offline.

At first, leaders of this nexus of NGOs utilized preexisting circuits of communication that were developed through a rigorous organizing process that started in the 1990s and linked NGOs and citizens across Mexico.[10] These online networks cohered to support anti-NAFTA organizing, as well as the indigenous rights organizations based in the region and globally (Collier 1994; Cleaver 1998a).

Over time, a computer-mediated social network developed specifically around the Zapatistas and the situation in Chiapas. Through listservs and archives, people shared information, read statements from the Zapatistas, and organized around the conflict (Cleaver 1998a). Through this social/computer-mediated network, the EZLN garnered unparalleled presence on the Web, which enabled the movement to endure future onslaughts from the Mexican army (Ronfeldt and Arquilla 1996). It became clear in this process that the key to this form of organizing was the free flow of information, a communications infrastructure that was fast and wide-ranging, and a social network that was poised to take advantage of these tools. The embrace of new media by the informal EZLN support network was distinctive precisely because it occurred alongside the rise of the Internet and digital technologies. In this sense, the informational technologies that enabled NAFTA and other globalizing economic trends also facilitated the shift in strategy by this Marxist-Mayan movement.

Going Global: Building a Network of Struggle

In the years following the initial conflict, the Zapatistas and the struggle in Chiapas dominated the political landscape of Mexico, but the impact of this conflict reached far beyond the borders of Mexico. The EZLN became an international cause célèbre, cultivating networks of support while inspiring movements across the world.[11] Channeling this newfound attention, and heralding what they believed was the coming of a new global wave of resistance, in 1996 the Zapatistas sent a message to the world inviting all—"with no matter of color, race, or borders, [who] make of hope a weapon and a shield" (Zapatistas 1998, 15)—to come to Chiapas to start a global dialogue about equality, dignity, and social transformation. The weeklong Intercontinental Encounter for Humanity and against Neoliberalism, known as an *encuentro,* was attended by thousands of people from over forty-four countries. At the end of the weeklong conference, the EZLN put forward a vision that directly linked the creation of an alternative communications infrastructure to the formation of a global social movement. EZLN members appealed to encuentro attendees:

> We will make a network of communication among all our struggles and resistances. An intercontinental *network of alternative communication* against neoliberalism. This intercontinental network of alternative communication will search to weave the channels so that words may travel all the roads that resist. This intercontinental network of alternative communication will be the medium by which distinct resistances communicate with one another. (Zapatistas 1998, 53; italics added)

The core of their vision was that communications, and particularly new-media tools, should play a central role in connecting points of struggles across the world, cultivating a global social movement.

The call for an alternative communications network that could catalyze a global social movement tapped into a preexisting sentiment regarding the limitless potential of the Internet. It converged with a series of concrete, activist-led experiments that took place through the 1990s focused on harnessing new-media tools to advance social struggle, as I discuss in the next chapter. Thus, the EZLN blueprint for communications channels linking struggles and movements from Seoul to São Paulo seemed a distinct possibility and became a rallying point for organizers and activists across the globe, leading to the formation of the indymedia movement.

One of the first opportunities to build on the EZLN's 1996 proposal for a global communications network materialized in New York in 1997. Three organizations—the Learning Alliance, Paper Tiger, and Fairness and Accuracy in Reporting—organized the Freeing the Media Teach-In, which was focused on critiquing corporate media while exploring ways to strengthen progressive communication. Greg Ruggiero, a writer and activist who worked with the Mexico Solidarity Network and eventually helped organize the first Independent Media Center in Seattle in 1999, explained the planning process for the New York City–based conference. He highlighted a conversation he had with DeeDee Halleck, a professor of communications at the University of California–San Diego and longtime media activist:

> We were standing on Lafayette Street asking ourselves, "Well, who should we get to open up this gathering in New York?" And DeeDee Halleck said,

"Why don't we try to get Subcomandante Marcos?" And I thought, "Oh, that's a great idea!"—by way of video message.

. . .

So I sent a message down to Mexico . . . and Subcomandante Marcos agreed to do it. . . . We received a ten-minute message on the importance and power of independent media in movement building, and we aired this at the Freeing the Media conference of the New York Society of Ethical Culture.[12]

In the now-famous address to the Freeing the Media Teach-In, which is still cited as a foundational moment by indymedia activists, Marcos referred to the 1996 encuentro and made a direct call to his audience: "In August 1996, we called for the creation of a network of independent media, a network of information. We mean a network to resist the power of the lie that sells us this war that we call the Fourth World War. We need this network not only as a tool for our social movements, but for our lives: this is a project of life, of humanity, which has a right to critical and truthful information" (Marcos 2001, 181).

Reflecting on the impact this message had on U.S.- and Canadian-based activists, Ruggiero explained: "The link from Chiapas to New York and to the Freeing the Media movement was enormously influential; it was enormously energizing and inspiring for us; and we felt a connection, and continue to feel a connection, with the indigenous struggle in Mexico for democracy, for dignity, for autonomy, for alternative sovereign networks—and that language really shaped and directed our vision for independent media."[13] The Zapatistas gave their northern counterparts the political framework and a language that catalyzed the development of a new type of social movement that had media and communications at the core.

Marcos's appeal to U.S. and Canadian activists to build a network of independent media traveled across vast space, embedding itself in the oppositional resistance that developed in Seattle. And while indymedia was the physical embodiment of the EZLN vision, the institutions shared more than a fragile history and vaguely shared goals. Jeff Perlstein, another founder of indymedia, argued that the Zapatistas were offering "a lot of the ideological frame, a lot of input on process, and the importance of process, . . . and also a reclaiming of space and the importance of a decentralized network."[14] Here, Perlstein begins to lay out some of the core dynamics that came from the EZLN and framed the indymedia movement, from democratic process to the decentralized network formation and the use of media. These ideas became the bedrock for organizing the first independent media center.[15]

The unique characteristics of Zapatismo, as a theory of revolution, prefigured many of the structures, principles, and strategies of the indymedia movement and the broader Cyber Left: the Mayan substratum of patience and democracy; the focus on neoliberal globalization; the appropriation of new technologies for social change; the shift in organizational forms; and the strategy of creating a multiscalar movement that operated both across Mexico and globally[16] all became inherent elements of the indymedia movement.[17] To better understand how the Zapatistas influenced indymedia, it is instructive to look at the parallel governance, structure, and strategy of these movements as they laid the basis of the Cyber Left.

Zapatismo and the Cyber Left

1. STRATEGY: ONE NO, MANY YESES

In their bid to overthrow the Mexican state, the Zapatistas worked to forge unity across the different sectors of Mexican society. Their objective was to lead all dispossessed into an open battle with the dominant social forces in the country. Capturing this aim, the third EZLN communiqué, released in January 1995, reads:

> For everyone, everything, nothing for us! . . . We call upon the workers of the republic, the workers in the countryside and the cities, the neighborhood residents, the teachers and the students of Mexico, the honest artists and intellectuals, the responsible religious members, the community-based militants of the different political organizations to take up means and forms of struggle . . . incorporating themselves into the National Democratic Convention. (Qtd. in Marcos 2003, 657–58)

The central intention of the message was to call the different social forces of Mexico into one historical bloc that would fight for control of the country, exemplifying the Zapatistas' attempt to forge unity through communication.

The opening sentence of the communiqué, "For everyone, everything, nothing for us!" echoes Marx's insights on the necessity of a particular class to take leadership on behalf of all of society in "Contribution to a Critique of Philosophy of Right." In this early manuscript, Marx characterizes the generosity of spirit of a truly revolutionary class, writing, "I am Nothing and I should be Everything" (1978, 63). Explaining this outlook, Marx contrasts social movements in France and Germany. In Germany, he argues, each "class lacks the logic, insight, courage, and clarity" (63) to fight for complete human emancipation and therefore advocates only for its own material necessity, leading to isolation and fragmentation of the different classes. In France, however, each class is idealistic and believes itself to be a general representative of society and thus fights not for itself, but for complete emancipation.

Like the social classes of France, the EZLN is politically idealistic and therefore aimed to become a voice for all deprived people of Mexico, not only for Mayan peasants. From the first communiqué and throughout the EZLN conflict, the Zapatistas characterized the dispute with the Mexican government as a fight for universal emancipation. This logic is symbolically communicated as all members of the EZLN wear masks, hiding their faces and their particularities. It is also communicated through the enigmatic figure of Subcomandante Marcos, the spokesperson of the EZLN. In one of his statements, in response to an accusation that he is gay, Marcos captures the idealistic nature of EZLN political strategy:

> Marcos is gay in San Francisco, black in South Africa, an Asian in Europe, a Chicano in San Ysidro, an anarchist in Spain, a Palestinian in Israel, a Mayan Indian in the streets of San Cristobal, a gang member in Neza, a rocker in the National University, a Jew in Germany, an ombudsman in the Defense Ministry, a communist in the post–cold war era, an artist without gallery or portfolio. . . . A pacifist in Bosnia, a housewife alone on Saturday night in any neighborhood in any city in Mexico, a striker in the CTM, a reporter writing filler stories for the back pages, a single woman on the subway at 10 P.M., a peasant without land, an unemployed worker . . . an unhappy student, a dissident amid free-market economics, a writer without books or readers, and, of course, a Zapatista in the mountains of southeast Mexico. So Marcos is a human being, any human being, in this world. Marcos is all the exploited, marginalized and oppressed minorities, resisting and saying, "Enough!" ("Subcommander Marcos Is More Than Just Gay" 1994, 1)

In this communiqué, Marcos is emptied of particular meaning, standing in symbolically for all of the oppressed in Mexico and beyond.

In many ways, the indymedia network operates in a parallel fashion. The aim was to forge a communications infrastructure that allows dispersed points of struggle to speak and listen and see their commonalities across space and issue. An important point, however, is that indymedia does not see itself as representative of the "class" or community-in-creation, like the EZLN, but rather as the *medium* through which "gay[s] in San Francisco," "black[s] in South Africa," or "Palestinian[s] in Israel" come together to say "enough!" In this sense, indymedia plays its role as a *switchboard of struggle*, or a social relay bringing these different communities and antagonisms into contact to create collective understanding. The question that comes to the fore is whether or not this model can work without a group, like the EZLN, that exercises moral and political leadership. As we see in the case of indymedia, the lack of leadership makes it difficult for the movement to build proactive struggle that leads to tangible collective action.

2. ORGANIZATIONAL STRUCTURE: NETWORKS

The Mayans, Marxists, and the transnational NGOs all use networked arrangements to organize themselves. Members of the EZLN live in geographically bounded communities in southeast Chiapas called *caracoles*.[18] Caracoles ("snail" in Spanish) are the community-based structures for the EZLN. There are five caracoles across the state of Chiapas. As autonomous zones outside the Mexican governance structure, they house, educate, and care for all members of the movement within these communities. The caracoles are networked together into one larger body, which is elected and acts as the EZLN leadership or the Indigenous Revolutionary Clandestine Committee-General Command.

Correspondingly, the NGO leaders who supported the EZLN utilized computer communications to connect vast numbers of people within Mexico and beyond, using listservs and other newly developing tools, including Peacenet[19] (e.g., carnet.mexnews), the Internet (e.g., Mexico-L, Native-L, Centam-L), and Usenet (e.g., soc.culture.mexican, soc.culture.Latin-American) (Cleaver 1998a; Martin-Torres 2001). The new digital technologies facilitated a distinctive organizational network structure. As Harry Cleaver (1995) puts it, "[T]he process of alliance building has created a new organizational form—a multiplicity of rhizomatically connected autonomous groups—that is connecting all kinds of struggles throughout North America that have previously been disconnected and separate" (para. 7). Multiple autonomous organizations were linked together through a loosely shared commitment to the EZLN, the transmission of massive amounts of information, and the development of tools for online dialogue. These communication practices blurred the boundaries between the Zapatistas and their supporters, creating the building blocks of a broader movement.

Most importantly, the model worked, as the NGO network successfully interceded in the Mexican government's ability to exercise its right to *use physical force* against the EZLN. Specifically, the network did two things: (1) broadcast a message sympathetic to the Zapatistas across mass media (through *La Jornada* and other newspapers), and (2) used communications to inspire direct action in real space by mobilizing thousands of activists to converge on Mexico City and Chiapas, creating what some have called a swarm or cyberswarm.[20] Activists also posted online petitions that were made public through the press and publicized phone numbers of politicians so that people would call them directly and voice their concern over the conflict. Some parts of this spontaneously formed network became the Zapatista National Liberation Front (FZLN) in 1997. The FZLN were supporters of the EZLN, but not members of the army; they lived throughout Mexico and the world, and they were linked principally through the Internet, though they had a founding conference in Chiapas in 1997. The FZLN foreshadowed indymedia's organizational structure of a network of local collectives and individuals bound together through information and communications, as well as a loosely shared set of objectives.

3. GOVERNANCE: COMMAND-OBEYING

The final element of the Zapatista movement that became a foundation for indymedia and other Cyber Left movements has alternatively been called direct, participatory, or radical democracy. Of course, the EZLN is not the first revolutionary movement to employ direct democracy. This form of governance was employed by the workers' councils during the Russian Revolution in 1917[21] and was also the basis of the prefigurative,[22] participatory politics central to many 1960s New Left movements, such as Students for a Democratic Society.[23]

Despite these parallels, the Zapatista concept of democracy comes from centuries of Mayan tradition. The Marxist revolutionaries, who expected to develop a hierarchical army based on the principles of *focalism* and Maoism, had to accept this nonhierarchical mode of decision making if they were to build a shared movement with the people of Chiapas. Marcos relayed the spirit of this process of decision making as he explained the community's decision to go to war in 1994:

> Antonio son of Antonio returned with the minutes of the agreement that said: "Men and women and children met in the community school to look into their hearts to see whether or not it was time to initiate the war for liberty, and they divided into three groups—of women, of children, and of men—to discuss this, and then we came back together in the school, and the thinking of the majority was that the war should begin. . . . This thinking was confirmed by 12 men and 23 women and 8 children who have clear thinking and those who could sign did so and those who could not stamped their fingerprints." (Qtd. in Lorenzano 1998, 130)

Within the EZLN, direct democracy goes under the names "command-obey-ing" (*mandando obedeciendo*) and "walking while asking" (*caminando pre-guntando*).[24] The idea of command-obeying is that decision-making power accorded to leaders is revocable, and those in leadership positions serve at the will of the community, in essence obeying the community. Thus, command-obeying places the power of governance in the community. It is not a party or guerilla army in revolt, as was the case in Cuba, but rather a community in revolt. This distinction is vital, as the locus of power in this movement, at least in theory, is situated not in a military body or party hierarchy but rather in the entire polis.

While structured in a different form due to a global geographical composi-tion, indymedia and other Cyber Left organizations are deeply influenced by the EZLN's concept of direct democracy and the correspondent horizontal organizational structures. Founders of indymedia point to the EZLN's demo-cratic processes as the bedrock of indymedia and look to the practices of the EZLN for guidance. Within indymedia, however, as I discuss in chapter 4, direct democratic practice comes into conflict with local autonomy of nodes within the global network structure, which makes democracy within the movement different and arguably less effective than it is within the EZLN.

As I outlined in the introduction, the strategy, structure, and governance that emerged as elements of the EZLN ultimately became the core attri-butes of the Cyber Left's cultural logic of resistance. It is important to mark, however, that this was largely an interpretation of the Zapatista struggle by northern intellectuals. This interpretation was partly accurate, but in many ways it missed the substance of the EZLN struggle and strategy of resistance.

Zapatismo and the Problems with Making Virtue of a Necessity

In a trenchant critique of the theoretical and political misapprehension of the EZLN, the anthropologist David Nugent (1995) wrote:

> Focusing on, even celebrating, the EZLN's use of modems, fax machines, and e-mail suggests that their most distinctive feature as a political move-ment is to have shifted the object of struggle from control of the means of production to control of the means of communication; revolutionary ideals are to be advanced by the free exchange of rebel-friendly software and com-munications packages. But this way of thinking about the rebellion tends to block out the years of organizing that preceded January 1, 1994. To assert the

> fundamental "postmodernity" of the EZLN is not really to analyze "actual events" in Chiapas. It is more a way of allowing some intellectuals to appropriate these events, to situate these complex historical developments on their own (intellectual) terrain, to assimilate them to a discourse that permits computer-literate academics to feel good about themselves. (128)

While Nugent was writing on the eve of the digital revolution, and therefore seems to undervalue the role of media and communications in contemporary life and struggle, his main thrust is to challenge what he sees as a political misinterpretation or appropriation of the EZLN by northern activists and intellectuals. Running parallel to Nugent, I argue that a similar appropriation of the EZLN history has taken place within the Cyber Left and many theorists of this new form of social movement. While this appropriation of the Zapatista experience has been useful in placing communications at the core of struggle, and in offering a vision for the role of democratic governance and networked structures in contemporary social movements, the appropriation of Zapatismo by early Cyber Left institutions has ignored or misinterpreted some of the key insights of the peasant army while extending other aspects beyond useful limits.

As crystallized through the historical development of the EZLN, the key contribution of their political praxis is flexibility—flexibility that comes because of the clarity of the EZLN mission, which is grounded in the political interest of the Mayans and the entirety of the dispossessed in Mexico. The EZLN rose up and declared war because NAFTA was a death sentence to the peasantry. This focused political objective allows for tactical adaptability to respond to shifting everyday concerns in Mexico. This flexible engagement was exemplified when the EZLN negotiated and won communal autonomy—the ability to independently govern Zapatista communities—through the San Andreas Peace Accords in 1996. The decision to fight for autonomous communities, however, was not the initial goal of the EZLN but instead became an objective once the Zapatistas were unsuccessful in their bid to take state power. Autonomy was not seen as an abstract political good but instead was a tactical response to the conditions of warfare. Along these lines, the political praxis of the EZLN resembles Lenin's notion of dialectical politics. As the political theorist Robert Mayer (1999) argues: "Lenin insisted that a dialectical politics demands tactical flexibility. . . . [N]ew circumstances require new tactics, and nothing could be more undialectical than to deduce policy from fixed rules" (42).

Along these lines, the essential elements of Zapatismo are not democracy, autonomy, communications, or networks, which are the principal vectors through which the EZLN was interpreted and put into practice by indymedia and other Cyber Left institutions. Zapatismo comes from a clear political line and consequently an adaptable strategy of confrontation. These aspects of Zapatismo, however, are not apparent in indymedia and other Cyber Left institutions. So, while the political line of the EZLN is embedded in the interests of Mayans and the dispossessed of the country, there is no clear political line in indymedia and other Cyber Left institutions. The closest expression of a mission statement is the slogan "don't hate the media, be the media," and accordingly there is no shared doctrine or goal for the movement. Consequently, while Zapatismo is defined by adaptability and process, the core dynamics that were harnessed in indymedia and the Cyber Left have become "fixed rules" and orthodoxy.

To give an example, the ideal of patience and direct democracy makes sense within a Mayan movement, where it is a cultural practice that has a long history. Further, the EZLN is a geographically bounded movement, based in the rural poor communities of Chiapas. People make decisions in face-to-face meetings and often share a history, a set of traditions, and a vision of social change. Finally, this direct form of democratic decision making is fused with hierarchical, at times nondemocratic decision-making structures within the military configuration of the EZLN. In this sense, a full picture of the EZLN governance structure is variegated with horizontal and vertical decision-making structures, which were developed to most effectively represent the interests of the Zapatistas. Thus, the concept of direct democracy was part of a dynamic process in Chiapas and was not considered an a priori good but instead a response to the history of the region. However, within indymedia and across the Cyber Left, the idea of direct democracy and egalitarian structures is understood as orthodoxy or an absolute political value.

Of course, it is hard to quarrel with democratic processes in social movements. At the same time, however, the ideal of direct democracy has not worked within the context of a global social movement like indymedia, where people are attempting to make clear decisions across space, time, and language barriers. As I discuss in chapter 7, while indymedia has been able to make a few democratic decisions, especially when the organization is forced to find resolution for the sake of survival, for the most part the decision-making apparatus of the indymedia network does not facilitate proactive decision making or collective identity. In this sense, the principle of democracy plays out very differently within the EZLN than it does for a globalized, deterritorialized, movement-based institution, like indymedia, that has a thinner, more spread-out base of support. So, while theories of networked organizational structure and direct democratic governance were necessary, contextual responses to real conditions in Chiapas, they became rigid virtues within indymedia.

A similar argument about orthodoxy could be raised around the role of media and communications in movement building. The intersection between the EZLN and indymedia brings to the fore the role of media in building contemporary social movements. For both the EZLN and indymedia, communication tools have been reconsidered as constitutive of movements, playing a central role in cohering people and organizations across space and struggle. In this sense, communication technology is one of the key factors for building networks of struggle, becoming a seminal conduit that links otherwise disparate elements of the contemporary working class, facilitating the development of collective identities across autonomous movements, divergent living conditions, and vast geographies (Wolfson and Funke 2012).

However, while the Internet was key as an accelerant, getting the message out about the struggle in Chiapas and organizing networks of people throughout the world to take action, the Internet itself was not the resistance, nor the base of resistance, in Chiapas. The base of resistance came from an organized community that was in struggle because of a set of social and economic conditions. The Internet and the social networks connected to the EZLN overlay this already existing powerful social bloc and amplified the struggle in Chiapas.

In this sense, the role of media and communications in Chiapas was not fixed but rather was conceived in response to situations like the early military defeat of the EZLN, which forced the army to retreat and make an appeal to global civil society to survive. Thus, while the EZLN and indymedia have made important breakthroughs regarding the role of media and communications in struggle, as Nugent argues, the role of media and communications in struggle has been taken too far by cyber-optimists who see in new-media tools and communicative networks the unmuddied reflection of an egalitarian, democratic future (Shirkey 2008; Rheingold 1993). In reviewing the role of media in social-movement building, it is important to have a nuanced view, recognizing the possibility in new-media tools and grounding their use in the lives of communities, but not extending those possibilities too far.

Conclusion

This chapter has argued that indymedia and the Cyber Left generally understands themselves to be rooted in the Zapatista revolt and the corresponding strategies of social struggle developed in Chiapas. This adaptation of EZLN praxis has led to important insights and new ideas about the structures, strategies, and governance of social movements in the era of informational capitalism, playing a key role in the development of the Cyber Left logic of horizontality. At the same time, the interpretation of EZLN praxis by northern intellectuals and Cyber Left institutions has been partial, seizing on novelty while missing history, as well as the flexible nature of EZLN strategy. It is fair to say that this logic led to the rapid growth of Cyber Left organizations and a swift political impact. At the same time, this misapprehension of the EZLN model has led to a rigid orthodoxy about the role of democracy, networks, horizontality, and media within Cyber Left institutions, not allowing for adaptive, dynamic institutions that can effectively make long-term change.

2

Activist Laboratories
The Road to Seattle

IMC didn't just come out of nowhere. You read [about] it
everywhere from Radio Venceramos to Liberation News
Service in the sixties here in the states to the Zapatistas'
use of the Internet in '94 and since then to a project called
Counter Media. . . . So all of those—the groundwork that
they laid over the years really paved the way for the IMC
model, which was really tying all of these people all over the
country and internationally together in a network that would
be powerful and vibrant.

—Jeff Perlstein, a founder of indymedia

Activist Laboratories: Indymedia
and Its Forerunners

In the 1990s, as the Internet went public, a throng of technological utopianists
began declaring the coming of an authentic social, political, and democratic
revolution. In the reflection of instantaneous, unregulated flows of information and countless self-generating channels of communication, a growing
group of pundits saw the promise of an empowered and engaged citizenry
that could rewrite the balance of power in society. Their faith in the revolu-
tionizing potential of technology has many roots, but one important point of
origin was the perfect future world predicted by the prophets of postindustrial and informational society a few decades earlier. Led by the sociologist
Daniel Bell, postindustrial theorists in the 1970s began to forecast, evocative
of Marx, that technological advances were changing the nature of production
and cultivating a new professional class that would become the central protagonist of history. Harnessing this new postindustrial mode of production,

an emergent "creative class" would create profit through knowledge—instead of control over property or the means of production—and abandon a fixation with capital accumulation. As a matter of course, as Bell (1973) and others argued (Toffler 1970; Brezinski 1970), the technological transformation of the economy would lead to the peaceful transcendence of capitalism, rewriting a history of inequality and eliminating stark class divisions in society.

While the statistics on poverty and inequality since the postindustrial transformation belie Bell's thesis, it has not prevented a new and diverse faction of New Age seers from proclaiming that technology is once again the panacea to our sociopolitical ills. From Bill Gates and Howard Rheingold to Nicholas Negroponte and Clay Shirkey, scholars and commentators have pronounced that with the rise of the Internet, true democracy and a new, more just society are on the horizon. Their argument: with the explosion of new-media tools and other communication technologies, we are on the verge of a true democratic age, where networked organizational structures and new forms of participatory culture will correct for historical imbalances and entrenched power.

Breathing life into these quixotic visions, young, white, college-educated men across North America, Europe, and Australia flocked to the Internet in the 1990s. These computer programmers-cum-activists took to the Internet with the vision of protecting the nonhierarchical nature of this new communications medium, while harnessing its powers to support a myriad of political organizing projects. Some of these experiments developed in conversation with events in Chiapas, taking cues from the EZLN. Other projects began autonomously, as activists took advantage of this relatively cheap, accessible communication platform.

This period of experimentation with the Internet led to the creation of open Web-based forums for information and dialogue, media platforms that highlighted perspectives otherwise submerged from view, and democratic communication infrastructures that could support the creation and distribution of media and information during heightened periods of protest. The ideas, experiences, and relationships that materialized through this process led to the development of the first IMC in Seattle, while arguably playing a role in shaping the future of the Internet itself. In this regard, while the inspiration and ideological roots of indymedia came from Chiapas, northern activists translated the EZLN vision for a communications network into this new context, forging the nuts and bolts of indymedia praxis.

In this chapter I look at three of the most critical new-media projects, all of which played an important role in the birth of indymedia. I begin with

BURN!, a project initiated by undergraduates at University of California–San Diego (UCSD). BURN! launched during the initial stages of the Internet, and it was one of the first experiments where activists developed their own semi-autonomous Web-based infrastructure. BURN! technologists also created one of the first platforms for controversial groups to tell and share their political outlook, bringing forth some important lessons on the role of the Web in circulating information about political struggles across borders. Because BURN! was established early on, the site attracted high-profile militant groups such as the Revolutionary Armed Forces of Colombia (FARC) and Basque Homeland and Freedom (ETA), which led to backlash against BURN! and UCSD. The experiences and lessons of BURN! underscore many of the central questions, practices, and tensions that come up around the logic and practice of new-media activists, and for this reason it is the cornerstone of this chapter.

Following the discussion of BURN!, the chapter foregrounds the Z Media Institute (ZMI) in Cape Cod. ZMI, which still exists today, is a think tank and leadership institute for radical politics and alternative media. The cofounders of *Z Magazine* and South End Press founded ZMI in 1994 to "teach radical politics, media and organizing skills, the principles and practice of creating non-hierarchical institutions and projects, activism, and vision and strategy for social change."[1] In the mid 1990s, ZMI enrolled many of the eventual founders of indymedia, and it was at ZMI that many of the critical ideas about the importance of participatory democratic governance structures within independent media networks began to take form.

Finally, the chapter details the short history of the independent journalism project CounterMedia. CounterMedia was a temporary tactical media-convergence center established in Chicago during the 1996 Democratic National Convention. As the name suggests, the founders launched CounterMedia to challenge the bias of the corporate media's reporting of the 1996 DNC. The aim of CounterMedia was to create a physical and virtual space for the production and distribution of alternative journalism during the Chicago-based convention. The development of media-convergence centers in times of protest and the production of independent journalism took root through the CounterMedia experiment.

While I focus on BURN!, ZMI, and CounterMedia, it is important to note that in the 1990s there was a general feeling of excitement and an air of innovation regarding the possibilities of the Internet. This fertile atmosphere led to dozens of new-media projects across the United States and beyond, many of which played important roles in the development of indymedia. This includes projects like the U.S.-based Direct Action Media Network, the Tao

Collective in Toronto, Community Activist Technology in Australia, Don Hazen's Media and Democracy Conference, Geert Lovink's Next 5 Minute Festivals (N5M) in Amsterdam, and the transnational Reclaim the Streets protests that took place annually throughout the late 1990s. The breadth of projects and experiments that were taking place demonstrate the dynamism of the period, as the tools of new communication technology, which were just being realized, began to be utilized in social and political struggle.

Looking at these projects as precursors for indymedia and the Cyber Left, in this chapter I make two interrelated arguments. The first is that BURN!, ZMI, and CounterMedia, as well as other activist laboratories, were the central sites where the cultural logic of indymedia began to take shape, particularly as this logic was actualized through technology. Second, I argue that the class position of the new-media activists led to a specific understanding of resistance and, correspondingly, the role of technology in social change. Thus, while the activist laboratories of the North created critical new-media tools and open, participatory communications platforms, there was a tendency for technology itself to become the answer to social ills. This led the projects and activists to become detached from local struggles and the real material concerns of those most oppressed. The upshot is that instead of technology becoming embedded as a critical element in struggle, new-media activists tended to lift technology out of social context. In this process, the technology itself became the instrument of change, not the social appropriation of that technology by oppressed communities. This technologically deterministic tendency is one of the reasons these activist laboratories and, later, indymedia have had trouble connecting to local communities, or building long-term powerful social movements.

BURN!: Using the Web to Circulate Stories of Struggle

In April 1993, while the Internet was in its infancy, a small group of students at the University of California–San Diego launched a digital-media project to support radical political activism. The ten students in this collective—including one of the eventual founders of indymedia, Chris Burnett—were interested in the connective potential of the Internet and wanted to create a Web site that would link political struggles throughout the world. The students came together, as many of them frequented the alternative student center Che Cafe, which included Germinal, a computer lab modeled after anarchist infoshops.

As the students began the process of creating a new Web site, they quickly realized that if they wanted autonomy on the Internet, they needed a Web server[2] to host the new site. So, in true DIY style, they pieced together a couple of old computers and built their own Web server. As Chris Burnett explained, the students recognized that with a server came a greater degree of independence to create their own Web presence and support other groups in taking advantage of the Internet.[3]

After months of tinkering with the new machine, the students connected it to the university's broadband network, and one of the first radical political Web-based media projects went live. The group of student technologists dubbed the server and the Web site BURN! and dubbed themselves the BURN! collective. As the Internet had not yet emerged from its long gestation, the act of creating a Web site and building a server to host information on the Web was radical and innovative. Over time, as the students began to better understand the possibilities of the Internet, their goal was to create an independent, accessible archive for radical politics as well as a communications platform that could cultivate dialogue and disseminate information, tactics, and stories of political activism around the world.

The BURN! Web site was hosted by the UCSD communications department and supported by DeeDee Halleck, a professor in the department. Halleck was the ideal advisor, as she was a longtime documentary filmmaker and media activist. For over thirty years, Halleck was a leader in the independent media movement, helping to found projects like Paper Tiger TV in 1981 and Deep Dish TV in 1986. Like BURN!, Paper Tiger and Deep Dish utilized media tools, and specifically video, to tell stories and offer alternative perspectives otherwise hidden from view. Moreover, both projects harnessed new technologies, like satellite TV networks, to more effectively create and distribute media. In many ways, UCSD students reinterpreted the vision embodied in the work of Paper Tiger and Deep Dish in the context of the Web and the emergent information revolution.

Understanding the BURN! Model

Members of the BURN! collective saw the new Web site and server as a tool to circumvent the monopoly over information and knowledge held by corporate media. On the "About BURN!" Web page, the founders explained:

> We are working to build a society without hunger or fear, where people have real control over their own lives. Participating in this type of primary source

media instead of passively accepting what we are told by the corporate media is part of our praxis. We provide access to information so that people can make up their own minds about it. As part of our efforts in effecting radical social change, we are making radical social media by publishing primary source materials, mostly from other groups working toward radical social change.[4]

Members of the BURN! collective express their belief that free access to information is a direct challenge to corporate media's monopoly over the means of communication. Consequently, they argue that a free and open media system is a necessary ingredient to radical social change. This recognition of the central role of participatory media in the digital age is a clear precursor to the indymedia model of creating open platforms that call people into the media-making and -sharing process. Further, it captures a consistent premise held by new-media activists that open access to information and the free ability to communicate is a critical if not preeminent political value.

This vision is further articulated in the founding manifesto of BURN!. Here drafters define the project in the following manner:

- A freely-available collection of texts by groups excluded by the present global political order that have been censored or are unavailable elsewhere
- A laboratory for studying distributed (post-geographic?) social and political organization, publication, new forms of journalism, and other cool stuff
- An experiment in cross-cultural communication and social organization
- A friendly place to experiment, learn, create, and publish with computer communication technologies
- A group of activists working to prevent the enclosure of cyberspace and the domination of its inhabitants. (Halleck 2003, 20)

Beyond the vision of a free and open media infrastructure, the manifesto highlights the innovative and playful spirit that motivated organizers to utilize "computer communication technologies." The manifesto also expresses the experimental nature of the BURN! laboratory and the "post-geographic" social network that the students wanted to create with the BURN! server.

The closing point of the manifesto foregrounds an important theme that emerged among new-media activists with the rise of the Internet. Drawing parallels to the English peasantry's long battle with industrial capitalists over the enclosure (read: privatization) of public lands or commons from the sixteenth to the nineteenth century, BURN! founders understood themselves as protecting the Internet, a cyber commons, from corporate control and privatization.

As Dorothy Kidd discusses in her research on indymedia, this sentiment came from a recognition among early digital activists that while the Internet plays a key role in facilitating a new informational stage in capitalism, its open, socialized, nonhierarchical nature has important radical political potential that must be protected. Detailing the work of digital activists to keep the Internet open, Kidd (2003b) argues: "Regardless of their self-definitions, the open-source movement, the hackers, and file-sharing 'pirates' have had a profound effect on the global net, challenging new corporate enclosures and attempting to keep the open architecture and free flow of information" (57). Members of BURN! were part of this digital ecosystem and specifically fought, through their open server, to promote the free flow of information, an aim that incurred the fury of state governments, leading to the eventual closure of BURN!. The aim of BURN! members to protect the cyber commons helps to highlight a change in strategy as activists begin to see technology itself as a key site of struggle, accentuating the shift away from the more material concerns of poor and working people.

BURN! and the Early Internet

The BURN! Web site went live in 1993. At the time there were less than two hundred active Web sites on the Internet, compared to the nearly two hundred million sites today (Gray 1995). Hence, BURN! did not look nor act like the thousands of polished Web sites we encounter in cyberspace today. In the contemporary Web environment, most sites are anchored by image and/or sound, and the structure and wireframes that hold a site together are largely invisible, making the Web experience more dynamic and more carefully managed. Part of the first generation of Web sites, and without the flood of programmers and designers that have emerged in recent years, BURN! and its counterparts had a flatter, more monotonous look and feel. As users went online, through dialup modems that made each mouse click a serious investment, they would land on Web sites that were principally straightforward text-based pages with hyperlinks. If there were images, like the billowing orange and yellow flames set against BURN!'s black background, the graphics were clumsy, giving the Web page an artificial feel and highlighting the virtual nature of the Internet. And it wasn't only the look of the Internet that felt primitive by today's standard, but also the functionality. Dominated by blocky discussion boards, unwieldy mailing lists, less interactivity, and a smaller constellation of destinations, the Web experience at the time was comparatively prosaic.

It was in this environment that BURN! existed and ultimately thrived. Because it was one of the first radical political projects on the Web, the site filled a niche. In a relatively short period of time, BURN! became a popular destination among a diverse array of audiences. In an article about BURN!, DeeDee Halleck (2003) detailed the enthusiastic growth of the Web site: "[T]he site (Burn.ucsd.edu) became a sort of underground wildfire: picking up anarchists, rebels, and a wide variety of international activists" (20).

Based on the vision of creating an open media system, the BURN! approach was to give audiences direct access to primary source material from groups involved in radical social change. The BURN! site was the anchor for the different Web sites and information that the BURN! server hosted. To this end, the homepage was a map for accessing a variety of material, including twenty Web sites, five to ten mailing lists and their archives, a discussion board, information manuals on consensus decision making, links to dozens of anarchist Web sites that were "useful in our struggle for self-determined life," and a sizeable archive of images from periods of social resistance, including May '68 in France and the Spanish Civil War.

Perhaps the most important function of BURN! was hosting radical political Web sites. This was particularly important in the early days of the Internet, because there was a scarcity of servers, and few were willing to host controversial sites. For instance, the Web site for the Revolutionary Armed Forces of Colombia (FARC-EP; Fuerzas Armadas Revolucionarias de Colombia–Ejercito del Pueblo) was kicked off numerous servers because of the violence associated with the ongoing civil war in Colombia. In this void, the BURN! server was a vital resource. BURN! hosted the FARC site for free for many years, along with a number of other sites that were controversial, including the American Kurdish Information Network and the Basque separatist newspaper *Egin*.

Alongside Web sites, the BURN! server also hosted mailing lists such as CHIAPAS-L, which was devoted to the Zapatista struggle, and RAZA, which was dedicated to "the struggle of Chicanos for justice and self determination." In all, BURN! hosted about eight mailing lists, which allowed people to circulate and archive information in the form of news, commentaries, and alerts. Mailing lists, like CHIAPAS-L and RAZA, were a key ingredient in the ability of transnational advocacy networks to effect politics (Keck and Sikkink 1998). After the Mexican government shut down an EZLN listserv hosted by the National Autonomous University of Mexico (UNAM) in the mid 1990s (Oleson 2004), the CHIAPAS-L listserv became the central nerve center of the transnational activist community supporting the Zapatista movement. In this role, Chiapas-L distributed messages and connected thousands of users throughout the world, playing a key infrastructural role for the vast activist and NGO community supporting indigenous resistance in Mexico. Listservs like CHIAPAS-L enabled the EZLN to take their struggle to the global community and receive support from an emboldened NGO network in key moments of conflict.

In parallel fashion, the biggest innovation and arguably the most controversial aspect of the BURN! site was the focus on publishing primary source materials from radical political struggles worldwide. As BURN! members explained on their Web site:

> BURN! started as a student project in the communications department in the early 1990s as an experiment in a new type of media. Instead of publishing information written *about* various social protagonists, BURN! publishes information written by them. Primary source media eliminates the go-between because the best way to learn about what's going on is to hear it from the people who are actively involved. The information that we publish is used for research by academics and journalists throughout the world. A lot of the information that we publish is unavailable elsewhere. In the interest of preserving academic freedom and availability of information, we publish information that is censored by various governments. Our information is also used by people who live in the countries where it is coming from, because of how difficult it is to get this information there.[5]

The significance of the BURN! model crystallized in late 1996 when the Tupac Amaru Revolutionary Movement (MRTA) stormed the residence of the Japanese Ambassador in Lima, Peru. Members of the MRTA, a Marxist revolutionary group that operated in Peru throughout the 1980s and 1990s, took six hundred hostages in a standoff with the Peruvian military. During the six-month standoff, the Peruvian government attempted to control the flow of information about the hostage crisis by limiting the ability of the press to access information directly from the MRTA.

One way that the MRTA was able to circumvent this information blockade was by using computers at the Japanese ambassadorial residence to send out primary source documents in the form of daily, and at times hourly, communiqués. Frustrated that they couldn't stop the MRTA from disseminating information through the Internet, a Peruvian official explained, "We can't very well cut phone lines and confiscate computers" (Vogel, Moffett, and

Sandberg 1997). Once the communiqués were sent out, the Toronto-based anarchist solidarity group Arm the Spirit (ATS), a member group of BURN!, posted the messages to the BURN! Web site and sent the communiqués out on mailing lists hosted by BURN!. ATS eventually developed a MRTA solidarity page, hosted by BURN!, which included background information on the revolutionary group as well as sixteen communiqués spanning from the day the hostage situation began in December 1996 until the day it ended in April 1997. During the standoff, BURN! received a great deal of Web traffic from journalists and other individuals eager for primary source information that was not filtered through the Peruvian government. According to political scientist Michael Dartnell, the BURN!-based MRTA solidarity page received close to seven hundred hits per day during the standoff, a sizeable number in 1997.[6]

BURN!'s use of the Internet to circumvent the media censorship of the Peruvian government was innovative, and as the Web site gained exposure, BURN! itself quickly became a story. In 1997, toward the end of the MRTA standoff, *TIME* ran an article on "The Real Revolution: Net Guerillas."[7] In the story, the journalist Elizabeth Frantz highlighted BURN! as an example of a young student-led project where the Internet was harnessed to disseminate information on "terrorist groups." Frantz quotes Jim Phillips, a terrorism expert from the Heritage Foundation, voicing the concern that public university resources and taxpayer dollars should not subsidize the "propaganda" of "groups that have attacked Americans in the past." Countering this position, UCSD administrators came out in support of the students and BURN!. Dan Hallin, chairman of the communications department at UCSD, was quoted as saying, "We're proud that our students are part of that communications network . . . we don't see any reason to get rid of it because it's controversial."

The BURN! site became the center of attention again a year later when the collective published an issue of the separatist newspaper *Egin,* which was closely associated with Basque Homeland and Freedom (ETA), the armed Basque nationalist organization. Earlier that year, the Spanish government forcibly shut down *Egin* and arrested some of its high-profile members, including the editor, on charges of direct association with a terrorist organization. While the Spanish government successfully closed down *Egin,* the transnational character of the Internet made it difficult to censor the Basque militants. Once the Spanish government realized that BURN!, via UCSD, was offering *Egin* server space to publish the newspaper, the Spanish government retaliated with a cyberattack directed at UCSD. This attack came in the form of a coordinated email campaign, which, according to DeeDee Halleck (2003), almost crashed UCSD's internal email system (21).

Similarly, the Turkish government initiated an email campaign against UCSD because of Kurdish nationalist Web sites that the BURN! server hosted. This included the American Kurdish Information Network, which advocated secession or "the right of Kurds to self-determination." The forceful reaction of the Spanish and Turkish governments to a relatively small Web site in the United States draws attention to the ability of the Internet to disrupt borders and traditional models of sovereignty.

BURN!'s support of different revolutionary groups throughout the world and the increased attention raised the stakes and forced BURN! into the spotlight. In the period after the article ran, the issue of whether UCSD should support BURN! began to escalate. Threats were directed at members of the UCSD administration, and the administration put pressure on the communications department to shut BURN! down. On June 1, 2000, the new chair of the communications department reversed the department's earlier position and disconnected the BURN! server from the UCSD broadband network. To explain the actions, the new chair addressed a letter to the communications department:

> Last week and through this week, we have had an unusual barrage of complaints about the Burn! Page. We've had them for some time, often as frequently as once a week, and as they came in, I would try to deal with them, or direct them to someone who could. But last week some individuals started sending e-mail messages complaining in particular about the FARC page to a list of UCSD administrators. . . . I got a specific call from certain top university officials to either respond or disconnect the site. I have chosen to disconnect it. . . . As a chair dealing with an anonymous site, with little connection to individuals who actually run the site and who decide its content, I have lost the ability to stand in front of it. (Halleck 2003, 25)

Because BURN! developed a following and was a unique site of political expression used by journalists, scholars, and activists, the university's decision to cut the flow of information and expression was significant and was met with protest. DeeDee Halleck wrote a public response, arguing that, "as the faculty member who has been most directly concerned with the Burn! website, I am disturbed that the site was closed without first contacting me." She continued, "I realize that this sort of access to a variety of political views and news will often provoke reaction and dissension, but I hope that in the interest of supporting open communication, our department can speak up for open dialogue and free speech." Halleck concluded, "I am requesting that the server be immediately reinstalled" (Halleck 2003, 26). The server, however, was not reinstalled and instead was given back to the students, who were instructed to find a new broadband connection, which they did, and BURN! continued operating for a few more years.

After BURN! was kicked off the UCSD network, Halleck wrote the essay "The Censoring of BURN!," in which she argued that the decision to shut down the server went against one of the central principles of the university system: to protect free speech. In an effort to illustrate the broad appeal of the project, at the end of the essay Halleck published numerous messages sent to the chair of the department of communications in support of BURN!. One such letter came from leaders of the Revolutionary Armed Forces of Colombia. The FARC's response focused on the right of communities to inform themselves.

> The presence, on said server, of the homepage of the Fuerzas Armadas Revolucionarias de Colombia-Ejercito del Pueblo (FARC-EP) was supposedly rejected via telephone calls by a few people who claimed to be students, and via e-mails from a few people who claimed to be Colombians. Let's assume that these claims are true. Do these people represent anything among the millions of Colombians who are suffering the rigors of the war that the State has imposed? . . . Independently of whether or not one agrees or disagrees with the just and necessary struggle of the Colombian rebels, what is above discussion is their right to inform, and the right of the community to inform itself with their version of the Colombian reality so that with at least the two versions the community can build its own criteria and opinions. (Halleck 2003, 27)

Mirroring the FARC response, a Colombian-born student at CUNY made a similar argument:

> I want to convey to you the practical implications of your decision. . . . Your decision to disconnect the BURN! server will . . . effectively grant one side of the debate a monopoly on the means of communication. Whatever you may think about the FARC (and I am not a fan), they command the allegiance of several million very poor people in Colombia. Their views must be made accessible to people who are debating the merits of waging war on them. (Halleck 2003, 34–35)

The messages from the FARC and the UCSD student capture the promise of the Internet as a new tool for the dissemination of information that is otherwise censored. They also highlight the stakes associated with the Internet in the early stages of development. The Web, and BURN! specifically, offered a highly sought-after venue for groups and people to disseminate their message and circumvent either a corporate or state-based information blockade.

Along these lines, one of the critical lessons that BURN! offered activists was early insight into the ways the Web could be appropriated to freely circulate information that was otherwise suppressed, creating a community of interested people across borders and boundaries. In this sense, like indymedia after it, the BURN! project foreshadowed the explosion of social media and the potential role it can play during times of political conflict. Through the BURN! server, activists used the Web to interact and build relationships while creating networks of support for groups like the EZLN, MRTA, and the FARC. In this sense, the practices that BURN! and indymedia established prefigure the prominent role of social media in recent revolutions from Eastern Europe to North Africa and the Middle East.

At the same time, while BURN! was a support for global political and revolutionary struggles, examining the Web site and server makes it clear that there was little connection between the students that created BURN! and the myriad of local struggles in San Diego or California, and to a lesser extent the United States.[8] In this sense, it is hard not to detect in BURN! and the model a prioritization of struggles in other parts of the globe. While the Internet was used to circulate messages across national boundaries, there was little experimentation with the role of the Internet in local struggle. This tendency to prioritize struggles in other parts of the world has real ramifications, as new-media tools were not crafted in the midst of and as part of communities fighting for social change but rather in isolation or in support of distant communities. This flaw in new-media activists' connection and relationship to local struggle has been a constant point of tension for indymedia and the Cyber Left generally.

The BURN! phenomenon also illustrates the complicated function universities played in the development of the Internet in this period. While UCSD acted as an incubator, offering a well-resourced and protected space for the development of BURN!, university officials ultimately shut down the server because of mounting pressure. Thus, while universities were seen as critical, open spaces for the development of the free open-source software movement (Moore 2001), the BURN! episode brings up new questions regarding the role of the academy as a site of freedom of thought and expression, especially in moments of duress. It also illustrates that while BURN! members built their own server in order to have a greater degree of autonomy, they were still dependent on the broadband infrastructure provided by UCSD and therefore only had partial independence.

The BURN! project served as a vital laboratory for young activists to experiment with the possibilities of digital technology to transmit information across national boundaries, building transnational forms of political solidarity linked through the Web. Halleck and Burnett argue that through learning to build a server and create the tools that enabled the free flow of information about political struggle, BURN! became a central testing ground for the development of indymedia. For Burnett, the main lesson was that "the Internet was a powerful tool for new forms of struggle and experimentation enabling people to share stories and perspectives that without this new technology were hidden and silenced."[9] Burnett took these lessons and experiences to indymedia a few years later.

Z Media Institute: Developing a Generation of Media Activists

At the time that BURN! was establishing itself as a communications hub for political radicalism, journalists, social-justice organizers, and media activists from across the United States converged on Woods Hole, Cape Cod, to take part in a workshop on media and political organizing at the Z Media Institute. Michael Albert and Lydia Sargent, founders of the independent monthly *Z Magazine* and the nonprofit book publisher South End Press, founded ZMI in 1994. As Albert explained, "[T]he idea was to offer a way people could share and learn about political thought and activism generally, and specifically about creating alternative media."[10]

Each year, ZMI opens and closes with the same passage from Noam Chomsky, which is meant to capture the role of mass media in "manufacturing consent": "To keep the rabble in line . . . to make sure that we are atoms of consumption, obedient tools of production, isolated from one another, lacking any concept of a decent human life. We are to be spectators in a political system run by elites, blaming ourselves, and each other, for what's wrong" (qtd. in Sargent 2003). In a video about ZMI, Lydia Sargent explains that the rationale for bookending the conference with Chomsky's quote is to make sure that workshop participants recognize the true role of the mass media to control and pacify the masses. In the ten days that follow, ZMI is punctuated by guest lectures from left intellectuals like Amy Goodman and Barbara Ehrenreich, as well as daily workshops on different aspects of media, politics, and skills building. Michael Albert outlines the diverse components of the institute: "In addition to classes on radio, print, online, finances, promotion, and other media-skill areas, and classes on the broad issues of mainstream and alternative media, including structure, motives, etc., we also had many classes on economic and social vision and strategy, on international relations, and so on."[11]

Toward the Development
of a Democratic Media Infrastructure

ZMI was constructed around the ideas articulated in a highly circulated essay Albert penned in *Z Magazine* in the mid 1990s, "Mass Media: Theirs and Ours" (Albert 2006). Albert argues that the "existing mainstream mass media systematically deadens minds and obscures truth . . . because the mass media is owned and run by the beneficiaries of the institutions we oppose." Consequently, one of the critical tasks of the left is to build its own mass media. Albert then outlines a detailed plan for building an extensive alternative media network—print, radio, magazine—that would be coordinated and span across the United States. Albert describes this alternative media network as a necessary step for social movements to "eliminate oppressions of all kinds."

The vision of ZMI was to create a dedicated space for activists to study the intersection of media and politics and, correspondingly, to build a new generation of leaders interested in the role of the media in movement building. In fact, the founders saw ZMI as a vehicle to bridge the experiences and lessons of the New Left, of which they were a part, with the emergent leaders of the Cyber Left:

> We had lived through a time of incredible social change, from civil rights and black power movements to student and antiwar movements to counter-culture, women's, and gay and lesbian movements to labor, Native American, and ecology movements. A new politics was developing, and we felt left media had to relate this politics to existing movements, to those just becoming radical, and to a larger public. Otherwise, they would be ignored, revised, or misrepresented by mainstream media outlets. . . . In 1994 we decided to pass along what we knew, partly to encourage others to start radical, self-sustaining institutions that could educate, inspire, and organize; partly to meet people interested in creating and joining a future larger left media network; partly to teach a democratic, participatory, radical politics and a democratic workplace structure and process.[12]

One of the key purposes of ZMI was to share the history and experiences of some organizers involved in the New Left with younger activists. Accordingly, over the course of the first ten years, ZMI enrolled many of the eventual leaders of the indymedia movement, from Jeff Perlstein and Jay Sand to Evan Henshaw-Plath. Sand and Perlstein attended ZMI in the summer of 1996. They were habitual readers of *Z Magazine* and saw the announcement in its pages and decided to apply. At the time, Sand was living on the East Coast and working as an independent journalist and activist. He "was drawn to ZMI" because he wanted to learn more about the potential role of the Internet in activism.[13]

Perlstein was living in Seattle in 1996 and was involved with a host of political-organizing projects focused on issues of workers' rights and the death penalty. While organizing, Perlstein saw the importance of building an alternative media infrastructure that countered the narrative of mass media, and he and some friends began building a pirate radio station in Seattle. To further this project, when Perlstein attended ZMI he took part in the radio track, to get the pirate radio station "off the ground" and help him "be more thoughtful and strategic about it."

The structure and content of ZMI was stimulating, as Perlstein explained:

> Getting on site kinda blew my head apart. The conversations and people I was meeting there . . . the way they structured it, not just being about a skills piece. Every morning was grounding in political theory, and then there were sessions on process, then the afternoon was hands-on media, making projects. And I had David Barsamian as a mentor. . . . And I was having inspiring discussions with peers. . . . The mix was very forward-pushing.[14]

As Perlstein and Sand attest, the stimulating atmosphere led to a vibrant environment where many new projects were workshopped. Both the Direct Action Media Network, which Jay Sand helped to found, and CounterMedia were discussed at ZMI in the summer of 1996 and launched thereafter.

With the growing popularity of the Internet, new media was at the heart of the camp in 1996. Jay Sand was struck by the focus on new technologies and the innovative strategies people were discussing: "I was at Z Media Institute in 1996, and he [Michael Albert] was talking . . . he was working very hard on some Internet-based projects, and he was really very completely on top of the effect that the Web would have and the way that it would help build movements."[15] Along these lines, one of the tracks of the camp was experimentation in the use of digital technologies. This track became a place for leaders to consider the possibilities of using digital technologies to create a distinctive media system that took advantage of new tools.

While experimentation with new media was key, it was not the central goal of the school. The founders of ZMI had two integrated purposes for the summer school: to train leaders who could help build an alternative media network to support left-based social movements, and to develop a democratic infrastructure for this network. As Albert explains, he believed it was critical that these new-media institutions develop radically democratic governance structures. In his analysis, this democratic governance was the only way alternative media infrastructures could last and create real change: "For alternative media to be really alternative, beyond having radical content it needs to have radical structure. It can't incorporate the kinds of oppressive race relations or gender relations we see all around us, but more controversially, nor can it incorporate the kinds of oppressive class relations—the typical corporate ways of defining and remunerating and deciding on labor—that we see all around us."[16] The core component of this argument is Albert's vision of oppressive class relations. He further elaborated on this point:

> If you adopt capitalistic corporate divisions of labor and modes of decision making in your operations, that choice would both call into question your seriousness when criticizing capitalism, and, even worse, it would by the alibis and rationalizations involved diminish the depth and range of your critiques. We in fact go beyond this injunction at ZMI, to propose how alternative media and other institutions can organize and structure themselves to be very effective and yet not mimic oppressive class relations.

His argument, which became a central tenet of indymedia, was that it is not enough to report on issues of social justice that the mainstream media ignores or distorts, or offer a venue for silenced perspectives. Much like the prefigurative practice of the New Left, Albert believed that alternative media institutions must go one step farther, and independent reporting must be coupled with a consensus-based governance system that brings new voices into leadership of the alternative media organization itself. It is this practice, Albert argues, that challenges the value structure of a capitalist system.

Sand and Perlstein saw the development of prefigurative structures as a critical component of the school, and it was one of the reasons they both attended. In reflecting on ZMI, Jay Sand explained how the workshops around democratic governance worked:

> It was ten days of workshops about making alternative political . . . alternative media entities, but also doing it structurally within a political context. So you would form . . . an independent newspaper, but you didn't want to replicate capitalist structure—and just make it independent news. It would just fall flat, it wouldn't work. . . . I mean, the example the people from *Z Magazine* used was *The Nation*, and how *The Nation* had done some credible journalism, but the critique of it is that it is run in a hierarchical manner.[17]

ZMI leadership used the example of a progressive magazine that they argue replicates the for-profit model of journalism to illustrate the alternative praxis they wanted ZMI attendees to consider.

To reckon with the difficulties of building and sustaining a prefigurative political infrastructure, workshop attendees were asked to create their own independent media institutions. However, as they were building these organizations, they were forced to wrestle with difficult questions: How do you democratically determine what stories and issues should be covered and highlighted? How do you develop an efficient editorial system within a democratic media infrastructure? Should independent journalists be paid for their work? Will your media organization take paid advertisements? All of these questions and many others helped ZMI participants imagine a new collective way of creating media. Ultimately, the ideas that emerged around democratic praxis, decision making, organizational structure, and the role of volunteers became a set of principles that informed the development of many new projects, including indymedia.

The focus on democratic structure is the most obvious legacy of ZMI; however, the think-tank atmosphere also helped forge important relationships that led to a series of media-activist projects. Through the nexus of ZMI, a group of media activists in Canada and the United States started to discuss the creation of a network of alternative media centers in cities across North America. The first center was established in Toronto and was called the Tao Collective. Following this, other collectives were established across North America. ZMI's role in laying the groundwork for this new-media network, and eventually indymedia, was not lost on Michael Albert: "Yes, I have been told many times that in a very real sense indymedia was spurred and facilitated by lessons from ZMI. . . . It is very nice to hear and is certainly the kind of thing we hoped for."[18]

CounterMedia: The Birth of Web-based Independent Journalism

A few months after ZMI, Sand and Perlstein, among others, took their recent education into the world, initiating the experimental journalism project CounterMedia. CounterMedia was launched in Chicago during the 1996 Democratic National Convention and was conceptualized as a short-term, independent newsroom for the creation and distribution of alternative reporting. The project was defined as "a coalition of political organizations, media groups, and individuals dedicated to providing alternative coverage of the Democratic National Convention and community struggle in Chicago."[19]

The idea of developing an alternative media project began taking shape in early 1996, while activists were putting together plans for a DNC counter-conference called Active Resistance. During the planning process, a group—including one of the eventual founders of CounterMedia, Jim Wrecks—decided that it was important to create their own independent media presence during the DNC (Huebner 1996). A few months later, Wrecks moved to Chicago and began organizing CounterMedia. As he explains, the organizing process was easy, as people were excited by the concept of a grassroots journalism project: "Basically the energy of all the people who got involved offered more resources. . . . The whole thing exponentially grew. . . . We now have over fifty volunteers—it just exploded" (Huebner 1996). Once a strong and growing contingent of local volunteers was established, Wrecks and others put out a national call on activist listservs like AUT-OP-SY, inviting people to come to Chicago and take part in the CounterMedia experiment:

> If you have experience in video, photography, radio, journalism, or the internet, Countermedia needs you—to help document the issues that concern you most, from affordable housing and immigrant rights to safe abortion on demand and the right for a living wage. . . . Help organize the Countermedia information net that will provide activists, the media, and individuals with news about breaking events through daily updates and press releases, web sites, and phone banking. Help schedule coverage or post news to our alternative wire service to get the word out about breaking actions and local struggles. Don't have a particular skill? There's ways for you to volunteer from working the office to delivering tapes by bike.[20]

This extensive organizing set the stage for a week of action in Chicago, where multiple CounterMedia journalists were arrested, and CounterMedia mobile media vans were raided by Chicago police. The launch of CounterMedia at the 1996 DNC was symbolic, as twenty-eight years earlier Chicago had hosted the infamous 1968 Democratic National Convention. At the time, with intensifying combat in Vietnam, the convention was met with massive anti–Vietnam War demonstrations that culminated in riots between protestors and police and the trial of the Chicago Seven. CounterMedia organizers recognized the historical significance of the 1996 DNC and saw the event as an ideal springboard. At the foundation of the CounterMedia experiment was a distrust of the mainstream media and a recognition that evolving movements and struggles need their own communications infrastructure. Along these lines, the CounterMedia Web site proclaimed:

> CounterMedia will focus on the protests, actions and issues ignored by conventional media sources, during this summer's Democratic National Convention and beyond. We'll document community struggles and protests as they occur, help reporters find out about demonstrations and local organizing campaigns, and make video images, photographs and reports available to mainstream media outlets and the alternative press, both locally and nationally. This summer, make sure the City of Chicago and the Democratic Party tell the truth.[21]

The CounterMedia approach to the DNC was fourfold: (1) create an autonomous space for the production of news; (2) develop a streamlined production process for independent journalists and activists to cover stories; (3) collect and share information about the DNC and counter-demonstrations with journalists and activists; and (4) establish a distribution strategy to circulate stories to a wider audience.

Prefiguring the Seattle Independent Media Center, CounterMedia organizers raised money and built an extensive community newsroom in Chicago using space that was donated by a local Teamsters union. Jeff Perlstein was not involved with preplanning, but when he arrived in Chicago to volunteer, he was amazed by the infrastructure that CounterMedia organizers built.

> They put together this functioning newsroom. They had a sign-in table where you got credentials, and you were asked questions to make sure you were legit in some form. They had all these people working at an editing base, they had a briefing team, they had a story assignment team. All the kind of stuff you would expect in a functioning newsroom. . . . These were people that I was aligned with politically, and they were making this happen.[22]

At the heart of the grassroots newsroom was a streamlined coverage strategy and a process for reporting on the events in Chicago. Organizers kept a detailed calendar of all of the protests and events that were taking place during the DNC, and, as Perlstein explains, organizers were constantly updating "whiteboards all around the main room" to track fast-moving situations. In a sense, the CounterMedia office acted like a war room, or a netwar room, where massive amounts of information were collected, tracked, and shared with CounterMedia journalists and protestors. Much of this information was shared through a two-way radio system. When "hot" information came in, the story assignment team identified a mobile media team to cover the story. Evidence points to the fact that this strategy of information tracking and sharing infuriated the Chicago Police Department. Over the course of the week, CounterMedia journalists claim that the CounterMedia vehicles were raided twice and police confiscated at least one of the two-way radios. Following the DNC, CounterMedia members sued the Chicago Police Department, and during the court case members of the department claimed that CounterMedia members used the two-way radios to track and confuse police operations.

While information tracking was a critical part of CounterMedia, organizers were also concerned with reaching a broad audience. CounterMedia was set up to create media in multiple platforms (print, video, Web). For instance, the newscasts that video journalists produced during the DNC were uplinked to satellite and, with the help of Deep Dish TV, broadcast on public-access TV stations across the country. Ultimately, all of the CounterMedia video was compiled into a single program called *Off the Record*. The hour-long documentary highlighted issues "left out of the conventions agenda,"[23] focusing on footage of protests and interviews with community activists.

Alongside the video newscasts, CounterMedia journalists filed about forty stories from July through November 1996. The majority of the stories focused on issues of police brutality and repression, which became a central theme of the 1996 DNC. However, reporters also filed dozens of stories focused on the different protests taking place in Chicago, as well as a few stories focused on broader social and political issues.

One of the central differences between CounterMedia and the Seattle IMC was the distribution strategy and the role of the Web. The founders of CounterMedia were experimenting with the Internet, but they did not expect the Web site to be visited by many people; instead, they expected to use the CounterMedia site as a storage/archival space for stories. Thus, unlike indymedia, there was no participatory open-publishing aspect to the CounterMedia Web site. As Sand explains, "We had a Web site, and we posted stories, but there wasn't an interactive component, and also people really weren't paying attention to the Web."[24] Without the networking and circulatory capacity of the Web, in order to distribute the stories and get attention, CounterMedia organizers took a more traditional approach to distribution. The Counter-Media briefing team organized daily press conferences and press releases in which CounterMedia stories were highlighted, in an attempt to convince mainstream news organizations to cover these stories.

Repression in Chicago

CounterMedia organizers framed their mission as oppositional to the DNC and the mainstream media; however, they did not expect actual conflict with Chicago authorities. During the course of the DNC, six different CounterMedia videographers, including Jeff Perlstein, were arrested, and their equipment was confiscated and at times destroyed. The clashes between protestors and police culminated in a series of raids on Active Resistance, the counter-conference organized in parallel with CounterMedia. Organizers of CounterMedia and Active Resistance reacted to the raid by calling a press conference the following day, while issuing a press release.

The attacks on Active Resistance protestors and CounterMedia journalists during the 1996 DNC has direct parallels with the violent clashes between police and protestors in the 1968 DNC. In fact, CounterMedia photographers captured photos of police officers wearing shirts that read: "We kicked your father's ass in 1968 . . . wait 'til you see what we do to you!" The odious humor of the Chicago Police Department aside, there were serious differences between 1968 and 1996. In 1968, the Democratic National Convention was an important link in a period of heightened protest against the Vietnam War and U.S. imperialism. The organized resistance during the 1968 convention led to massive battles between police and protestors over control of the Chicago streets and was organized by New Left organizations like Students for a Democratic Society, the Black Panther Party, the Youth International Party (YIPPIE), and the umbrella group National Mobilization Committee to End the War in Vietnam (MOBE). During the DNC, Chicago was in mayhem, and it culminated in the famous trial of the Chicago Seven, which was a symbolic moment capturing the tensions and struggles of the late 1960s.

Unlike 1968, the 1996 DNC was not an important event in a growing cycle of protest. For this reason, the demonstrations in Chicago in 1996 were considerably smaller. However, while the 1996 DNC did not draw massive protest, the Chicago Police Department consistently targeted members of CounterMedia and Active Resistance. One reason the CPD may have targeted CounterMedia was their innovative use of communication tools to track the protests, surveil the police, and share the information with journalists and protestors, none of which was illegal. The tension between the Chicago police and CounterMedia also highlights the growing hostility between police and independent journalists and media makers that has emerged with the onset of the information revolution, as Brad Will's death so poignantly illustrates.

In the aftermath of 1996, CounterMedia continued to report on stories connected to the convention and Chicago politics more generally, but by the end of the year the CounterMedia experiment folded. Looking back, Jay Sand explained that CounterMedia "was a really inspiring thing that helped us build our understanding of the role of media in conflict, and I think it was an essential precursor to the birth of indymedia."[25]

Along these lines, there are two core lessons that organizers of CounterMedia were able to draw on in establishing indymedia three years later. First, CounterMedia was a barometer that signaled the eagerness of activists, independent journalists, and everyday citizens to take up the tools of journalists and "be the media." The model of independent journalism that CounterMedia pioneered was the cornerstone of the indymedia model and arguably inspired the larger public, civic, and community-journalism movements that have emerged in recent years.

Second, CounterMedia participants like Jeff Perlstein and Jay Sand developed expertise in building short-term community-media infrastructures that could function as convergence centers and newsrooms during periods of heightened protest. The CounterMedia model of establishing a community newsroom during a period of heightened protest was the blueprint for the development of the Seattle IMC during the Battle of Seattle and many of the Independent Media Centers to follow. As Perlstein explained, he was amazed by CounterMedia, and three years later, he and others re-created that infrastructure in Seattle.

The Road to Seattle Was Paved

The 1990s saw an explosion of new-media activism. Students and professors, programmers and activists, writers and protestors came together to develop experiments and classrooms that aimed to harness the Internet to build a new world. These experiments offered important insights into the ways new information and communication technologies can be harnessed in social struggle. While BURN!, ZMI, and CounterMedia each played critical roles in developing strategies and practice around the formation of indymedia, if we look more generally, it is clear that the social and technological innovation of indymedia and other Cyber Left institutions took time and came from multiple people and organizations. In this sense, the social and political possibilities of the Web did not emerge suddenly, like a lightbulb that went on in someone's head; rather, innovation came from a series of experiments across the world, which then informed the development of indymedia and other subsequent projects.

Another lesson of BURN!, ZMI, and CounterMedia is that the social position of activists impacts the ways technology is utilized. For the most part, BURN!, ZMI, and CounterMedia attracted white, middle-class activists focused on freedom of expression and building an open media system. The class position of these activists as well as their focus on communication technology led to important innovations around the Internet. At the same time, their distance from direct everyday struggle had an impact on their vision of the role of technology in struggle and has led to a technologically oriented social movement.

3

The Battle of Seattle
and the Birth of Indymedia

The proliferation of Independent Media Centers (IMCs) since
Seattle has become the trademark of the antiglobalization
movement and has shaped its organizational forms and
modes of communication in profound ways.

—Eddie Yuen

On the eve of the 1999 World Trade Organization ministerial meetings in Seattle, two software programmers, Matt Arnison and Manse Jacobi, posted the
first message to the newly created, open-publishing indymedia.org Web site:

> Welcome to indymedia. The resistance is now global . . . a trans-pacific col-
> laboration has brought this web site into existence. . . .
> The web dramatically alters the balance between multinational and activist
> media. With just a bit of coding and some cheap equipment, we can set up
> a live automated website that rivals the corporates. Prepare to be swamped
> by the tide of activist media makers on the ground in Seattle and around the
> world, telling the real story behind the World Trade Agreement.

The post concluded with what later became a classic indymedia prompt:
"Add a comment on this article."[1]

Arnison and Jacobi's prophecy turned out to be on target. In the days to
come, thousands of journalists, activists, organizers, and concerned citizens
responded to the call, and the new Independent Media Center, as well as the
city of Seattle, were "swamped by the tide of activist media makers." With
hundreds of volunteers on the ground and millions of visitors turning to the
new participatory news portal, a truly open, democratic newsroom was established, and the indymedia movement was born. As the previous chapters
detail, the road to Seattle was long and circuitous and was paved by many
hands. Likewise, the creation of the first open and democratic newsroom in

Seattle involved a great deal of planning, proselytizing, and programming by countless people. This chapter provides an account of the organizing and vision that went into establishing the Seattle Independent Media Center in two short months before the WTO meetings. It also focuses on the work that went into establishing the first IMC, the innovations and possibilities that emerged during the Seattle experiment, and finally, some of the problems that surfaced in this new model of movement-based communications.

Organizing for Seattle:
Building an Infrastructure

In the months leading up to the World Trade Organization Millennium Round meetings, energy began to mount as activists and labor leaders saw a significant opportunity to challenge the WTO agenda of establishing rules on global free trade. The 1999 WTO meetings came shortly after successful protests in France halted the ratification of the Multilateral Agreement on Investments, which, like the WTO, aimed to establish rules on international investment. Building on the success in France, Seattle became a target of activists because the meetings were being held on U.S. soil, and because the WTO represented a wide range of concerns and therefore became a convergence point for a varied community of protestors.

The broad coalition in Seattle came out of a diverse base of interests. The U.S. labor movement, for instance, was largely concerned with the growing trend of offshoring U.S. jobs to foreign countries with lenient labor laws, a pattern that was promoted by the WTO's free-trade agenda. Likewise, movements of poor people from the developing world, like the EZLN, opposed the WTO for multiple reasons, including a belief that global free-trade agreements would flood markets in developing countries with cheap, genetically modified food, making it difficult for peasants and farmers to make a living. The environmental movement saw the WTO's free-trade agenda as restrictive on individual states' ability to legislate robust laws that would protect the environment against pollution. Finally, a diverse group of citizens were concerned with the opaque, undemocratic fashion in which supranational organizations like the WTO made decisions. This litany of concerns, as well as a growing wave of transnational protest against capital-driven globalization (Tarrow 2006), set the stage for the Seattle protests, which were the largest demonstrations and mass action in the United States since the 1960s.

On the ground in Seattle there was extensive organizing for the WTO protests. The planning began in January 1999, when Seattle was chosen as the site for the Millennium Round meetings. A broad array of groups, including the Rainforest Action Network, the National Lawyers Guild, Art and Revolution, Earth First!, Ruckus Society, and Global Exchange came together during the summer of 1999 to form the Direct Action Network (DAN). In an initial flyer, the DAN defined itself as "a network of local grassroots groups from Los Angeles to Vancouver BC formed . . . to creatively resist the WTO and to organize large scale street theater and mass non-violent direct action at the WTO ministerial."[2] Shortly after DAN was established, the coalition put out a global call, through the diverse networks of member-groups, for a Direct Action Convergence in Seattle for ten days prior to the WTO meetings. The convergence was to be followed by four days of action during the WTO meeting to "creatively and nonviolently shut it down."[3] Following this ambitious call, DAN organizers held a series of meetings and established a coordinating body that would prepare for the WTO protests. DAN member groups, like Ruckus Society and Art and Revolution, focused on organizing for the WTO. Both groups undertook "road shows" and "action camps," where they traveled around the country and held workshops explaining the problems with the WTO and the strategy of nonviolent protest and direct action. These educational tours were meant to educate, cohere, and prepare the newly minted coalition for Seattle.

Alongside the diverse social-movement organizing, John Sweeney, then president of the America Federation of Labor–Congress of Industrial Workers (AFL-CIO), announced that fifty thousand workers would demonstrate during the Seattle meetings. The newsletter *Labor's Voice,* of the AFL-CIO King County Labor Council, put out a call for the mobilization prior to the WTO: "Join workers' rights advocates from across the country on November 30th, the opening day of the World Trade Organization ministerial, to march from the Seattle Center to the Convention Center in support of reshaping the global marketplace to protect workers' rights and the environment."[4] To make Sweeney's vision of fifty thousand workers marching in unison a reality, unions across the country, from the International Longshore and Warehouse Union to the Teamsters and the United Steelworkers, and importantly, the King County Labor Council, began to organize in an effort to bring out the rank and file. Much like the organizing that happened within DAN, labor organizers aimed to educate members on the problems with the WTO and prepare protestors for the events in Seattle.

The goals of the Direct Action Network and the AFL-CIO were different, with the AFL-CIO looking to "reform the rules of trade," while DAN took a more radical position, aiming to shut down the WTO and prohibit the global body from setting new trade rules. With differing aims, DAN and the AFL-CIO organized independently and had different plans for challenging the Millennium Round meetings. However, while DAN and the labor movement had different agendas, leaders of these two networks came into contact at an annual Jobs with Justice conference the summer before the WTO meetings and were in close dialogue through the planning process and during the protests. This dialogue allowed for cooperation between labor and the social-movement left, and the loose coalition between the two formations raised the stakes and laid the groundwork for what became the Battle of Seattle.

A Humble Media Project

In the shadow of DAN and AFL-CIO organizing, the growing media-activist community, which had been primed by the EZLN experience as well as the work of BURN!, ZMI, and CounterMedia, rapidly coalesced into a unified front. Sensing the importance and possibility of the upcoming protests, their aim was to create the first Independent Media Center to report on the supranational meetings and counter-demonstrations. Jeff Perlstein, who lived in Seattle at the time, explained the rationale behind developing the first IMC: "I began to recognize, as someone who has done independent media projects and activist media projects, that we couldn't just let CNN and CBS be the ones to tell these stories, and so that we needed to develop our own alternatives, and our own alternative network. That's really where the idea came from . . . just the necessity for communities to be controlling their own message. . . . So we set about to create a community-based people's newsroom."[5]

Perlstein and a growing group of Seattle activists saw the development of a "noncorporate," open, democratic newsroom as a conscious effort to challenge the ideological frame of mass media, offering new perspectives on the WTO and beyond. In a strategic fund-raising document created in the runup to Seattle, the coalition of organizations convening the first IMC detailed the extensive role they envisioned for it:

> Grassroots media organizations including Free Speech TV, Deep Dish TV, Radio for Peace International, Paper Tiger TV, Free Radio Berkeley, and others are putting together an *Independent Media Center (IMC)* to serve a number of purposes:
> - *coordinate coverage* among teams of independent video, still camera, print, and audio journalists coming from around the world

- *document* direct actions, discussion of economic alternatives to globalization, and progressive analysis by under-represented voices
- *produce audio, print, and video* documents for distribution
- *host an interactive speaker's bureau* (live on-site and virtual on the Web) for grassroots community and labor leaders from around the world—those most directly impacted by globalization—to provide their voices to the coverage and productions
- *create a "WTO Police-Watch"* working with community groups in Seattle, a live Web-cam monitoring system to protect citizens' First Amendment rights
- *distribute productions* via website-based streaming and indexed archives, satellite uplinks, tape distribution, and "rip 'n read" text digests
- *deliver content to global mainstream media* via Web push, computer faxing, and email
- *strengthen and link existing networks* of alternative media and community organizations to maximize the impact of the content produced
- *emphasize results to date* of international conferences and civil society dialogues, including workers' trade agreements, the Kyoto Climate Treaty Rio Earth Summit, Beijing Women's gathering, International Encuentros hosted by the Zapatistas, etc. (Independent Media Center 1999, 1–2)

The agenda that organizers set for the emergent IMC was extensive and focused on creating a movement-based media center that could coordinate coverage and broadly distribute media in multiple formats while becoming a hub or link among alternative media and community organizations. To accomplish this ambitious agenda, the underlying strategy was to create new spaces, online and offline—or, as Perlstein said, "both virtual and physical"—for citizens and journalists to produce independent news stories of the WTO meetings, creating a counter-narrative to that of the mass media.[6] To this end, IMC organizers focused on three interrelated tasks: (1) establishing multiple open and democratic communication platforms (radio, video, print, Web); (2) developing a physical media center or newsroom where people could come to produce and distribute reports; and (3) building support in Seattle and among the national groups organizing against the WTO in an effort to bring activists, organizers, and journalists into the media-production process.

Putting out the Call
and Building a Coalition

With the vision of an alternative media center in mind, the organizers in Seattle wanted to build links to national organizations devoted to independent-media production and organizing. In the informal role of evangelist, Jeff Perlstein began meeting with a network of media activists in New York, Boulder, San Francisco, and other independent-media hotbeds to build support for the project. Perlstein's work was successful, and as he and others detail, assistance flowed from over thirty different organizations across the country to the new IMC, in the form of equipment, staff time, money, and advice. Perlstein described the "all hands on deck" mentality that made the Seattle IMC possible: "Everybody was doing their little piece so that in an amazingly short amount of time, with, like amazingly little resources, we were able to do a significant amount."[7]

Indeed, support for the center grew so rapidly that the second annual Grassroots Media Conference held in Austin, Texas, in the fall of 1999 essentially became a planning meeting for the new Independent Media Center, bringing together longtime media activists. Perlstein attended the conference on behalf of the Seattle Independent Center:

> It was actually a . . . pivotal moment, because it was the only face-to-face opportunity that we had to meet up between the time of the idea and the WTO, with independent media makers around the country. . . . Essentially this project [Seattle IMC] became the talk of the whole weekend. It was basically like this, we ended up workshopping on how we could make this a go with all of these people that had done these things for years.[8]

Eric Galatas, a programmer with the national cable-news channel Free Speech TV, played a critical role in the initial stages of the indymedia movement and organized a special track focused on the Seattle IMC at the Austin Conference. He explained that the aim of the Seattle IMC track was to bring together people that had solid experience with media-activist projects to help plan the nuts and bolts of the first IMC. Galatas invited a mixture of software programmers, videographers, and other media makers as well as organizers. Many of the individuals involved in the Austin-based conference formed a core collective working on the project, offering the funds, skills, and connections necessary to assist Jeff Perlstein and other Seattle-based organizers in developing the IMC in the final weeks leading up to the WTO meetings.

Building Local Networks

In conjunction with the development of a national network of media activists and alternative media institutions supporting the IMC, organizers focused on raising awareness within Seattle. The first step was to develop a group of committed media activists who could help run the IMC on the ground.

Starting two months prior to the WTO meetings, first Perlstein and eventually other IMC organizers held weekly open meetings in Seattle to inform people about the new media center. Each week, the number of participants attending the meeting grew. In the first meeting there were about ten people, but by mid-November Seattle IMC meetings consisted of hundreds of participants. In fact, people who came to the initial meetings, such as Dan Merkle (a social-justice lawyer) and Sheri Herndon (a local independent journalist), eventually played key roles in organizing the IMC.

As Merkle and others involved in the early organizing argued, the idea of a people's newsroom attracted an extensive network of social-justice activists, trained "techies" from local companies like Microsoft, and activists and artists from micro radio,[9] community TV, zines,[10] and the independent press.[11] Along these lines, Evan Henshaw-Plath, one of the critical members of indymedia's tech team, contends that Seattle was an ideal place for the initial IMC, because Microsoft and Boeing were headquartered in the city. These companies were doubly significant, he argued, because they lobbied to bring the WTO meetings to Seattle, and at the same time their employees offered a significant class of tech-based workers that desired transparent government and had resources and skills that were vital in supporting the IMC's development. Media-studies scholar Dorothy Kidd (2003b) concurs with this assessment:

> The IMC was no historical accident, but the result of the historical conjuncture of an emerging global social movement, and two groups of skilled workers both operating with heritages of collective intelligence, and using the new digital technologies. Since its birth in the high-tech incubator of Seattle, home of Microsoft and others, the IMC has enlisted many young, talented techies from around the world who developed their expertise in the high-tech centres and in the peer-to-peer networks of the Open Source movement. With sophisticated problem-solving skills, and as importantly, an ethos of collaboration, they built a digital environment featuring free software and open source code, which, in large measure, spurred the Network's rapid growth as centers everywhere could quickly share the resource. The global tech crew remains indispensable, sharing the support and improvement of sites and the network as a whole via cyberspace, and often from day jobs in the corporate world. (Kidd 2003c, 6)

This distinctive coalition between a new type of politically active computer engineer, traditional social-justice activists, and independent journalists was the foundation of the Seattle IMC, locally and nationally. It was on the basis of this largely middle-class, tech-savvy grouping that indymedia began to develop as a movement that employed technology to develop innovative communication platforms in an effort to open new fronts in political activism.[12]

While this vision of the role of technology began to emerge, and the Seattle IMC began attracting a large base of people from the middle class to volunteer as members of the project, organizers also recognized the importance of building a relationship with the local and national groups organizing around the WTO meetings and social justice in Seattle. In an effort to do outreach, Perlstein organized meetings with a network of local and national groups like Public Citizens, the People's Assembly, the Basement Collective, and the Bayan Philippines group, to build bridges and gain support. He explains: "I was one of the people who was kind of a liaison with different community organizations here in Seattle. . . . I was checking in with them about how they wanted to play a role, or how we could support the work they were doing." The attempt to build strong social relations with local groups was perhaps the most difficult part of creating the first IMC. In reflecting on this difficulty, Perlstein said, "We did a shitty job of building on-the-ground relationships that were really real, you know, with preexisting organizations. I am not talking about media organizations. I am talking about community-based organizations. And I think it was through the efforts of a handful of people who had some local relationships that there were some modest collaborations."[13] The inability of organizers in the Seattle IMC to establish deep relationships with other local organizations and social movements and the distinctive middle-class coalition of the IMC set the course for this new social formation. At the same time, organizers successfully built a newsroom and created an infrastructure for people to create their own news.

Building the First "People's Media Center"

In order to create a robust media infrastructure, IMC organizers were working hard to raise funds and find a space for the new IMC. Through a rapid and extensive pre-event fund-raising campaign,[14] organizers found a central space for the IMC in downtown Seattle. They also raised over one hundred thousand dollars, in both in-kind donations and cash, to create the newsroom they envisioned. Dan Merkle, a lawyer in the Seattle community, was one of the organizers responsible for finding the physical space. He explained:

> It was our job to go find a venue to create an infrastructure that would allow hundreds of media activists around the country to come in and have a place to work and just be able to "plug in" to a system. Whether it was the computers

we got donated, or the DSL line, or we rented a church with seven rooms and each room was set up as the editing suite for the video folks . . . and then we had a photography gallery nearby where we had interviews for quiet space, and we had a dark room where people could do some of their photography work. . . . But our main venue was right in the heart of downtown Seattle.[15]

Ultimately, the Seattle IMC consisted of four spaces. The headquarters was a 2,400-square-foot space on Third Avenue in downtown Seattle. Three other spaces were utilized for media production during the WTO meetings: a video-production space in the Queen Anne neighborhood, an audio-production space in Belltown, and the Benham Gallery for photography on First Avenue in downtown Seattle. Beyond physical space, the donations included equipment, as well as a considerable amount of money, which was used to purchase a satellite feed from Free Speech TV, media and office equipment, printing runs for the newspaper, and money to compensate a select group of organizers and media makers.

While activists were establishing the physical infrastructure, they were also debating the mission and aims of the IMC. One discussion of particular importance was whether indymedia should be a closed newsroom for radical media makers, or an open space for all citizens, regardless of political affiliation. Sheri Herndon explained:

Early in the fall, on the organizing email list, some people wanted to see this communications space be only for the radical activists. Others argued that it needed to be open; there shouldn't be a limit on who could walk in the door. In the end, the philosophy of openness guided us, and people signed up and we didn't ask them about their political affiliations—we were facilitating a space less than deciding what should be produced in that space. This has been the guiding principle with strong roots in that first IMC, and our openness is one of the core principles that gets at the heart of our success and our uniqueness. When we speak of open publishing, it is not just a technological phenomenon, it is a philosophical underpinning that forms the foundation of policy and praxis.[16]

This preference for openness meant that the IMC would not cater to any particular political positions but instead create an open infrastructure for noncorporate media makers to utilize the newsroom. As Herndon notes, however, openness as a political value was not naturally ingrained in these new digital communication technologies, but instead was something activists fought for. Following Seattle, the political preference for openness became a guiding philosophy of the indymedia network and has been both a strength and weakness, allowing indymedia to be a space for many to engage, while diluting the role and function of the movement.

Developing Working Groups

The basic building blocks of the Seattle IMC were independent collectives that operated within the broader IMC structure and took on discrete tasks to make sure the center ran effectively. These collectives—or working groups, as they were called—became the central human infrastructure of the IMC. This configuration was exemplified in the plan around media platforms. Organizers divided the working groups across the different forms of media, establishing a video team, radio team, Web team, and print team. The different working groups established a point person and began organizing a plan for the protests. Beyond the media collectives, there were many other working groups, including the physical-space team, database team, and media and organization outreach team, among others. Dan Merkle estimates that twelve different working groups were established to plan and run the IMC in Seattle.

The starting point for each working group was determining the process of decision making. Building on Z Media Institute's vision of a democratic media infrastructure, the goal of each working group was to establish a participatory decision-making structure as the basis of a layered democratic form of governance for the IMC. To do this, organizers used a decentralized, consensus approach, where individuals broke into nonhierarchical teams to develop the structures and practices of the particular working group. Each of these working groups formulated a specific strategy for building a decision-making process, and the different working groups operated as autonomous nodes in that they were part of the overall IMC, but they worked independently.

The video team, for instance, developed specific working rules and goals that made sense in the context of video and documentary work. Michael Eisenmenger, one of the point people of the video collective, explained the democratic process of creating the media and the different roles people took within the Video Working Group:

> We did a lot of discussion beforehand—I mean, I think in projects like this, obviously the people who commit to editing the segments, they become content creators. . . . The trick or the balance is having consensus in terms of who those people are—how they're chosen, if they have to be chosen. This isn't a case where we had too many people and had to say no to anybody. . . . I mean, we were scrambling to fill a half hour, which, now it seems easy—then it was

... it was the first time any of us had ever tried this. And I mean, anything like this . . . especially back staff—it wasn't like we had reporters in the field, or careers in the studio.[17]

The basis of the video working groups was allowing those who took initiative to have more decision-making responsibility. However, this unspoken rule about taking initiative was in productive tension with the desire to create space within the working group for new people to take initiative so one or two people did not control the group. In the case of Seattle, for the most part, this strategy was successful.

While the working groups were the basic building blocks of the Seattle IMC, they folded into a spokes-council that was the central decision-making structure. One member of each working group sat on a spokes-council, so there was coordination across the working groups. The spokes-council also operated by consensus, and as Merkle explained, this layered decision making formed "the governing structure of the Seattle IMC."

Building a Web-based Open-Publishing Infrastructure

Alongside the decision-making infrastructure, the Web team was working to create a technological infrastructure and Web site for the new IMC. Since Seattle, the cornerstone of indymedia has been the open-publishing platform that programmers developed, which allowed for the creation of participatory journalism at a grand scale. Harnessing the interactive nature of the Web itself, this approach to media production prefigured YouTube, Facebook, Twitter, blogging, and the citizen- and community-journalism movement. The development of open-media platforms for IMC, however, was not the original intent of indymedia organizers.

Building on the BURN! experiment, organizers of the Seattle IMC recognized the archival potential of the Internet as well as its ability to support other media formats. For this reason, they designated the IMC Web site as the central distribution backbone of the indymedia center. In the original model, however, the Web site was not conceived of as an open-publishing newswire. Instead, much like other Web sites at the time, the plan was to have centralized control over what was published on the IMC site.[18] In this sense, the social and political decision to create an open IMC laid the groundwork for the technological innovation of open publishing that developed later in the process.

Because organizers did not conceive of the Web site as open and interactive, they also did not think it would be a sufficient platform for distributing media. Along these lines, to distribute the media produced at the IMC, organizers developed a speakers' bureau where people involved with the IMC from disenfranchised communities could give their perspective on the WTO protests to traditional news sources. Correspondingly, Perlstein and others created a "Web push" strategy, utilizing press releases and press conferences and passing the stories covered by IMC journalists to mainstream news sources for wider distribution. The model came directly from CounterMedia's work and strategy during the 1996 Democratic National Convention.

While the details for the distribution model were being discussed within the IMC, the creation of the IMC Web site—or, more specifically, the software program to support the site—was also progressing. The development of Seattle IMC code was a global project that brought together programmers as far afield as Australia, Palestine, and the United States in an effort to create an innovative software code. Two of the core programmers for this project were Mansur Jacobi and Matthew Arnison. Jacobi worked at Free Speech TV and was recruited by Eric Galatas to come to the Grassroots Media Conference in Austin to help plan the Web development. After Austin, he became one of the point people for the Web working group.

Arnison was from Australia, and in the years leading up to Seattle he had been involved with the Sydney-based project Community Activist Technology (CAT), which used new-media tools to build local, national, and transnational organizing projects. In the summer of 1999, Arnison was traveling in the United States for a graduate-school research project in Colorado when he stumbled on the Seattle IMC organizing process, as one of his colleagues in Australia participated in the Grassroots Media Conference in Austin. He explains: "There happened to be another activist from CAT . . . from Sydney, who had actually went to some Texas grassroots media conference. And he emailed back to Sydney about it, and I picked up that email in Colorado and saw this media-activist project was starting up."[19] Once Arnison learned about the project, he visited Galatas and Jacobi at Free Speech TV in Boulder, and thereafter, Jacobi and Arnison played the central role in developing the code for the first Web site.

The core of the software code Arnison and Jacobi used came from the Reclaim the Streets (RTS) carnival/protest, which was held on June 18, 1999. The slogan of RTS was "Our Resistance Is as Transnational as Capital," and true to the slogan, RTS organizers aimed to coordinate a worldwide protest using the newly created J18 Web site. Announcing this intention, the site read:

The Internet is a powerful tool: electronic communications will allow us to know what is happening everywhere on the day through the main site www. j18.org. This site will have a continuous feed of text reports, photos, video, and audio from as many places as possible. It will also be an invaluable tool for media work, prisoner support, and a future archive for inspiration as well as a breakthrough in setting up our own direct communication channels. Send in what you want to say about your group or action to the June 18th website—*www.j18.org*—it belongs to all of us![20]

J18 organizers used webcasting to synchronize actions and events in London, Nigeria, and India, and they developed a Web site where pictures and stories from across the transnational protests could be uploaded to the J18 site. The vision for creating a transnational resistance and using the Web as a mediator of that resistance was the basis for open-publishing and participatory news creation within the indymedia movement.

Members of CAT developed the software code for J18, and Arnison recognized that it could be utilized for the IMC:

I saw this media-activist project was starting up around Seattle, and I thought, "Hmmm . . . this is similar to some of the stuff we've been doing with J-18 and webcasts and stuff." And I remember seeing the difference between what we did in Sydney, because we had managed to automate some of the stuff—some of the coverage that day. . . . And I wanted to see all those stories, I wanted to feel all those stories coming through from London and Nigeria, so I thought there was a huge opportunity there. So I got chatting to Manse [Jacobi], and I saw that they were working on some software that . . . the software that we'd done in Sydney was further ahead, so I offered . . . maybe we could work together, and so it sort of took off from there.[21]

Taking the basic rubric from CAT, Arnison and Jacobi developed the framework for an open-publishing newswire where people could instantaneously upload their stories, reports, photographs, and audio/video clips. This open newswire offered immediate transparency: journalists would see their message on the Web site directly after they posted it. Capturing the engaged nature of the open newswire, the software program that undergirds the Seattle IMC Web site was named Active.[22] While the central innovation of Active was the open-publishing newswire, the program was also written to meet the need of synergizing and supporting other media formats so reporters could upload the video, audio, and digital photography captured in Seattle.

The creation of Active and subsequently the Seattle IMC Web site was the crowning achievement leading up to the WTO meetings. By the time the WTO meetings arrived, organizers in Seattle had successfully set up the Seattle IMC. In two short months, organizers successfully raised over one hundred thousand dollars; established a network of physical spaces to house the first people's newsroom; developed a video team, a pirate-radio team, a photo team, a print team, and an innovative Web-based platform; and created the human infrastructure and capacity to effectively manage hundreds of visitors who descended on the newly minted IMC. On November 29, a new Independent Media Center was in place to welcome thousands of people who were arriving in Seattle as friends and foes of the WTO.

The Battle of Seattle

Arnison and Jacobi's christening message to the indymedia movement: "Welcome to indymedia. The resistance is now global." This message went out on November 29, the night before the commencement of the WTO meetings. In the days that followed, Seattle was turned upside down as protestors and police battled for control of the streets and the city. As the events in Seattle escalated, the police and mayor lost control of the city, and likewise WTO leadership lost control over the global body. The social upheaval in Seattle forced the WTO proposals into the spotlight, and some of the world-trade body's proponents, like President Clinton, were forced to distance themselves from the global free-trade agenda. Ultimately, with the mayhem, the rules for global trade were not written at the Millennium Round meetings, as leaders of the Direct Action Network predicted. Activists and organizers pounced on the situation and claimed a rare victory that many believed was a critical moment in a growing wave of protest challenging neoliberal globalization.

During the Battle of Seattle, the Seattle Independent Media Center called hundreds of volunteers into the process of making media. Organizers granted over 450 press passes, offering people the capacity and platform to document their worlds. By building a significant cadre of grassroots "citizen journalists" to report on the protests, the Seattle IMC became a vehicle of expression for the manifold counterhegemonic struggles and perspectives confronting the WTO formation. DeeDee Halleck, one of the organizers of the Seattle IMC, described this sundry mix of people as "teamsters and turtles, hackers and tigers," coalescing into what she saw as "a formidable force" (Halleck and Kovel 2000).

Expanding the possibilities of the Internet as an interactive communications medium, the IMC Web site crystallized the media-democracy or media-empowerment ethic of the movement. When the site was unveiled, community journalists used it to offer up-to-the-minute coverage of the protests. The time it took for someone to call in a blockade, make a report, or upload a picture of a clash between police and protestors was the length of time it took for information to be mediated through the Internet to an extensive audience. This immediacy and transparency through which dialogic information was produced and disseminated marks one of the cornerstones of indymedia philosophy.

Thus, the Web site became a media forum itself, offering a new space for activists and citizen journalists to post their messages on to the open-publishing newswire, while simultaneously reading messages and stories posted from other users on the site. As Arnison put it: "It seemed like we were opening up this huge flower, and all this passion and energy and stories and ideas were just pouring through because they'd been locked for so long. And it was like just opening up the gates and letting a whole bunch of these ideas and passion flow through."[23] In much the same way that Michel de Certeau (1984) saw "readers as poachers" or walking in the city as an agent-based reappropriation of social texts, users of the open-publishing software adapted technology to innovative uses that were different from the original intentions. The energy that developed from open publishing was a surprise for the organizers, but it quickly became one of the central components of the site and the Seattle IMC more generally.

Due to successful organizing, the experimental indymedia Web site received over 1.5 million original hits in its inaugural week, outpacing CNN[24] for the same period. Amateur journalists posted hundreds of reports and personal accounts of the WTO protests. The sheer number of posts and the diverse perspectives on the IMC offered audiences a richer and deeper understanding of the WTO and Seattle protests, while offering up-to-the-minute information which enabled protestors to quickly respond to the Seattle police, bringing to life James Surowiecki's (2005) theory on the wisdom of the crowds.

The popularity of the indymedia Web site is magnified by the fact that the IMC embarked on no official advertising campaign, and the Web site and organization were entirely new entities with no preceding identity or relation with media consumers. As Perlstein explained, because of the interactive nature of the site and the volume of reporting during that week, knowledge of indymedia spiraled outward to protestors and observers mostly through word of mouth. The IMC also received attention from "corporate" media, as a host of mainstream media journalists visited the IMC and interviewed different indymedia activists. In the wake of the IMC's early success, stories on the new-media center appeared in the *New York Times, Wired,* the *Washington Post,* the *Christian Science Monitor,* and on CNN.

While the Web site was the backbone of the Seattle IMC, indymedia journalists created media in a host of formats. The members of the video collective created five video newscasts, one per day, focusing on different aspects of the protests and the broader policies of the WTO. There were dozens of IMC journalists in the field each day with cameras. These videographers were connected to a dispatch center at the IMC headquarters, where they would get tips about protests, confrontations, and other events. At the end of each day, all the video captured would be brought to an editing team, who would work all night to edit hundreds of hours of footage into a thirty-minute segment that was aired the following morning.

Michael Eisenmenger described the frenzied yet exciting atmosphere of the video-production process:

> It was mostly shoot all day . . . and we had people dubbing all day, because people were out in the field shooting in BETA and DV, you know, Hi8 . . . so we had a range of decks to get dubbed from. They were dubbing everything in BETA . . . by the end of the week we had a few hundred BETA masters, like four hundred hours of tape! It was just madness! You know, just the truckload of tape . . . but that was the only feasible way of doing it. . . . So we had people all day kind of dubbing, and there was sort of like assistant editors too . . . and then at night . . . you know, the editing teams would come through—usually around between 8:00 and 10:00 we'd have a meeting inside about what the segments were going to be for the show the next morning, and how long they were. . . . My job was kind of the line editor, sort of coordinator. So, once other assignments were done, everyone's people agreed they were going to stay up all night and do this . . . they'd start editing. . . . And in a lot of cases, it was footage they had shot that day, but they needed a lot of film. In some cases, some of the camera people in the field shot something really good, they found a way to work it out. . . . So that's where other people were getting footage, they were like assistant editors, you know, like, "I need a shot of this . . . oh yeah. . . ." So, it was kind of like back and forth, and then . . . everybody would stay up all night. . . . We never output before 10:00, usually it was like 10:15, then 10:20, you know, so we'd be waiting for the tape. . . . We had this guy who was a volunteer who was a bike messenger, and he would take the tape every day to the uplink because you couldn't drive—the streets were closed.[25]

Following this rigorous process, with the help of Free Speech TV, the daily newscasts the video team produced were uplinked to satellite and broadcast around the country. In a report made by Free Speech TV at the end of the protests, organizers boasted that the video newscasts were screened in community centers, university dorm rooms, union halls, and churches.[26]

Similar organizing and development went on in photography, audio, and print collectives. Leaders emerged, and a working set of practices was developed that fit the particular communications medium. Consequently, along with the daily video newscasts, Seattle citizen journalists produced hundreds of articles and reports, countless hours of radio programming, as well as a daily newspaper. The newspaper *The Blindspot* was distributed throughout the city while being posted each day online as a pdf file. The audio team had a daily radio program that was streamed live on the Web.

High/Low Technologies and the Role of the Web

As the diversity of the media produced attests, from the beginning organizers in Seattle recognized the importance of creating multiple communication platforms to deal with issues of access. Along these lines, in an attempt to bridge the digital divide, the indymedia Web site enabled what Perlstein saw as a "high and low," or "old and new," technology strategy. Practically, this meant that by synergizing different media, the Web site cultivated new distribution tactics. Perlstein notes:

> We were really concerned with what's been called the digital divide, and the question of access. Who's getting access to the Internet? How does that play right into a lot of the things we were trying to be an alternative to? . . . So we set about to really do this somewhat innovative, what we're calling linking of high and low technologies. . . . For example, we would post audio files, video files, text, and photos, all these different mediums on the site, then we hooked up with, like, a community radio station, cable-access station, even community-based organizations internationally who . . . had an Internet connection.[27]

During the WTO meetings, the Seattle IMC newspaper was put online. In Belgium, organizers downloaded the newspaper, and eight thousand copies were given out on the streets of Brussels to people who did not have Internet access. Accordingly, in Cuba, producers for Radio Havana pulled down the audio-stream of different interviews and programs the indymedia audio collective produced and rebroadcasted them in Cuba so people across the country who did not have Internet access could hear about the actions in the United States. This practice of synergizing different forms of communication to maximize distribution still operates in indymedia. Perlstein explained his hope for this strategy: "It's really about finding out where these different points, these nodes, are around the world and nationally, who do have Internet access, and they can ripple out the impact wider and wider . . . [and] be accessible to the majority of the world's people."[28]

From Seattle IMC to the Indymedia Movement

The energetic inauguration of the indymedia movement presaged a new era of grassroots citizen journalism and digitized, networked resistance, which has grown into an expansive communications network after Seattle. Jill Friedberg, a documentary filmmaker and the co-organizer of Seattle IMC's video team, visualized the prospective evolution of the indymedia movement. In the five-part documentary, Showdown in Seattle,[29] Friedberg explained that during the week of the WTO protest, activists "started to talk about using this model and going around the world to help people set up similar centers so there really could be an alternative network throughout the world."

The aftermath of the Battle of Seattle saw IMCs quickly germinating throughout the industrialized nations—first in Washington, D.C. and London, then Philadelphia and Los Angeles, followed by Prague (IMF/World Bank), Davos (World Economic Forum), Genoa (G8), and Cancun (WTO). The early IMCs were launched in conjunction with the protest circuit of the burgeoning Global Social Justice Movement. Activists involved in Seattle and the broad network connected to the alternative media movement targeted cities with major protests and made plans to create IMCs. Perlstein explained this growth:

> What we've seen since Seattle, I think, is the growth of these international mobilizations and confrontations with these transnational corporations. So, for example, the IMF and World Bank actions of confronting them in April in D.C., the Republican National Convention here in the States, in L.A. and Philly, the actions recently in Prague in September. In all these places, people have seen it appropriate to carry the IMC model on. Actually, we've been overwhelmed by the interest and demand by people to really make use of this tool and to plug in and keep this dialogue and these connections going.[30]

In time, however, the idea reached a tipping point, and communities wanted to develop the tools to tell their own stories. Much of this growth was completely decentralized, with no connection to the original founders of the Seattle IMC. Jay Sand described learning about the birth of the London IMC:

I got an email, or an email came across an IMC listserv from someone in the U.K., and they said, "Hey! We just had this big Mayday thing, and we formed an IMC—take a look!" And so they did it all internally on their own. . . . I'm sure they were communicating with someone, but there really wasn't an entity there to communicate with. . . . And that was the first time I really felt that this was actually something people wanted to do.[31]

By the end of 2001, two years after the Battle of Seattle, there were over sixty Independent Media Centers across the world. As they emerged, they formed a loosely federated noncorporate media and communications structure. From 2000 to 2004, in the height of the movement's development, an IMC was developed once every seven days. The Seattle IMC grew into a broad-based indymedia movement as foreseen by the EZLN about eight years earlier.

Conclusions

The events leading up to Seattle, from Chiapas to Cape Cod, and the birth of the indymedia network bring to the fore the complex, entwined relationship between new information and communication technologies, a shifting economic order, and the promise and practice of social and political resistance in the information age. Many of the innovations and concerns of Seattle set the course for the Cyber Left and the new logic of political resistance. To conclude, I want to enumerate three outcomes and practices that grew out of the organizing practices of Seattle and beyond: (1) the technological innovation of indymedia led to true participatory media; (2) the resulting media practices and platforms led to new possibilities in the structure, strategy, and governance of political resistance, and (3) the inability to connect with communities of struggle on the ground in Seattle was a problem rooted in the foundation of the movement and has plagued the network since.

A few years after Seattle, Matt Arnison argued that the Seattle IMC "revolutionized the way media works,"[32] as it was one of the first Web experiments where hundreds of users were actually generating content as opposed to merely receiving or retrieving content. He continued: "The flow of information was stood on its head. Instead of corporate media moguls telling people what was important, information was created from everyday people, and it bubbled up, in effect giving people new tools to express themselves and importantly to impact political life."[33] Although the claim is bold, others have corroborated the fact that indymedia technology—and the way that people have used it—was a central precursor of the social-media revolution popularized in 2006, when *TIME* proclaimed "You" as the Person of the

Year for "seizing the reins of global media . . . and framing the new digital democracy" (Grossman 2006).[34] How activists and organizers approached and utilized media transformed as communities fighting for social change began to recognize that the corporate mass media was a critical part of the problem. This recognition led to a strategic shift away from fighting for the mass media, toward building an alternative media infrastructure. DeeDee Halleck (2002) captured this shift in ideology when she declared of indymedia: "This is not an attempt to 'get on TV,' but a commitment to create new forms of information sharing using new spaces and technologies and new ways of collaboration. . . . [T]his time the revolution is not only televised but digitized and streamed" (416). This strategic decision to create an alternative infrastructure in turn led to new technological innovations, which have impacted the Internet and larger society.

The multitude of perspectives cultivated by open publishing and the Seattle IMC had real political outcomes, approximating Manuel Castells's "creative cacophony" (1996a). Castells argues that in the Information Age, diverse communities use new technologies to transform the relationship between space and information flows, creating a contested civil society from multiple places and experiences. In the same moment, however, the experience of open publishing during the WTO extends Castells's idea, as the focus of the IMC was not on an unrestrained burgeoning of a "plurality of views and interests," as his "cacophony" suggests, but rather on diverse but convergent reckonings with a singular interest: the problems of the WTO and the global economy. In this sense, it is more apt to understand this phenomenon that grew out of indymedia not as an overpowering disharmony, but as something more akin to a patterned mosaic. This patterned mosaic, channeled through a shared communications infrastructure, was the underlying strategy of indymedia.

Finally, while open publishing represented a new way for people and communities to speak and listen, the process of establishing Independent Media Centers in local communities is often fraught with tension. The obstacles to gaining traction with the Seattle community were a problem that has continued to plague the indymedia movement. Directly after the WTO meetings, Perlstein discussed the reasons that the IMC did not integrate into the community completely. With regard to local organizing, he contended: "Frankly, that didn't happen as much as it needed to in retrospect. . . . The relationship with local organizers and local organizations wasn't as strong as it could have been and in my mind should have been. . . . The reality was that most of those organizations were maxed out running their own projects."[35] A few years later, however, reflecting on this assessment, Perlstein argued that it was more complex than groups being overextended: "It was an oversim-plification by me and not complete. . . . It is true [that] organizations were overextended. We did go, and they were maxed out and we were maxed out, but it is also true that if we had a deep relationship over time they might not have said, 'We are busy, go away,' so it is more complex than what I said in the past."[36] It is this complexity and, importantly, the hard work of building real local relationships that was a problem in Seattle and has continued to plague the indymedia movement since. So, while the hard work of technological development and the creation of new open-communication platforms were achieved, building trust, particularly among the most oppressed, is a much more difficult task that was not achieved in Seattle. Along these lines, another founder, Dan Merkle, argued, "Indymedia has done a poor job of trying to figure out how to reach out to other communities. Particularly poor com-munities and communities of color."[37] Merkle marks this inability to build alliances with communities of struggle as one of the failings of the indymedia movement in the long run, and one of the reasons he left the project a few months after the WTO. This disconnection from the materially oppressed or "deprived" has been a problem at the root of the Cyber Left in general.

Figure 1: Storefront of Seattle IMC, November 2000. (Photo courtesy of Jonathan Lawson.)

MONDAY NOV 29 ISSUE NO. 1

BLIND SPOT
A DAILY BULLETIN OF UNDERREPORTED ANTI-WTO ACTIVISM

INSIDE

KOMO news blackout

Copwatch: National Lawyers Guild, arrest report, finding friends

Mothers stand up for Mother Earth

Wild ride on the planet bus

Bringing the noise

State Department denies visas

Squatters occupy abandoned building

"We are reclaiming what was private property and making it community property," exclaimed Hagbard, one of over 75 people who took over an abandoned building downtown that was recently affordable housing for artists.

The occupation began around 8pm on Sunday night. After the initial break-in, people began crawling through a small space left open from the boarded up staircase leading from the front door. People immediately got to work.

Within an hour people had covered the windows with black tarps. The electricity and water were hooked up and running. The cooking crew was busy cutting vegetables, preparing spaghetti for the first community feast to celebrate their action. Makeshift stoves were fired up and water was boiling.

"As anarchists, we are working together to create a place without hierarchy, coercion, or centralized power. Unlike people from the WTO we believe that people are good and they don't need masters," explained Hagbard, a Eugene, Oregon, based anarchist.

"Each person is equipped to govern themselves," added Cat.

After about an hour and a half, a police officer arrived. Alex, the police liaison stationed across at a bus stop across the street spoke with him. A list of questions was communicated from inside via walkie-talkies. The cop gathered some information and left.

"The risk of being put in jail should not deter people from feeding people and putting a roof over their heads," remarked Hooch, in town from Idaho. "Everyone deserves a place to live."

"Every form of protest that says No to the existing order is necessary," commented Cat.

"Barricading is going on for our safety," said one of the new residents.

"But I am not interested in a march that begins and ends at a certain place and gets us nowhere. This form of nonviolent direct action is not about just saying No! It is about saying Yes! And creating a real alternative. We are turning this into activist housing during the WTO and hope to keep it as housing for the homeless once we are gone."
—*scott winn*

Protest no mystery for People's Assembly

"How the WTO raised the ire of such a wide group of protestors remains somewhat of a mystery," reported the Sunday November 28 edition of the Seattle Times.

It is no mystery to Ace Saturay, convenor of the People's Assembly and chair of the Seattle division of the Filipino organization Sentenaryo ng Bayan. His organization has been planning the People's Assembly for over a year. It is taking place Sunday November 28 and Monday November 29 at the Filipino Cultural Center in Rainier Valley at 5740

(continued on back page bottom)

Figure 2: The first issue of the Seattle IMC newspaper *Blindspot* during WTO protests, November 29, 1999.

Figure 3: One of the founders of the Independent Media Center of Philadelphia, Alec Meltzer, during the 2000 RNC protests. (Photo courtesy of Independent Media Center of Philadelphia.)

Figure 4: Philly IMC journalists with the fifth issue of *The Unconvention*, August 2000. (Photo courtesy of Independent Media Center of Philadelphia.)

Figure 5: A videographer capturing images during the International Wages for Housework Campaign march at the RNC, when Philly IMC was established. (Photo courtesy of Independent Media Center of Philadelphia.)

Figure 6: Edinburgh IMC Convergence Center during G8 protests in Scotland, July 2005.

Figure 7: Indymedia activists set up the Edinburgh IMC Convergence Center during G8 protests in Scotland, July 2005. (Photo courtesy of Erin Siegel McIntyre.)

Figure 8: Brad Will working on a farm in southern Brazil with the Landless Rural Workers' Movement in 2003. (Photo courtesy of Dyan Neary.)

Figure 9: Family, friends, and indymedia activists come together to celebrate the life and commemorate the death of Brad Will in New York City, fall 2006. (Photo courtesy of Erin Siegel McIntyre.)

Figure 10: IMCistas create a banner honoring Brad Will. (Photo courtesy of Erin Siegel McIntyre.)

PART II

The Logic of Resistance

> In the face of the totalitarian features of this society, the traditional notion of the "neutrality" of technology can no longer be maintained. Technology as such can no longer be isolated from the use to which it is put; the technological society is a system of domination, which operates already in the concept and construction of techniques. . . . Technological rationality has become political rationality.
>
> —Herbert Marcuse, *One Dimensional Man*

Critical Theory of Technology

In "The Work of Art in the Age of Mechanical Reproduction" (1969), Walter Benjamin famously wrote, "To pry an object from its shell, to destroy its aura, is the mark of a perception whose 'sense [is] of the universal equality of things'" (225). In this poetic turn, Benjamin impels the reader to reckon with the irrevocable (progressive) changes to social life that came with the technological advances of industrial capitalism. A friend of Bertolt Brecht and an admirer of Charles Baudelaire, Benjamin saw art as a primary medium through which subjectivity is fashioned. In particular, he saw bourgeois art as a hegemonic instrument reproducing social hierarchy. This power is rooted in the ways works of art are at once embedded in history and tradition, while holding a magic or "aura" that enables those same works to stand out, maintaining authority over the viewer, thus reproducing social order.

Hailing the birth of popular culture, Benjamin believed that with the technological advances of the Industrial Revolution would come the capacity to mechanically reproduce art, which in turn would lead to a fundamental change in the distance of art from the masses. With mechanical reproduction, "aura" would be ripped asunder, creating a more egalitarian engagement or a "proletarianizing" effect on cultural production and analysis. This transformation, however, was not purely aesthetic, leading to an immutable, emancipatory change in human consciousness and ultimately the revolutionary subject.

Appraising "The Work of Art in the Age of Mechanical Reproduction," Theodor Adorno[1] took issue with the revolutionary power Benjamin accorded technology. Adorno countered that Benjamin's belief in the "proletarianizing" effect of mechanical reproduction was naïve, as technology is deeply entwined with power relations and the mode of production.[2] In a letter to Benjamin, Adorno wrote, "The idea that a reactionary is turned into a member of the avant-garde by expert knowledge of Chaplin's films strikes me as out-and-out romanticization" (Adorno, Benjamin, Bloch, Brecht, and Lukacs 1999, 123).

Marked by the rise of Nazism and his experiences in the United States shortly thereafter, Adorno had a more measured outlook on the role of technology in the development of popular culture and mass society. In 1944, Adorno worked with fellow Frankfurt School scholar Max Horkheimer to write *The Dialectic of Enlightenment* (Horkheimer and Adorno 1972). The book's foremost chapter, "The Culture Industry: Enlightenment as Mass Deception," was a direct response to Benjamin's "The Work of Art in the Age of Mechanical Reproduction."[3] Horkheimer and Adorno advanced the now-famous culture-industry argument, which holds that new industrially produced art forms, like film, manipulate the masses into passivity. Reflecting on the culture-industry argument some years later, Adorno summarized his view on the intersection of art and technology: "The progressive technical domination of nature becomes mass deception and is turned into a means for fettering consciousness. It impedes the development of autonomous independent individuals who judge and decide consciously for themselves" (1991, 106). Analyzing the correspondence between Adorno and Benjamin on aesthetics, technology, and politics, Fredric Jameson contended that while on the one hand, "it is clear that Benjamin, following Brecht, tended to hypostatize techniques in abstraction from relations of production . . . on the other hand, Adorno's analysis of jazz was notoriously myopic and rearguard" (Adorno, Benjamin, Bloch, Brecht, and Lukacs 1999, 107). The conflict that emerged in the exchanges between these titans of art and literary theory parallels the central contradiction Marx foresaw in capitalism between the forces of production (technology) and relations of production (social/class relations in society). For Marx, social relations within society cannot keep pace with the advancement of technology, which is propelled by the needs of capitalism. This ultimately leads to struggle and transformation. In this sense,

Adorno and Benjamin represent the different poles of this contradiction as it concerns technology and social relations. Benjamin is focused on technological advancements that can transform society, while Adorno is focused on the social relations of domination that mediate technological advancement.

We can see reflections of Adorno and Benjamin in the contemporary debate regarding digital technology and social movements. On one side of the contradiction are the contemporary technological utopianists who ruminate on the power and potentiality of the Information Age, with digital media as the precipitate for a new dawn of democracy. Scholars like Manuel Castells, who, upon evaluating the "multifaceted rebellion" characterized by the Arab Spring and Occupy Wall Street, argues that while new communication technologies do not necessarily foster rebellion, there is a profound relationship between the Internet and a progressive society. The Internet "creates the conditions for a form of shared practice that allows a leaderless movement to survive. . . . There is a deeper, fundamental connection between the Internet and networked social movements: they share a specific culture, the culture of autonomy, the fundamental cultural matrix of contemporary societies. . . . This is because the technology of the Internet embodies the culture of freedom" (Castells 2012, 229–31). Explicit in Castells's argument is a belief that the Internet "embodies a culture of freedom" and is therefore structured to cultivate this culture of freedom in humanity. A similar outlook regarding the intrinsically progressive nature of new communication technologies is offered by media-studies scholar Joss Hands (2011), who observes "that there lies at the heart of rebellion a kind of thinking that entails the mutual recognition of others, and of solidarity and openness. . . . It is my contention that the digital networked age is one that can be, and is, amenable to just this kind of horizontal communicative action" (17–18). In a similar vein, the anthropologist Arturo Escobar (2009) argues:

> The approaches discussed here aim at making visible a different logic of social organization that resonates clearly in two domains of concern to this book: digital technologies (cyberspace, as the universe of digital networks, interactions, and interfaces), and social movements. . . . I argue the model enabled by ICTS is based on an altogether novel framework of interaction—a relational model in which all receivers are also potentially emitters, a novel space of dialogic interaction. . . . [S]uch a vision resonates with the principles of complexity and self-organization, which emphasize bottom-up processes. (273–74)

Finally, consider the words of the contemporary political theorists Michael Hardt and Antonio Negri (2004): "We might understand the decision-making capacity of the multitude in analogy with the collaborative development of computer software and the innovations of the open-source software move-ment. . . . [O]ne approach to understanding the multitude, then, is as an open-source society, that is, a society whose source code is revealed so that we can all work collaboratively to solve its bugs and create new, better social programs" (339–40).

In all of these arguments there is a similar two-layer structure. At the first layer is a celebration or at the least an uncritical confirmation of the contem-porary cultural logic of resistance, which calls for horizontal organizational forms and eschews power structures and details practices of resistance or-ganized around autonomy, mutual recognition, dialogic interaction, self-organization, and collaboration. At the second level is a concomitant belief that this logic of resistance is bound up in the nature, structure, or interface of new communication technology. Sometimes technology compels this new logic of resistance, sometimes it is a mere mirror of this logic, but in all of these cases there is a presumed homology between the structure and poten-tialities of new technology and the prevailing logic of social movements.

On the other side of this dialectic between technology and social relations are the neo-Luddites[4] who warn of the increasing disenfranchisement that comes with the capture of these new technologies by the powerful. On this side of the ledger, scholars have written about the way technologies have been appropriated to enable neoliberal globalization,[5] to create automated production processes that exclude or deskill workers,[6] as a security apparatus that heightens the state's ability to suppress resistance,[7] and as a dominant mass media that disseminates hegemonic control and the reproduction of social relations.[8] In this vein, Jodi Dean (2009) has developed a theory of "communicative capitalism" to challenge the techno-utopian visions of new technologies:

> Communicative capitalism designates the strange merging of democracy and capitalism in which contemporary subjects are produced and trapped. It does so by highlighting the way networked communications bring the two together. The values heralded as central to democracy take material form in networked communication technologies. Ideals of access, inclusion, discussion, and par-ticipation come to be realized through expansions, intensifications, and in-terconnections of global telecommunications. . . . Expanded and intensified communicativity neither enhances opportunities for linking together political struggles nor enlivens radical democratic practices—although it has exacer-bated left fragmentation, amplified the voices of right-wing extremists, and delivered ever more eyeballs to corporate advertisers. Instead of leading to

more equitable distribution of wealth and influence, instead of enabling the emergence of a richer variety in modes of living and practices of freedom, the deluge of screens and spectacles coincides with extreme corporatization, financialization, and privatization across the globe. Rhetorics of access, participation, and democracy work ideologically to secure the technological infrastructure of neoliberalism. (22–23)

For Dean and others, new communication technologies do not enhance "opportunities for linking together political struggles nor enliven radical democratic practices." Dean challenges the presumption that technology is structured in a way that enables it to cultivate the emergent cultural logic of resistance. Much like the techno-utopianists, there are two layers to Dean's argument; however, in her case the process is flipped. She argues that there is a double capture. At one level, capitalism has captured new technology as the communication infrastructure enables global financialization, privatization, and many of the central attributes of a neoliberal economy. At another level, Dean argues that informational capitalism and the communications infrastructure capture the rhetoric of democracy and all of the attributes that orbit around the logic of the Cyber Left, from access and inclusion to participation and collaboration. It is within this double capture that subjects are produced and trapped, particularly because they hail strategies and attributes that are embedded in, and ultimately empower, contemporary capitalism. Thus, whereas the techno-utopianists discuss a homology between the logic of resistance and the structure of new technologies, Dean discusses the capture of the technological infrastructure and the logic of participatory democracy by capitalism.

While it is attractive to take one or the other side of this debate, and much of what I have seen in my research parallels Dean's critical analysis, I argue that we must take a different approach to technology, not assuming either its inherent revolutionary character or its complete capture by capital. Concerned with many of the same issues, Paolo Gerbaudo (2012) argues for a "cultural and phenomenological interpretation of the role of social media as a means of mobilization" that attends to the concrete media practices "activists develop in their use" (9). Building on this perspective, and following the philosopher of technology Andrew Feenberg (1991), I argue for a dialectical approach to technology—an approach that places technological practices and relations of domination and resistance into conversation with one another. This dialectical approach does not hold that technology is neutral, as it was produced and reproduced with social intention by those with power; but at the same time, technological practice is a site of contested struggle, and technological tools can be utilized to create social change.

This dialectical approach to technology avoids a techno-utopian outlook that imputes naturally given revolutionary character to the Internet. At the same time, this dynamic approach recognizes the critical and likely realist analysis of technology embodied in Dean's work, while not seeing the capture of technology as complete or given. In this sense, as other research has shown, "if capital 'interweaves technology and power,' this weaving can be undone, and the threads can be used to make another pattern" (Dyer-Withford 1999).

This reweaving of technology is illustrated by Frantz Fanon in *Studies of a Dying Colonialism* (1965), when he famously described how the Algerian National Liberation Front (FLN) reappropriated the radio, changing it from a tool of French colonial domination to a fundamental weapon of resistance. As Fanon argues, "[T]he creation of a *Voice of Fighting Algeria*" (93) and the correspondent construction of an Algerian version of truth put the French truth, which for so long was unchallenged in Algeria, on the defensive. Thus, while in the hands of the French, the radio served to further French domination, obscuring social relations and isolating "natives" from one another, whereas the FLN's reappropriation turned the radio into a tool of information, connection, and unification by creating a new language of Algerian resistance and nationhood. Thus, it was not radio alone that produced change; in fact, Algerians would not adopt the radio while it was a tool of French domination. It was the social use of radio by the FLN that made it a revolutionary tool in Algeria.

Fanon's dialectical analysis of radio in Algeria offers an entry point into this complex discussion of technology and social movements. Along these lines, the birth of the Internet serves as a useful example of the dialectical interplay of technological tools and social relations. By all accounts, the development of the Internet as a communications tool was financed, and at times led, by the U.S. Department of Defense, through the Advanced Research Project Agency (DARPA). DARPA created the predecessor to the Internet, ARPANET, in order to decentralize command and control in case of nuclear attack.[9] Developed at the height of the Cold War in response to the Russian launch of Sputnik in 1957, the technology had a singular military purpose. Scholars have shown, however, that in the research and development process, the tech laborers working on ARPANET appropriated the system to create a social-communications network. Correspondingly, much of the original intent was supplanted by the aim of creating a democratic, egalitarian communications network. In this respect, a technology that emerged out of the U.S. Department of Defense became the backbone for a worldwide-unrestricted medium for information and communication. As Hafner and Lyon explain: "The romance of the Net came not from how it was built or how it worked but from how it was used. By 1980 the Net was far more than a collection of computers and leased lines. It was a place to share work and build friendships and a more open method of communications" (1996, 218). In another account, speaking of social networking and successive layers of social usage that engulfed the new technology, Peter Childers and Paul Delany (1994) exclaimed, "The parasites took over the host" (62).

More recently, however, as the Internet has emerged as a central tool of social life, the forces of capitalism have successfully worked to co-opt it and create a technology that prioritizes profit over information sharing. In *Digital Disconnect: How Capitalism Is Turning the Internet against Democracy* (2013), Robert W. McChesney details how, for the last two decades, in every major fight that determined the direction of this new communication technology, the forces of capital have won: "The tremendous promise of the digital revolution has been compromised by capitalist appropriation and development of the Internet. . . . In the great conflict between openness and the closed system of corporate profitability, the forces of capital have triumphed whenever an issue mattered to them" (97). This appropriation of the Internet for the interests of capital is not complete, of course, as there are a host of struggles that will determine the character of this new technology for decades, yet it does offer the central window through which to understand the Web in the second decade of the twenty-first century. In a broader sense, however, the conflict over the Internet yet again illustrates that a dialectical approach to technology offers a framework for studying technological practices as they are tied to social relations and the mode of production, while leaving open conditions of possibility for contravening interests.

Digital Technology and the Cultural Logic of Resistance

Many techno-utopian scholars claim a congruence between what they see as the intrinsically cooperative nature of the Internet and the cultural logic of resistance for Cyber Left actors and institutions. However, while there is clearly a link between new digital technologies and the practices of contemporary activists, it is critical to disaggregate technology from political logic. As I discussed in the introduction, the cultural logic of resistance for contemporary social movements emerged not through a homology between activist practice and technological potentiality but rather in relationship to the nature of capitalism and the material (technological) environment, as well as the history of social-movement practice. Thus, in order to appreciate the social-movement logic of a particular moment, one must understand this triangulated interaction between social-movement actors and the material-ist present, on the one hand, and the long unfolding history of resistance, on the other hand.

Part I focused on the histories and influences that led to the birth of indy-media and this broader logic of resistance. The aim was to demonstrate how the contemporary logic of resistance is historically engendered as a response to informational capitalism, as well as the history of left-based organizing in the United States and beyond. In this sense, the Cyber Left's social hori-zon and the character of its movements for social change are bound by the political imaginary[10] of the period. In addition to responding to the social, political, and economic environment, I contend that each stage of the left is also reacting to previous generations and the historical legacy of movement building. As Karl Marx (1978) once remarked, "The tradition of all the dead generations weighs like a nightmare on the brain of the living" (595).

In part II, "Logic of Resistance," I focus on the core attributes that comprise this contemporary logic of resistance: the strategy, structure, and governance of indymedia. The strategy of indymedia and Cyber Left movements is to create platforms and processes where different fragmented struggles can be networked together, not in an effort to become one singular struggle but to become stronger together as a complex of struggles. Cyber Left actors and institutions presume that there are multiple, irreducible fronts of struggle that must exist independently and cannot be subsumed under one banner, framework, or organizational structure. Indymedia takes up this strategy, utilizing the local, national, and global communications infrastructure to link people and struggles across space and theme, becoming a platform for this diversity of struggle.

Indymedia and other Cyber Left institutions tend to be structured as global, decentralized networks. In the specific case of indymedia, this means that the network is composed of a collection of local Independent Media Centers, usually based in urban settings across the world. The local IMCs are part of one loosely shared network, but they have almost complete autonomy. This structure is in contradistinction to the past, where social-movement organizations were structured as political parties (Communist, Black Pan-ther), unions (IWW, Teamsters, AFL-CIO), or organizations (Students for a Democratic Society, Student Non-Violent Coordinating Committee), and the different parts of an organization were more closely tied to the whole.

The internal governance of indymedia is a form of direct democracy, enacted through a complex, consensus decision-making process at the local, national, and global scale. As a governing doctrine, this means that each member of indymedia has a right to equal participation in any decision affecting the organization. Accordingly, indymedia has no formally expressed hierarchy, there are no elections, and there is no president or executive director of the network. Everyone is considered a leader.

The three core dynamics of the Cyber Left—strategy, structure, and governance—form a discernable pattern of action, captured by the desire to build a new world order without hierarchy or entrenched forms of power. The Cyber Left cultural logic of resistance is defined by a desire to build a movement, and ideally a world without hierarchy. This logic of horizontality is clearly present in the strategy, structure, and governance of the Cyber Left, as each of these aspects of contemporary movements is marked by an aspiration to create open, flat, nonhierarchical arrangements.

4

Structure: Networks and Nervous Systems

The Che Guevara of the twenty-first century is the network.
—Alec Ross, Hillary Clinton's Senior Advisor
for Innovation at the U.S. State Department

On February 15, 2003, I followed Mia out into the brisk winter day. We hopped on an eastbound trolley and headed toward Center City, Philadelphia. As we got off the trolley and walked across the concourse of City Hall, I began to hear the faint murmur of people chanting and the unmistakable din of a momentous gathering of people. Walking a few more blocks, we joined a colorful mass of ten thousand protestors, marching to the strident beat of a Korean drum troupe and a makeshift samba band. As we made our way east on Market Street, toward Philadelphia's famed Liberty Bell, Mia whipped out her video camera (on loan from a local university) and began capturing footage of giant puppets and members of United Food and Commercial Workers Local 1776 holding signs proclaiming, "No Blood for Oil" and "Wage Peace." As Mia and I joined the surging crowd, our voices and bodies merged with the largest coordinated global protest in history—with estimates of around sixteen million people protesting in eight hundred cities around the world.

Throughout the march, Mia and other members of the nascent indymedia movement were busy taking notes on the action, photographing the surging crowd, recording the fiery words of renowned speakers, and interviewing impassioned demonstrators. I watched this new breed of "independent journalists" performing the same tasks as the seasoned reporters from the *Philadelphia Daily News* or the local ABC-TV affiliate. The chief difference, besides the quality of equipment and the existence of a press pass, was that Mia and the other Philly IMC journalists saw their documentation of "F15" as a vital part of the worldwide day of protest. They did not understand their task as detailing the day from an objective, impartial vantage; rather, much like an ethnographer, they saw their role as capturing the day from inside, as both reporters *and* participants.

Encapsulating the participatory impulse of this new-media project, for every photograph or interview Mia captured, she handed out a pamphlet declaring, "Don't hate the media, be the media." The quarter-sheet she gave out invited demonstrators to visit the Philly IMC Web site and use the open-publishing platform to tell their stories of the day. People responded. Within hours of the protest, indymedia Web sites across the world were adorned with thousands of photos, hundreds of written reports, and dozens of videos, offering audiences expansive, unmediated coverage of F15.

The stated aim of F15 was to consolidate the broad but dispersed antiwar sentiment into a powerful political force that could preempt the impending U.S.-led war with Iraq. The historic nature of the transnational antiwar protest, and the new political formation it epitomized, was not lost on the mainstream press. The journalist Patrick Tyler (2003) of the *New York Times* envisioned F15 as the dawn of an incipient "global civil society" that could potentially challenge U.S. dominance in the post-Soviet era. Meanwhile, the United States' foremost progressive weekly magazine, *The Nation,* hailed F15 as the materialization of the world's "other superpower" (Schell 2003). Jonathan Schell compared the growing peace movement to the singular force of the American-led military in Iraq. "Both are creatures of the Information Age," he argued, "which underlies the so-called 'smart' technology on display in the war as well as the Internet, which has become the peace movement's principal organizing tool." While the *New York Times* and *The Nation* captured the shifting dynamics of global protest, they did not account for the intricate network of social-movement organizations that cultivated and organized this massive public demonstration.

Networked Organizing and Transnational Activism

The size and scope of the F15 protests were historic, but the day of action was also notable because of how rapidly it was organized. Members of the British group Globalise Resistance first raised the idea of a European-wide antiwar demonstration during the European Social Forum in Florence, Italy, in November 2002.[1] The idea was embraced, and a council of European social movements issued a call to "citizens of Europe to start continent-wide resistance to war." The appeal concluded with a declaration that Europeans should "start organizing enormous anti-war demonstrations in every capital on February 15th 2003."[2] This appeal for a massive, continent-wide day of action quickly picked up steam and was endorsed by countries throughout Europe during a planning meeting in Copenhagen in December 2002. As energy for F15 grew in Europe, the call for a day of action spread to an international audience through the World Social Forum, which took place in Brazil in January 2003. The Belgian political scientist Joris Verhulst (2010) explains:

> Between January 23 and 27, 2003, the European Social Forum antiwar call was further disseminated on the third World Social Forum in Porto Alegre, Brazil. The World Social Forum Secretariat had set up a workshop exclusively devoted to planning the February 15 international day of protest. With some five thousand organizations present from every corner of the globe, the call was spread throughout the world. . . . These important face-to-face meetings were complemented by a second major mechanism favoring the massiveness of the February 15 protests, namely the intensive use of the Internet and e-mail circuits. All national peace movements and coalitions were linked to each other by joint mailing lists and cross-referencing each other on the Web. On an international scale, the exact same thing took place, allowing the different movements to act very fast. (11–13)

Building on the international call for a day of action at the World Social Forum, the idea of a globally orchestrated protest intensified and intersected with national activist networks around the world. In most countries, a temporary national coalition was established that consisted of a diverse array of antiwar organizations. To demonstrate the global alliance, these newly minted national coalitions created interlinking Web sites and jointly used the symbol of a missile crossed out by the words "Stop the War" to signify F15 (Walgrave and Verhulst 2006).

While there was substantial transnational coordination of F15, in each country the process for organizing the day of protest was different. In Great Britain, the Stop the War Coalition, an alliance of political parties and social-justice organizations, put out a call for a national demonstration in London. The Stop the War Coalition then partnered with other U.K.-based groups like the Muslim Association of Britain to publicize and plan for the demonstration. The London demonstration on February 15 turned out to be one of the largest in the world, with estimates of around two million protestors taking part.

In the United States, United for Peace and Justice and Act Now to Stop War and End Racism jointly called for a national day of action after the World Social Forum. These groups then coordinated protests in major U.S. cities, including New York, Los Angeles, and Chicago. In conjunction with these nationally organized events, groups and networks of groups planned over fifty protests in smaller cities throughout the United States. The Philadelphia Regional Anti-War Network, a coalition of thirty groups across the region, organized the Center City rally that I attended with Mia.

Indymedia and F15

Indymedia coverage of F15 began shortly after the World Social Forum, with a series of appeals from members of indymedia's global editorial team. In an attempt to organize and synchronize coverage of the day of action, the global editorial team put out a request to local IMCs in Europe and beyond:

> All over Europe, anti-war demonstrations are planned on 15 February.
> We want to give this a good coverage on www.indymedia.org, but we need the help of the local IMCs with it. Especially, from those countries where the features group is lacking the appropriate languages, like Finnish, Greek, or Hungarian. Therefore the following call to all local IMCs:
> Can you send us summaries (in English) from Saturday's events?
> Please include links to articles and pictures on your local Indymedia site. (Those countries that have several IMCs: could you combine your efforts and only send us one piece?) We will then compile them into several features. Of course you can also send us complete features.
> Please send them to www.features at lists.indymedia.org. Please put F15 and the country in the subject line. If you have questions: send us an email or come to #features in the Indymedia IRC.[3]

All told, community journalists and activists from local Independent Media Centers covered over sixty protests in almost every major region of the world. Indymedia's global editorial team collated the diverse coverage into one central feature on the day of the protest, "Millions March Worldwide to Denounce Bush's War Plan." This article, a simple inventory of over eighty F15 protests worldwide, included a link to a local indymedia story and an estimate of the number of people at each protest. Members of the global editorial team explained that the idea behind this coverage was to drive people to the local IMC Web sites across the globe to experience the breadth and richness of the day of action. Following the initial story, members of the global indymedia editorial team did roundup coverage of protests in major regions, including Europe, North America, South America, Asia, and Africa. This coverage went into more depth about protests in different parts of the world. Indymedia's global Web site received over eleven million hits on F15.

Like millions of others, at the end of the long day of protest, which ended at an informal gathering at a Quaker meeting house in Old City, I was eager to get home and read reports of the other protests that were taking place across the world. When I finally got to my computer, I went straight to the global indymedia homepage, and then visited the different local IMC sites located throughout the globe. I watched as reports came in across the network detailing protests that had taken place in Rome, Athens, Melbourne, Paris, Los Angeles, and São Paulo. Through globally networked reporting, the indymedia communications network became a switchboard, connecting different elements of the transnational social formation opposing the Iraq war.[4] I followed the path of these local reports and began to visualize the weblike communications network that was the nerve center of this global movement, offering a view of each particular demonstration, while depicting a world in protest.

In an attempt to synthesize the role of indymedia coverage of F15, New York City IMC members Josh Breitbart and Mike Burke (2003) wrote an article for *Clamor* magazine in which they outlined the role of indymedia in giving form to an inchoate global civil society. They argued, "Indymedia, with reports for all of the biggest demonstrations and many of the smallest, wove hundreds of separate actions into a single story. As popular uprisings from around the world begin to coordinate their actions, indymedia is proving to be an essential tool for imagining this new community" (Breitbart, Burke, and NYC IMC 2003).

*   *   *

While F15 has a great deal to offer scholars studying the nature of a cohering global civil society, or what one commentator has called "globalization from below,"[5] the worldwide day of action is also a window onto the "network" as an organizational form capable of cohering a globally articulated yet locally organized social movement. Following the original call for F15, activists operating through vertically integrated, decentralized networks at nested global, national, and local levels employed new communications technologies and traditional organizing to stage on-the-ground events in cities across the world. Consequently, antiwar organizers, first in Europe and then across the world, were able to establish a transnational, or more accurately, a rooted cosmopolitan political formation (Tarrow 2006) that could act at multiple scales, targeting national and global targets. In this sense, F15 demonstrates how new technologies and networked organizational structures can connect actors across space, underscoring new possibilities in the development of transnational collective action, while bringing into focus the shifting nature of the politics of scale.[6]

This nested, multi-tiered relationship among local, national, and global networks exemplifies the structure of indymedia and is the predominant structural configuration of Cyber Left institutions, which operate at similar levels from the local to the global. In the rest of this chapter I look at the globally networked organizational structure of indymedia to understand the strengths and weaknesses of this organizational form. First, however, I discuss how scholars have understood the intersection of contemporary networked organizational structures and social change to understand how indymedia fits into this story.

Social Movements and Networks

With the explosion of new technologies and the corresponding rise of global capitalism, the network has become a critical conceptual tool for understanding increasingly complex social arrangements as well as the role of information and communication within those arrangements. In the first volume of Manuel Castells's trilogy *The Information Age* (1996), he captures what has become a growing scholarly consensus regarding networks:

> Our exploration of emergent social structures across domains of human activity and experience leads to an overarching conclusion: as a historical trend, dominant functions and processes in the information age are increasingly organized around networks. Networks constitute the new social morphology of our societies, and the diffusion of networking logic substantially modifies the operation and outcomes in processes of production, experience, power, and culture. While the networking form of social organization has existed in other times and spaces, the new information technology paradigm provides the material basis for its pervasive expansion throughout the entire social structure. (469)

While few would deny the increasing importance of networks in the Information Age, scholars have presented diverging views on the role of networks in society and specifically in social movements. Within the social-movement literature, the network concept has largely been met with exuberance, as the majority of scholars have argued that networked organizational forms compel us toward more egalitarian social structures. For instance, Kathryn Sikkink (1993) argues that international advocacy networks are motivated by "shared values and principled ideas" and therefore are intrinsic "carriers of human rights ideas" (437–41). In a similar vein, David Ronfeldt and John Arquilla (1996) argue that one of the strengths of networks are their inherent tendency toward cooperation and equality, mitigating the unequal distributive effects of the market. While Jeffrey Juris (2008) cautions that networked social movements "should not be romanticized," he maintains that they "suggest a *potential* affinity with egalitarian values" (17).

Taking a broader theoretical approach to understanding networks, Arturo Escobar's *Territories of Difference* (2009) builds on the work of Manuel de Landa (2006). In his study of Afro-Colombian movements, Escobar makes the case that nonhierarchical social-movement networks, or what he calls "meshworks," are self-organizing structures that help us reimagine social theory. Escobar contends that meshworks are part of a larger shift toward "flat alternatives" and "flat approaches" that enable new possibilities for social change, while reintroducing "complexity into our intellectual accounts of the real" (309). What begins to materialize in Escobar's analysis of networks is the blurring between scholarship and activism. As he argues, the ideal of flat, nonhierarchical movements is an important strategy for social change and a new lens through which scholars can reinterpret the world.

Challenging the exuberance around network-based social movements, a few scholars and commentators have questioned whether networks are effective organizational structures or inherently democratic. One of the most fashionable examples of this contestation to social-media-based networks is Malcolm Gladwell's highly publicized article in the *New Yorker*, "Small Change: Why the Revolution Will Not Be Tweeted" (2010). Gladwell compares the leaderless, decentralized nature of contemporary social-movement networks to the "centralized organization" of the NAACP and "the unquestioned authority" of Martin Luther King Jr. and the Southern Christian Leadership Conference. Gladwell argues that decentralized, consensus-based network structures "have real difficulty reaching consensus and setting goals" because they "can't think strategically . . . [and] are chronically prone to conflict." Gladwell concludes that while social-movement-based networks can make the "existing social order more efficient," they do not have the capacity to challenge entrenched, structural forms of oppression like segregation.

Taking a more rigorous and cautious approach in her study of the operations of NGO networks in the lead-up to the United Nations Fourth World Conference on Women, Annalise Riles (2001) questions the academic fascination with networks. She argues that the network concept occludes other important perspectives, and correspondingly, she claims that there has not been enough attention within academic scholarship to what she calls "network failure."

While Gladwell and Riles question the effectiveness of network structures, in *The Exploit: A Theory of Networks* (2007), Alexander Galloway and Eugene Thacker challenge the assumption of democratic or egalitarian affinity within networks. They argue that "[t]he mere existence of networks does not imply democracy or equality" (13). They go on to claim that traditional forms of sovereign power (for them, this is the centralized state) have adopted the network form, creating a new "networked sovereignty," and therefore social movements and other forms of resistance must find new tactics, strategies, and organizational structures.

Building on this diverse research, in the rest of this chapter I examine indymedia's multiscalar network structure, and I make two arguments. First, the indymedia network is neither hierarchical nor flat, neither democratic nor authoritarian. Instead, the networked structure of the organization changes in different lights—from some vantages it is more vertical, and from others it is more flat or horizontal. I call this a "heterogeneous network" to emphasize the variety of arrangements and flows of power and decision making at different levels of indymedia.

Second, as other scholars have argued (Gerlach 2001; Bennett, Breunig, and Givens 2008), the multiscalar, networked organizational structure of indymedia allowed for rapid organizational growth, flexible adaptation, and more diversified pathways of engagement and mobilization of potential members. However, the strengths of the network also lead to vulnerabilities around shared political identity, organizational stability, and collective decision making.

I argue that the networked organizational structures of the Cyber Left have an immense capacity for self-organizing growth, but they are unable to make collective, long-term decisions. Thus, while the network form and particularly the self-organizing or autopoietic aspect of the indymedia network allows for tremendous expansion and the development of a global social-movement network, the same aspects hinder indymedia from becoming an effectual organizing structure for the long term.

I first look at the core dynamics and processes of the indymedia network at the local, national, and global scales to delineate the complex, byzantine nature of this transnational network. I then look at the attributes and processes of the indymedia network that allow this global, tenuous network to operate. I focus on the roles of communications and ideology in holding the indymedia network together.

Mapping the Indymedia Network

Rondfelt and Arquilla (1996) offer a useful starting point for understanding the structure of network-based social movements:

> An archetypal netwar actor consists of a web (or a network) of dispersed, interconnected "nodes" (or activity centers)—this is its key defining characteristic. These nodes may be individuals, groups, formal or informal organizations, or parts of groups or organizations. The nodes may be large or small in size, tightly or loosely coupled, and inclusive or exclusive of membership. They may be segmentary or specialized; that is, they may look quite alike and engage in similar activities, or they may undertake a division of labor based on specialization. The boundaries of the network may be sharply defined or blurred in relation to the outside environment. (280)

True to this definition, the indymedia network is made up of interconnected nodes or local Independent Media Centers, which are linked through an internal communications framework, a common goal of building an alternative media infrastructure, and a shared organizational charter. The nodes within the indymedia network are open so that anyone can join; they are specialized in that each local IMC has a specific geographic focus; and the sizes of different local IMCs vary, from five active members to two to three hundred active members. At its pinnacle in 2006, indymedia was comprised of approximately two hundred locally based IMCs worldwide, and between 1999 and 2006, a new local Independent Media Center was established on average once every nine days.

The indymedia network has global distribution, with collectives on every continent; however, industrialized nations and particularly the United States and Europe are the most heavily represented regions in the network. In 2006 there were sixty active local IMCs in the United States, twelve IMCs across

Canada, one center in Puerto Rico, and seven IMCs in Mexico. In Central and South America, there were forty-four IMCs spread across nine countries. In Africa, there were far fewer IMCs, with a total of seven across the continent. In Europe there were seventy-five IMCs in almost all major countries and an average of eight local IMCs in France, Germany, England, and Italy. There were twelve IMCs, located across East and South Asia as well as the Middle East. In Australia and New Zealand there were nine IMCs, primarily in urban centers. Along with these local, urban IMCs, there were dozens of nation-state IMCs like IMC-US and IMC-Brazil, and a global indymedia Web site (www.indymedia.org) that acted as the central node of the network.

Indymedia has the attributes of a network-based social movement; however, not all networks are the same. Scholars have identified three distinctive network typologies: star, chain, and all-channel (Evans 1972; Ronfeldt and Arquilla 1996). Each of these typologies differs in the manner through which power, decision making, and communication flow among the different nodes within the network.

The star network is the most centralized structure, consisting of one central hub that acts as a conduit for the network. The central hub can be active or passive, meaning that it can be an inactive repository for information or it can be an active creator of information. All information, and consequently relationships and decision-making power, passes through the central hub, which then governs the network. Alternatively, in a chain network, goods and information move along a line of separated nodes on a predetermined path; so while there is no central hub, there is no free association of nodes, and the pattern of association governs the network. Finally, in the all-channel network there is no central hub. Each node is connected to every other node, and there is free association among nodes. Because of the decentralized, flat structure, the all-channel network is considered the archetypical network form. All-channel networks are self-organizing or autopoietic, and consequently tend toward the most explosive growth, but they are also the most difficult to sustain because there is no central mediating node or predetermined pattern of association.

On the surface, as many scholars have noted, indymedia is structured as an all-channel network (Pickard 2006b; Atkinson 2010; Fontes 2010) wherein each local IMC, such as indymedia Colorado or indymedia Toruń (Poland), is potentially connected to each other node within the network with no central hub. However, within the indymedia network there are aspects of centralized decision making that more accurately reflect a star network, and there are also predetermined patterns of association between the nodes that more accurately reflect a chain network. In this sense, indymedia is a heterogeneous network, with multiple arrangements and flows of power and decision making at different levels. To illustrate this complex structure, I will examine the network from the different scales—local/urban, national, and global—detailing how the network operates across the scales.

Indymedia Network: Philly IMC and the Local Structure

The fundamental building block of the indymedia network is the local Independent Media Center. As an organizational structure, most local IMCs, such as Philly IMC, are both a node within the larger network and a network themselves. This self-repeating pattern is known as a fractal, where each fragment is a reduced-size copy of the whole.

During my research, Philly IMC (see chart 1), which is a fairly typical local IMC, had between twenty and thirty active members. In its most intense developmental periods, however, such as the Republican National Convention in 2000, there were over sixty active members who were part of the decision-making structure, and over two hundred people publishing on the site on a regular basis. Structurally, Philly IMC is organized into distinct collectives that manage the operation of different aspects of the organization, including a Web-streaming radio collective (Radio Volta) that consists of about twenty people, a Web-editorial collective of ten to fifteen people, an outreach collective of about ten people, and a tech collective of about five people. Each of the autonomous groups meet on their own schedule, and activists often play a role in one or more of the collectives. When I was doing my research, I was part of the Web-editorial collective and the outreach collective.

In addition to these collectives, Philly IMC has a general body that brings together leaders from each of the collectives. The Philly IMC general body holds monthly meetings where decisions are made on issues including finances and grant writing, Web site development, and editorial policy. With free association between the different collectives and the central body, Philly IMC is a hybrid between an all-channel network and a star network. Further, in that the local IMCs mirror a structure of the overall network, indymedia is a fractal network, with self-repeating patterns of organization and structure at all levels.[7]

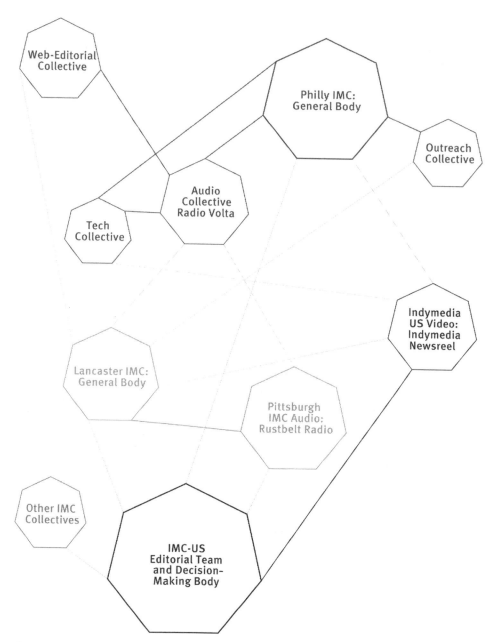

Chart 1: The local Philly IMC network, a fractal structure made up of self-dividing collectives at each level.

INDYMEDIA NETWORK: NATIONAL VIEW

While local IMCs are the foundation of the indymedia movement, in many countries indymedia activists create a nationwide network, with a national IMC acting as a central hub for local IMCs. The development of national indymedia networks has allowed local IMCs to establish a national presence, in effect collectivizing their infrastructure and focus. These national indymedia networks are often quite distinct from one another, offering a window onto the hybrid nature of the indymedia structure. During my research, I identified three separate models by which local IMCs in different countries are organized in relationship to a national IMC: (1) no national network, (2) weak national network, and (3) strong national network.

NO NATIONAL NETWORK: IMC-BELGIUM

In some countries where multiple local IMCs exist, there is no national indymedia collective or Web site, and therefore no coordination at the national level. This includes Spain, Canada, and Belgium. While each of these countries has an active indymedia presence at the local level—Spain (seven IMCs), Belgium (six IMCs), and Canada (twelve IMCs)—activists in these countries have not formed a national indymedia collective or decision-making body to collect information, coordinate coverage, or act as a mediator between local IMCs. This is the most decentralized national network, and in chart 2, Belgium IMCs are depicted to exemplify the decentralized national network. As chart 2 illustrates, because there is no national IMC, local IMCs interact directly with the global IMC network.

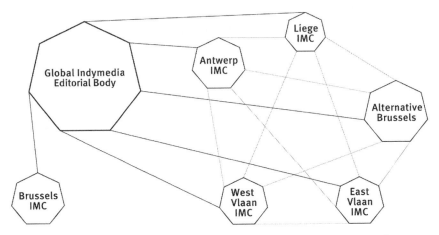

Chart 2: The Belgian IMC network is an example of how a network operates with no national collective.

This model approximates an all-channel network, with little coordination among local collectives and consequently little ability to create shared action or a shared perspective at the national level. It is important to note that this does not mean that the local collectives in a country do not interact, only that there is no centralized coordination or way to develop a national narrative among the different local IMCs.

WEAK NATIONAL NETWORK: IMC-UNITED STATES

A second model is the weak national network, and is exemplified by the IMC-US (chart 3). The local IMCs in the United States decided to form a national IMC in the summer of 2003 during a meeting at the Allied Media Conference (AMC). Members organized the meeting to discuss ways to better coordinate at the national level. At that time there were approximately thirty U.S.-based local IMCs. The activists at the AMC decided to create an IMC-US collective that could help with three levels of coordination: (1) create a national indymedia Web site, (2) coordinate technology needs for U.S.-based IMCs, and (3) organize outreach across all local IMCs in the United States. The mission statement of IMC-US is as follows: "Culling content from over 50 IMCs in the United States, www.indymedia.us is a critical tool for making local issues relevant to both a national and global audience and vice versa. While participating IMCs are U.S.-based, Indymedia.us remains firmly com-

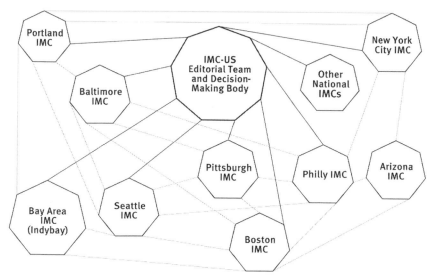

Chart 3: US IMC offers an image of how a weak national network looks and operates.

mitted to the ideas of international solidarity and mutual aid integral to the Indymedia network."[8]

While the IMC-US organizational structure offers more national coordination than a country with no national collective, it is important to note that within the IMC-US there is no national decision-making process except with regard to promoting stories onto the national IMC-US Web site. In this sense, IMC-US is, for the most part, a passive node in the network, with little decision-making power.

STRONG NATIONAL NETWORK: IMC-UNITED KINGDOM

A final model is the centralized national network, exemplified by the United Kingdom (chart 4), with variations across North and South America in Argentina, Mexico, and Brazil. In this model, local IMCs are nodes or collectives within a robust national network. There is a great deal more centralization of decision making at the national level. For instance, in Great Britain, the IMC-UK decision-making body decides what software and Web platform IMCs within the national network use, as well as the editorial rules for these collectives.[9] Due to the centralized decision making and shared outlook, local IMCs are closely aligned and tied to the national IMC. IMC-UK activists explain why they forged this structure:

> The first phase of imc-uk was marked by the specifics of an imc located in the metropolitan geography of London, the richness of connectivity and inspiration, the lack of space, and the offline-practices of blogging and sharing. The second, *post-decentralisation* phase points to the process of building a larger network, using more cybertools than before, and allowing for localised reporting.[10]

Drafters of the IMC-UK mission statement used the term "post-decentralisation" to characterize a move to a more centralized process with a shared communications platform and a more structurally cohesive national network. Much like the global network, the IMC-UK network has its own principles of unity, its own decision-making process, and its own process for determining new regional IMC-UK collectives. Further, new British-based IMC collectives are not listed on the global IMC and are not considered by the global IMC as specific nodes or collectives, as they are subcollectives of IMC-UK. In this sense, local collectives within IMC-UK, such as Oxford IMC, do not aim to be a direct node within the global indymedia network; instead, they are a part of a singular IMC-UK, which in turn is part of global indymedia.

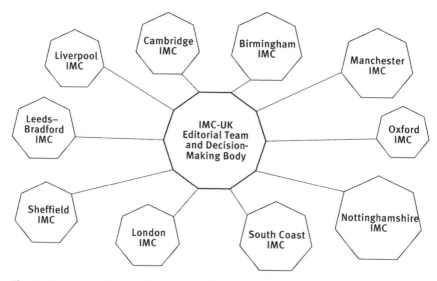

Chart 4: An image of how a strong national network looks and operates.

The IMC-UK model pushes against the decentralization of the indymedia network, attempting to create a hybrid form that mixes horizontal structures with more vertical organizational structures. It is important to note that while many IMCs in the United Kingdom are a part of the IMC-UK network, there are some local IMCs that want more autonomy and consequently have opted not to be a part of the network; these include IMC-Nottingham, IMC-Bristol, and IMC-Scotland. This rejection of the strong national network exemplifies a tension within indymedia between network centralization (star structure) and network decentralization (all-channel structure).

The diverse ways in which national IMCs coordinate with local IMCs illustrate the autonomous control at the local level that directs this global network. In looking at the network as an organizational form through the window of the national IMC networks, it also becomes clear that differently structured network systems create different communities, relationships, and ultimately capacities and strengths.

The Indymedia Network: Global View

Scaling up from the local and national indymedia collectives is global indymedia. In many ways, global indymedia is at the center of the network. Within global indymedia, I include the globally focused Web site and varied

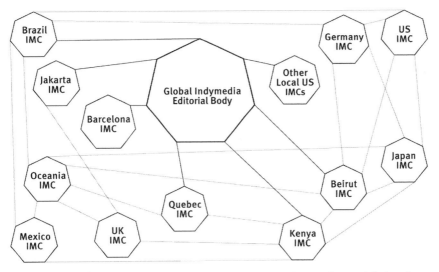

Chart 5: The global editorial body illustrates the all-channel network at a global scale.

collectives that play a role in coordinating the network. Global IMC consists of numerous collectives, but the most important collectives are Tech, Web Editorial, Finance, New IMC, Communication, and Process. Each of these collectives is comprised of activists from local IMCs across the world, and most of these collectives were developed to manage questions that were of network-wide concern, such as creating a process for admitting new local IMCs.

Chart 5 represents the flow of communication, news, and information across the indymedia network between the global indymedia editorial collective and the national or local IMC collectives around the world. As the chart makes clear, there is a decentralized, nonpatterned flow of information and communication between local and national IMCs and the global IMC.

While communication flows across indymedia are relatively decentralized, network-wide decision making is centralized, as illustrated in chart 6. Principal decisions for indymedia are made by the IMC-Process collective. There is one delegate from each local IMC collective in the IMC-Process collective. In this sense, IMC-Process is structured as a "spokes-council" where members represent their collectives in global decision making. However, while local IMCs have a representative in IMC-Process, the decision making of indymedia is centralized in this body and, along these lines, represents a star network structure.

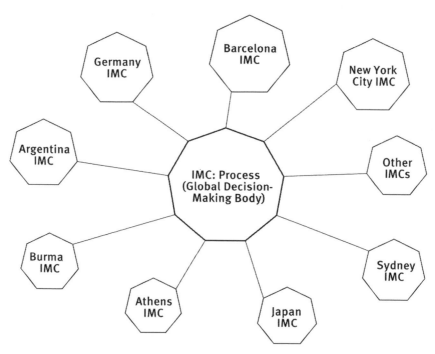

Chart 6: IMC-Process illustrates the more centralized decision-making processes across the global indymedia network.

As charts 5 and 6 illustrate, the relationship of global indymedia to local and national collectives is different in different situations. While information and communication flow within indymedia is akin to an all-channel network, with the global hub mediating information and communication flows, the decision-making body of global indymedia more closely represents a star network, with one representative from each local IMC sitting on the global decision-making body. Consequently, while each collective is represented in the global decision-making body, the global indymedia body has governance over network-wide decisions of finance, strategy, technology, growth, and structure.

As we look at the different layers of the indymedia movement, it becomes clear that the morphology of the network is complex, blurring spatial and organizational boundaries. More importantly, indymedia is not a simple, de-centralized all-channel network, as has been suggested. Instead, indymedia is a heterogeneous network, made up of hierarchical and nonhierarchical structures, decentralized and centralized authorities, and nonpatterned and patterned forms of communication and decision making.

While indymedia is not an idealized, flat, anti-authoritarian meshwork, it is a globe-spanning network with Independent Media Centers as far afield as Seoul and São Paulo. For this reason, space, time, and experience are obstacles that make it particularly difficult for activists across the world and the collectives they are a part of to hold together and remain a coherent formation. The glue of the global indymedia network is the communications/technological infrastructure, as well as the underlying ideology, which together establish a collective identity and sense of shared purpose.

Communication: The Nervous System of Networks

Historically, scholars and activists have understood media and communications as the arm of an existing social movement, giving voice to a preexisting organizational vision. However, in looking at the global indymedia network, it becomes clear that in the Information Age this metaphor is no longer suitable. Today, communication acts more like the nervous system of a network-based social movement, transmitting signals to different parts of the movement and thus coordinating its actions.

In fact, complex channels of communication in many ways chart the true shape of the global indymedia network. With local media collectives in all corners of the earth, the ability to communicate, instantaneously and relatively cheaply, across the globe is one of the central components of the indymedia movement. Without a rigid institutional backbone, the passage of information and capacity to communicate hold the local collectives together in a diverse but singular formation. Consequently, the technological infrastructure of indymedia is marked by a complicated communications arrangement that aims to cohere an otherwise decentralized global network.

Activists in indymedia use chatrooms, wiki pages, listservs, translation software, telephones, regular local face-to-face meetings, and occasional regional and global IMC meetings to communicate with each other. On the most overt level, because indymedia is a media-based movement, the Web sites of the different local collectives are a public level of communications for indymedia activists and for the broader public. This level of communication is the most transparent, and mostly focuses on stories of shared struggle.

INDYMEDIA LISTS

While the linked Web sites create an outward-facing, public domain of communication across the network, the indymedia movement is made up of a labyrinth of communication tools that support and complement the Web sites and facilitate the growth and coherence of the transnational network below the public surface. The most important channels of communication across the indymedia network are the hundreds of listservs that create flows of information across every vector imaginable. There were over six hundred operational listservs within the indymedia movement in 2009.

Shadowing the multiscalar nature of the network are local, national, and global listservs. For instance, there are about fifty different listservs to help manage different aspects of the work of the global network, from decision making (IMC-Process and IMC-Communication) and editorial decisions to spaces for women to discuss their experience in the movement, and places to discuss legal issues or software development.

It is also important to note that some listservs are decision-making domains, or what I call *strong discursive spaces,* and other listservs are primarily spaces for discussion, or *weak discursive spaces.* For the indymedia network to operate, both spaces are necessary, as the strong discursive spaces are critical for decision making, while weak discursive spaces allow for broad discussion and engagement for movement activists.

The relationship between strong and weak discursive spaces is exemplified by IMC-Process and IMC-Communication. Both of these listservs are meant to allow for the highest level of strategy discussion and decision making for the global network. IMC-Communication has the broadest membership of any indymedia list, with hundreds of members, and many of the most critical strategic issues are discussed there. However, IMC-Communication is only a space for discussion; decisions are not made on this list. Further, this list is open, and any member of a local IMC is given access to IMC-Communication. The IMC-Process listserv, on the other hand, is a decision-making listserv and therefore a strong discursive space. Most major network-wide decisions are discussed on IMC-Process, and this is the space where activists make proposals and attempt to reach consensus on issues. In contrast to the IMC-Communication list, the IMC-Process list is closed, and only one activist from each local IMC is allowed membership. When important issues emerge, there is greater conversation on IMC-Communication, while decision making occurs on IMC-Process.

Along these lines, on each listserv there is a separate and specific protocol for membership. Some of the indymedia listservs are open, which means that all users are offered access, while other administrative indymedia listservs are closed, meaning that a moderator receives a request from a user to be a member of the particular listserv. The moderator must then approve the request. This approval process may entail a discussion between the moderator and subscriber regarding the reason the subscriber would like to be a part of the listserv, or it may entail a consensus decision by those already on the listserv to allow the new user access. On all listservs, however, once a subscriber has been approved, he or she is asked to do a "roll call," answering a few basic questions. The following is a standard introduction made by Tim from Sydney when he first joined the IMC-Communication listserv:

> hi indy people,
> Apologies for only now subscribing. I agreed to act as network liaison for the sydney indymedia collective back in April. I've been relying on the list archives. My politics has developed from involvement in the early seventies in gay liberation, anti-psychiatry, the sisters of perpetual indulgence, and anti-violence and the pro-feminist men's movement through to indymedia and *cat at lyst* (which wrote indymedia's launch technology). Andy Nicholson and I attended the San Francisco convergence which drafted the initial Principles of Unity. . . . I understand some Spanish & French but don't trust myself to write them.[11]

As comes forth in this introduction, the purpose of the roll call is to show the author's personal involvement with a local indymedia collective and the larger movement, as well as the new participant's potential role and relationship to the listserv. Tim notes his role as liaison for Sydney IMC, his political background, which grounds his indymedia work, and his ability with languages. These are vital points in building Tim's credibility on the listserv. Mentioning his ability with language is particularly important, as the global listservs are meant to be communication spaces that function across the different languages represented in the network, and consequently multilingual participants are important.

Beyond introductions, listservs periodically hold a listserv-wide roll call where all members are asked to publicly identify themselves. Those who do not respond to the roll call are purged from the listserv. The purpose of this, as Philly IMC members discussed during a meeting before they did a roll call on the local Philly editorial listserv, is both to reengage those members of the listserv who have disengaged and to make sure that unwanted elements, from *agent provocateurs* to unstable characters, are kept off the listserv.

The more than six hundred listservs of indymedia form the nerve center of the network. Information flows self-generate in a multitude of directions, creating the communication and information sharing necessary to keep this flexible network together. Discussions, development of best practices, strategy building, social networking, and major decisions across the network happen on these lists.

WIKI PAGES

Alongside listservs, the wiki is another important communication tool used by indymedia activists. Indymedia wiki pages employ the same social technology as the well-known collective Web-based encyclopedia, Wikipedia. Within indymedia, wiki pages are best understood as a shared editing and management tool, where groups of people can work together on a specific project. The indymedia wiki pages are used to internally document different aspects of the movement, from decision making to gender balance, while also acting as the central archival tool, preserving dynamic information about the history of indymedia.

For instance, in 2005, when U.S. indymedia activists held a conference in Austin, Texas, organizers of the conference created the wiki page indyconference.[12] The indyconference page was first used by IMC activists as a space to collectively share ideas about the structure and sessions of the conference. Once the conference organizers planned indyconference, the wiki pages were used by conference-goers as the central repository for documentation of the conference. Different people attended workshops, took notes, or recorded the sessions and posted these notes or audio/video files on the wiki page so other indymedia activists or researchers who did not attend the conference could see what happened in Austin. On the indyconference wiki pages, there are notes from over ten different conference sessions, including the opening plenary and keynote. Along with these notes, there are multiple audio files from different panels and space for dialogue about different aspects of indyconference, from the success of the conference proceedings to next steps based on conference-wide decisions.

CHATROOMS

Complementing the listserv system and wiki communications system, indymedia activists also use chatrooms, or Internet Relay Chats (IRCs). While the listserv is a space for decision making and discussion, the chatroom is principally a social space where indymedia activists congregate online to discuss different aspects of work. On the indymedia wiki page, focused on IRC, the authors argue that a chatroom "bears a huge, largely untapped potential. . . . Chatting with someone is a whole different level of communication than e-mail, a much more dynamic one."[13]

Some IMC collectives, such as global IMC-Tech, use a chatroom as a weekly meeting space. As one of the IMC-Tech organizers explained, "The chatroom is useful because we can speak in real time, delegate work, and make decisions."[14] In the early period of indymedia, this focused, formal use of chatrooms as online, real-time conference spaces where decision-making processes occurred was the norm. In fact, the early network-wide indymedia meetings were held in IRC chatrooms.

The first call for a global IRC meeting came in January 2001, fourteen months after the birth of indymedia in Seattle:

> In order to sustain Indymedia as a network and to create a sustainable organization of inter-IMC communications and decision-making, people on the IMC Communications list invite all IMC's to participate in this first of what will become many IRC meetings. . . . The goal is to begin to discuss IMC Network-wide decisions and issues that face us as a collective, in order that we can find ways to solve some problems, create greater potential, grow at a more sustainable rate, find a basis for unity, strategize for the long-term, and allocate some funds. As the people committed to finding channels of responsible, effective, efficient, and democratic channels of communication that are fully representational, we want to convene a meeting to bring together as many of the IMC's as possible. At the second of these meetings, it is hoped that there will be even more folks at the table. We are calling this (for a lack of a better word) the convening of the IMC Global Roundtable. . . . The aim is to design and implement a process and structure through which the IMC Network can keep in contact with each other's activities; where local IMCs could bring ideas to improve and strengthen the global network; and where collectively we would make IMC network decisions through active communication and participation from the local level. This is hard work. We are not just in a digital network hooked up by wires and computers and websites, we are also actively in a social network that is created through human relationships. The more we can talk to each other and develop processes to go from point a to b, the better we will be at the significant work we are trying to do.[15]

This call led to a meeting of forty activists from around the world; subsequently, organizers established a bimonthly, formal, network-wide meeting using a chatroom. These meetings did not last, however, as there was too much difficulty synchronizing a meeting time for people across time zones, and there was difficulty creating a space for dialogue and constructive decision making across diverse language communities.

Ideology: The Glue of Networks

Alongside the communication infrastructure, the glue of most networks is the doctrine or shared ideology, which places the autonomous nodes on a similar course. While indymedia activists share the aim of building an independent democratic grassroots media infrastructure, the globe-spanning network does not share a political ideology, beyond loose progressive principles. In fact, in my research I found that indymedia activists range from progressive and liberal to socialist and anarchist in their political leaning, which has caused rifts throughout the network.

A member of indymedia Romania, Ulle, addressed this lack of political coherence in detail during a discussion on the IMC-Communication listserv: "I think the strength of the IMC network is that it defines the unity of the movement(s) as sharing loose, background principles and NOT in terms of comprehensive world visions, homogenous practices and forms of behavior or aspiring toward identical goals. . . . I mention the indymedia POU as one example."[16] Ulle argues against "comprehensive world visions" and "homogenous practices and forms of behavior" such as using a specific software program, challenging a specific political group, or linking to a singular political philosophy. Instead, Ulle sees indymedia as united by an underlying sense of shared direction. In this discussion Ulle references the indymedia Principles of Unity (POU) as the document that best exemplifies this sentiment. Interestingly, the Principles of Unity are the only shared doctrine that unites the global indymedia movement.

The path toward developing an organizational charter or constitution for indymedia began to emerge in October 2000, when a group of seven indymedia activists from throughout the United States made a network-wide call for a global indymedia meeting. In the original proposal, the members of the newly formed *encuentro* group explained their perspective: "We agreed that we need to meet, not in a 'conference' style where 'experts' address 'audiences' who get to ask questions of panelists, but rather we need to meet as do the Zapatistas, in an 'encuentro' where all are invited to be participants in dialogue toward building decentralized networks of resistance and community."[17] The plan for an indymedia encuentro generated a great deal of excitement from activists across the network. Six months later, in April 2001, the first network-wide face-to-face caucus was held in San Francisco. While the decision to hold it in the United States was controversial, members of the network decided this was the best decision, as flights to the United States would be cheaper for folks across the network. At the meeting, about seventy-five to eighty IMC activists from around the world assembled, with a heavy emphasis on IMCs from the United States, Europe, and South America. The principal goal of the meeting was to develop a constitution for the network.

Chris Burnett, one of the founders of BURN!, played a lead role in this process and volunteered to aggregate the thoughts of indymedia activists and draft an indymedia charter for activists to review during the conference. The original document was twelve pages long and, as Burnett explains,[18] followed the same basic structure of the United Nations charter. Through six chapters and sixteen articles, Burnett laid out the structure of a global democratic independent media network called the Confederated Network of Independent Media Centers (CNIC). As the basis of the CNIC, the charter called for a global decision-making process, a decentralized but operative power structure, a functional spokes-council for network-wide decision making, and membership criteria. The document Burnett developed offered the basis of a strong working global media and communications network.[19]

While Burnett's document offered a great deal of structure, or glue, to the emerging indymedia network, during the caucus, the collective represented in San Francisco could only reach consensus on ten general points of agreement.[20] These points articulate underlying principles, or what have become known as the Principles of Unity. To this day, the Principles of Unity that were developed in San Francisco are the only shared document that sets the direction of the movement and ideologically connects activists and IMCs across the world. While the Principles of Unity did offer some basic rules by which all IMCs would abide, the new charter did not lay out decision-making functions, the role of the global indymedia structure, or the relationship of different nodes to the entire network. In fact, the first principle of indymedia enshrines autonomy and decentralization over collectivity:

> 1. The Independent Media Center Network (IMCN) is based upon principles of equality, decentralization, and local autonomy. The IMCN is not derived from a centralized bureaucratic process, but from the self-organization of autonomous collectives that recognize the importance in developing a union of networks.

Ultimately, the charter indymedia created is a short, relatively weak document, and the conference in San Francisco stands as an important moment in determining the future of the indymedia as a network.

By not laying out a strong vision for the network or establishing rules for collective governance, the Principles of Unity by any external analysis must be understood as a weak central charter. They do not express any shared ideological or political commitment; they simply enshrine the necessity of autonomous and democratic decision-making processes. The weakness of the charter and the lack of strong glue has made it difficult for indymedia to make proactive decisions or create coherent, shared plans.

The process of sanctioning the Principles of Unity stands in contrast to another big debate over democracy and decentralization, the U.S. government's transition from the Articles of Confederation to the U.S. Constitution. While admittedly it is a stretch to compare U.S. state-making to the governance of the indymedia movement, it offers a valuable point of contrast. In the case of the United States, the thirteen states ratified the Articles, but some of the leaders of the country (the Federalists) saw them as a weak document that did not guarantee the fledgling country's future and gave individual states too much power and autonomy without creating shared governance. While there was a contested political process between the Federalists and Anti-Federalists, the Federalists were able to draft a new charter, the Constitution, which was ultimately ratified by a majority of delegates at the Constitutional Convention in Philadelphia in 1787. The Constitution was by all measures a stronger charter, paving the way for the right of the federal government to levy taxes, create a system of federal courts, and ultimately invest more power in a centralized authority.

In the case of indymedia, on a much more modest basis, the organization was presented with a strong, or at least stronger, centralized document. However, through the ratification process, the indymedia collective rejected the original proposal and instead consented to a weak central charter. This has set the boundaries of the indymedia movement, creating a weak network that is not able to create proactive decisions and consequently produce shared political outcomes.

Conclusion

The network has become the predominant structure for contemporary social movements. Activists have built network-based social movements, as the structure corresponds to the cultural logic of the Cyber Left to build a world without hierarchy and power. What becomes clear upon a close inspection of the indymedia network, however, is that it is intricate and defies the analytic box that scholars of the network have developed. Indymedia is not simply democratic or egalitarian; it is a combination of vertical and hierarchical structures at the multiple levels of operation. I call this hybridized formation a *heterogeneous network*, blending decentralized and centralized processes, online and offline spaces, local, national, and global collectives, and patterned and unpatterned interactions.

Indymedia activists have faced the difficulty of holding network structures, particularly transnational structures, together. Without a clear pattern of authority or a shared political program, network structures often disintegrate. In this chapter I have attempted to show that while indymedia is not held together by a building or an organizational chart, it is held together by a rigorous communications infrastructure and by indymedia's Principles of Unity. However, because of the relatively weak nature of indymedia ideology, I argue that it is a relatively fragile network, a problem that has made it hard for the organization to make shared decisions or chart a collective path. In the next chapter, I continue this discussion, examining the democratic governance processes across indymedia.

5

Governance: Democracy
All the Way Down

Argentina's antipolitical social movements are
engaged in the politics of everyday life and have evolved
more participative and horizontal forms of decision-
making. These movements aim to create the future within
the present, through new directly democratic relationships. They reject hierarchy, bosses, managers, party
brokers, and *punteros* [leaders].

—Marina Sitrin, author and activist

It is now seared into the collective American psyche: hundreds if not thousands of people, packed tightly together in a park or church, working through an arcane, ritualized process to make both the most important and trivial collective decisions. These images of primarily young, white, middle-class urbanites, with their fingers "twinkling" in the air to signify agreement, have circulated across the Web, Comedy Central, Fox News, and every other outlet imaginable, emerging as indelible parts of U.S. political and cultural life.

Occupy Wall Street's modern expression of direct democracy is reminiscent of a previous era in U.S. history, illuminated by Norman Rockwell's famous painting *Freedom of Speech*. In the iconic image, a middle-aged man with the worn jacket, chiseled jaw, and rough-hewn hands of the working class stands out among a sea of older and wealthier faces and assertively states his view in a town-hall meeting. Rockwell's nostalgic editorial on local democracy as the bedrock of American life in the 1940s and the horizontal general assemblies of today's Occupy movement share an idealized belief in the possibilities of free, open deliberation as the foundation of a more perfect social order. And while Occupy is not the first social movement to operate through collective decision making, it has succeeded where others have failed, by compelling U.S. society to reckon with the political and moral urgency of direct democracy, within and beyond our movements for social change.

In this chapter, I examine indymedia's multilayered, transnational application of direct democracy, which in many ways anticipates and sets the stage for Occupy Wall Street. I focus on the ways that democracy is understood and enacted by indymedia activists—from the development of an open media system where anyone can speak (democratizing the media), to the preference for consensus-based decision making (democratic governance), and the belief that activists must develop the structures, processes, and relationships within the movement that they aim to achieve in the world (prefigurative politics). Seen from this vantage, for indymedia activists democracy is multivalent, standing in as the end goal of a new society, a revolutionary tool to remake that society, and the everyday practice that allows for innovation and new forms of collective power.

While democracy has become a powerful concept, diverse interpretations within indymedia and other contemporary social movements have led to tangible problems in democratic practice—from tensions between decentralization and participatory democracy, to a distrust of online decision making, and an inability to make proactive decisions. These challenges bring to the fore both the strengths and weaknesses of the logic and practice of democracy in contemporary social movements. In an attempt to foreground these issues, in this chapter I focus on two critical network-wide decisions that exemplify the conflicts around democratic practice within the indymedia movement. The first episode occurred in 2003, when indymedia activists were forced to reject a major Ford Foundation grant. The fight over this grant illuminates the tension between central decision making and autonomy within networked structures and highlights what I mark as a crisis of sovereignty in networked social-movement structures. The second episode this chapter details is the fight within the network to expel one of the first and strongest European Independent Media Centers, the Brussels-based Belgium IMC. Like the Ford Foundation decision, the drawn-out process around the Belgian IMC illuminates the difficulties of making online decisions as well as some of the problems of consensus-based process. Before looking at these episodes, however, I discuss the historical trajectory of democratic practice within left-based social movements, in order to chart how this logic of direct democracy became the dominant currency within contemporary social movements.

Democracy in Social and Revolutionary Movements

Martin Luther King Jr. once prophesied that the long arc of history bends toward justice. Across the twentieth century, however, social-movement leaders saw the arc of history bend toward direct democracy. This sweeping transformation in the logic, strategy, and practice of social-movement organizations is put in relief by two events that took place ninety-seven years apart, bookending the twentieth century. The first of these events was the publication of Lenin's famous pamphlet, *What Is to Be Done? Burning Questions of Our Movement,* in 1902 (Lenin 2005). In this polemic on the task of Social Democrats, Lenin argued for the development of a centralized organization of "dedicated revolutionaries" who could effectively bring the message of socialism to the Russian working class.[1] Challenging the solitary focus on trade unionism (economism), Lenin argued for a revolutionary organization that would focus on the broad interests of the class, not only the economic interests. This organization would be built around professional revolutionaries who could deal with the lack of political freedoms in tsarist Russia. Operating at the height of Russian autocracy, Lenin believed that under these repressive political conditions it was critical for revolutionary organizations to be both centralized and clandestine, which unfortunately allowed for less open deliberation. At the same time, Lenin challenged the concept of "primitive democracy," where all members make every decision, instead calling for an organizational structure that would allow for both democratic representation and specialization within the party. While Lenin's position on the relationship between democracy, class-consciousness, and organizational structure was not static, as recent scholarship powerfully illustrates (Lih 2008; Harding 2009), in the years that followed the publication of *What Is to Be Done?,* as the historian Lars Lih details (2008), a dominant, "textbook interpretation" emerged that cast Leninism as both antidemocratic and bureaucratic, making a direct link between his political praxis and the subsequent crimes of Stalinist Russia.

Developing in many ways as a direct response to Lenin's theory of revolution and the subsequent events of Soviet Russia, *The Battle of Seattle* was driven by a very different logic, a logic of direct democracy and consensus decision making that eschewed hierarchy and was suspicious of institution building. The author, Eddie Yuen (2001), explains that one of the most influential components of the protests in Seattle was "the commitment to direct democracy, specifically the organizational forms of the affinity group, decentralized spokes-council meetings, and consensus process" (Yuen, Katsiaficas, and Rose 2001, 8). Across the twentieth century, the practice within social and revolutionary movements transformed from representative forms of democracy and the decision-making apparatus of the Bolshevik party to the consensus-based horizontal networks of the antiglobalization activists.[2]

The transformation of social-movement actors and organizations toward less centralized and more horizontal and temporary participatory structures is keyed to two convergent phenomena. The first is the dramatic advances in information and communication technologies, which enabled the instantaneous passage of information and real-time communication capacity across the world. These technological advances have allowed for more expansive forms of organizing and globally networked organizational structures, which scholars argue tend toward flat or "egalitarian" decision-making arrangements (Ronfeldt and Arquilla 1996; Keck and Sikkink 1998).

Alongside these technological transformations, the second and more important factor that compelled contemporary movements toward participatory democracy was a concern with the perceived ills of hierarchical decision-making structures of previous stages of resistance. Witnessing the problems of the Old Left—from the degeneration toward a bureaucratic, totalitarian state regime, in the case of Soviet Russia, or the compromised trade-union apparatus, in the case of the United States—a generation of thinkers began to challenge the basic Marxist-Leninist tenets that dominated social and revolutionary movements for the first half of the twentieth century.[3] Scholars and activists began to consider different decision-making structures that would not devolve into what Leon Trotsky called "substitutism," where centralized authority structures substitute leaders for the party, and the party for the people (Deutscher 1963).

The most influential critique of Marxist-Leninism on these grounds grew out of France and the journal *Socialisme ou Barbarisme/Socialism or Barbarism*, published from 1949 to 1965 by Cornelius Castoriadis, Claude Lefort, and Francois Lyotard. While it transformed from a specific critique of Bolshevism to a general critique of Marxism, in the early years the central thrust of the journal was to challenge the Stalinist bureaucracy of the Soviet Union and to call for the development of new revolutionary theory. In this light, Castoriadis and Lefort wrote essays as part of *Socialisme ou Barbarisme* (under pseudonyms) in which they argued that in future movements there must be a more grassroots democratic structure that favors workers councils as opposed to large bureaucratic parties. The journal ultimately collapsed, as Lefort and Castoriadis pushed these questions to their logical limits, disagreeing over the relationship between organizational structure and worker spontaneity. Nonetheless, their ideas influenced a new generation of activists and scholars, including one of the leaders of the May 1968 movement in France and an icon of the New Left, Daniel Cohn-Bendit.[4]

Operating in parallel to the May '68 student movements in France, movements in the United States, such as the Student Non-Violent Coordinating Committee and Students for a Democratic Society, began experimenting with direct democracy. Activists and leaders like Tom Hayden, the author of the Port Huron Statement and president of the SDS, saw direct democracy as the foundation of a new world order because, as he explained, "real participating democracy rests on the independence of ordinary people" (qtd. in Breines 1989, 57). For Hayden and others, however, direct democracy was not only a moral and political vision of a new world; it was also a tactical foundation, because direct democracy built leaders, helped develop a deeper level of identification with the movement, and created innovation in movement strategy (Poletta 2001). This vision of direct democracy as *the* necessary ingredient for building a new world became the heart of the New Left (Breines 1989; Poletta 2001), at least in the early years, and subsequently became a central theme in U.S.-based movements in the 1970s and 1980s, like the nonviolent direct-action movement (Epstein 1991).

The practice of direct democracy that emerged across the latter half of the twentieth century became the accepted logic of the indymedia movement and subsequently Occupy Wall Street, with one vital difference: with the emergence of new technology and the growth of transnational organizing, indymedia activists translated the practices of direct democracy to the global scale, attempting to make consensus-based decisions with IMCistas[5] from all corners of the world, harnessing online tools like chatrooms, listservs, and wiki pages.

Indymedia-Style Democracy

At the heart of the indymedia experiment is the goal of democratizing practices and processes at all levels of the institution. As Jeff Perlstein explained in an interview shortly after the birth of indymedia, "IMC invites democratic participation in every aspect of the project. In an attempt to live up to these ideals, IMC has tried to create structures and nonhierarchical and consensus-based decision making."[6] This goal was similarly captured in a pamphlet written in 2001, *Hands On: Building a Local Indymedia Center.* In the introduction, the authors explain:

> Behind all the cool media IMC has produced it represents an authentic revolution: a revolution in the forms of public action and documentation, *the most*

radical aspect is its non-hierarchical nature. All participants are themselves empowered. IMC has emerged as a model not only for new ways of media making but as an example of collective production, a necessary step in an equitable society. (Halleck and Kovel 2000)

The pamphlet illustrates the belief in democracy and equality as the basis of all organizational processes within indymedia. As other scholars have discussed (Pickard 2006a; Halleck 2002; Kidd 2003a; Morris 2003), these democratic ideals can be seen in practices such as the development and use of open software, the focus on multiple fronts of struggle, and the seemingly nonhierarchical organizational structure of the movement. In this chapter I specifically look at democratic governance or the aim of building democratic structures and processes for decision making at all levels of the organization.

Within indymedia, direct democracy is enacted through consensus-based decision-making processes. In fact, the sixth principle of the indymedia constitution declares:

All IMCs recognize the importance of process to social change and are committed to the development of non-hierarchical and anti-authoritarian relationships, from interpersonal relationships to group dynamics. Therefore, they shall *organize themselves collectively and be committed to the principle of consensus decision making and the development of a direct, participatory democratic process that is transparent to its membership.*[7]

Indymedia activists see consensus-based processes as an egalitarian alternative to top-down decision making, because the process is open and seeks consent among all participants. Generally speaking, consensus decision making demands a spirit of cooperation, space for deliberation, and well-structured facilitation. As others have argued (Hartnett 2011), consensus decision making hinges on five precepts:

- *Inclusion*: As many stakeholders as possible should be involved in the consensus decision-making process.
- *Participation*: The consensus process should actively solicit the input and participation of all decision makers.
- *Cooperation*: Participants in an effective consensus process should strive to reach the best possible decision for the group and all of its members, rather than opt to pursue a majority opinion, potentially to the detriment of a minority.
- *Egalitarianism*: All members of a consensus decision-making body should be afforded, as much as possible, equal input into the process.

All members have the opportunity to table, amend and veto, or "block" proposals.

- *Solution-Orientation*: An effective consensus decision-making body strives to emphasize common agreement over differences and reach effective decisions using compromise and other techniques to avoid or resolve mutually exclusive positions within the group. (Hartnett 2011)

Throughout my research on indymedia, local and global collectives consistently used consensus decision making for virtually every major decision. Chris Burnett explained that indymedia activists believe consensus-based processes lead to a deeper sense of solidarity and community and also lead to smarter decisions, as more individuals are comfortable offering input. In the following section, I look at two of the most important network-wide decisions that indymedia activists had to make in the first four years of the movement's existence to illustrate the strengths and weaknesses of this process.[8]

The Case of the Ford Foundation

In September 2002, three years after the formation of the first IMC in Seattle, a discussion broke out on the global indymedia listserv IMC-Process, designated as the space to make decisions on network-wide governance. The argument began as the indymedia collective of Argentina wrote a lengthy letter that was translated into four languages. In the letter, members of IMC-Argentina entreated their fellow IMCistas to reject an impending Ford Foundation grant of fifty thousand dollars.

The money from the Ford Foundation was meant to help establish an Indymedia convergence fund to facilitate regional indymedia conferences, in an effort to build network-wide and regional solidarity. As one member of the "encuentro group," which applied for the Ford grant, explained, "The funding we are looking for would be utilized by multiple IMCs (at their discretion) to support regional gatherings of IMC participants, and in this way, would help strengthen the IMC Network as a whole."[9] The objective of the grant was to aid in the cohesion of the indymedia movement by cultivating face-to-face meetings, which would increase trust and communication across the global federated network, bringing members of different local IMC collectives together to discuss strategies and best practices.

Members of the Argentine collective only learned of the grant shortly before the money was to be accepted. In their initial letter to the indymedia network, they argued that they were strongly opposed to accepting the grant because the Ford Foundation was inextricably intertwined with the U.S. Central Intelligence Agency. Correspondingly, they argued that Ford was directly connected to much of the misery that occurred during the "dirty war" that took place between 1976 and 1983 under an Argentine military dictatorship. Drafters of the letter argued that if the global indymedia network were to accept a grant from the Ford Foundation, it would irreparably damage the role of IMC-Argentina with local organizations, as they would lose credibility with the communities in which they were working. The letter from the Argentine collective read:

> For indymedia Argentina, to accept a subsidy of that foundation would be in the first place a suicide; if everybody here would know it, the place that nowadays indymedia [has] here, based on a year and half of lots of effort, would be quickly [thrown] to the garbage. And with enough reasons. We believe that Argentina indymedia is a tool that is being used by many movements and that is playing a very important role in the last years.[10]

Making use of the research of the U.S. sociologist James Petras (2001), the Argentine IMC documented the relationship they believed the Ford Foundation had with the CIA during the "dirty war," where upwards of thirty thousand people were "disappeared." In the same letter, they went on to detail the role they believed the Ford Foundation played in destabilizing twentieth-century social movements from the Black Panthers to the antiglobalization movement. The latter argument allowed the Argentine collective to move beyond self-interest, making the more powerful argument that a grant from Ford was not only perilous to indymedia activists in Argentina but imperiled the entire indymedia movement, as Ford would use the grant as a tool of control and/or surveillance. On these grounds, they asked local indymedia collectives to read their letter, do research, and respond in support of their proposal to reject the Ford Foundation's "compromised money." The email concluded with a powerful plea to the network:

> We, as the organizations of human rights that didn't negotiate the blood of their dead, as the organizations of unemployed and of [occupied] workers that maintain their autonomy, we reject to take a coin from those hands that are spotted with the blood of our comrades. The "Madres de Plaza de Mayo" think that they are not individuals' mothers, they are the mothers of 30,000 missing persons. We are also sons, brothers, grandsons, cousins, friends, and partners of the 30,000 desaparecidos [disappeared persons]. We carry the memory of all those comrades in our hearts. The force that comes from that

love [allows] us to continue fighting for a better world every day. We invite all our comrades of all the indymedias of the world to adopt in their hearts our missing comrades. We must reject any type of institutional relationship with the accomplices of the genocide of the military dictatorship, we must preserve the honor of Argentina indymedia and of the global net.[11]

Following the initial proposal from Argentina, there was a flurry of discussion on the IMC-Process listserv and the IMC-Finance listserv, as well as real-time computer-mediated discussion through IRCs. Suddenly, whether or not to accept the Ford Foundation money became a critical decision for the network to negotiate. From the impassioned responses on the IMC-Process listserv, it was clear that many collectives across the globe, such as indymedia centers in Greece, Cyprus, Melbourne, San Francisco, and Italy, not to mention Argentina, would most likely leave the young but growing indymedia network if the money from Ford was accepted. Faced with its own mortality, the indymedia network was forced to operationalize the tightly held belief in participatory democracy at the global scale, utilizing the global-communications infrastructure to make a significant democratic, consensus-based decision that would have serious repercussions for people and organizations across the movement. The stakes of this decision were heightened as IMC was a relatively resource-poor organization, and fifty thousand dollars was a substantial part of the global network's overall budget at this early point in the movement's development.

The money from the Ford Foundation was initially committed to indymedia through the newly formed encuentros working group. "Encuentro" is Spanish for encounter, and the aim of the group was to create a series of encounters modeled after the national and international Zapatista encuentros held in Mexico in 1996 and 1998. Following the initial proposal from the Argentine IMC to reject the Ford grant, one of the members of the encuentros working group, David Caruso from the Urbana-Champaign, Illinois, IMC, sent out a letter explaining that the grant was not officially in the name of the network but rather an autonomous grant for a local IMC collective applied for by the Urbana-Champaign IMC. The substance of his point was to argue that because it was not an IMC global grant, only this local body had a right to dictate whether the grant was accepted or rejected. Following this logic, he explained:

> I fully respect IMC-Argentina's desire not to accept funding because of the Ford Foundation's history in Argentina and will work to find other funding sources for those who do not wish to accept Ford Foundation funding; *but*

I think that it is inappropriate for individual IMCs to have veto power over the work and financial decisions of other IMCs.... [I]t is also a decision that should be left to the affinity group that has been working on this project for the past six months. If we do otherwise I fear we will seriously undermine autonomy and trust within the Network.[12]

Here, Caruso, a leader of the Urbana-Champaign IMC and a member of the encuentro working group, makes a claim to the a priori rights of the local collective and the encuentro working group to make autonomous decisions and to not have interference, democratic or otherwise, from the global network. The implication is that local collectives—or, in this case, "working groups"—should have autonomy to make decisions and not have an "external body" (the global network) interfere with these local, autonomous decisions. This argument and line of understanding defines in very weak terms the power of network-wide sovereignty within the movement. For Caruso and many others within indymedia, there is no shared governance, which calls into question what role, if any, there is in creating a democratic body. In a later interview, Caruso expands on this point: "Is it my business to say Brazil IMC shouldn't receive funding from X person or that corporation because I personally here in the United States disagree with it? Is that my right? Should I have veto-power over what other IMCs do? Global Indy Media—which has always been envisioned as a communications media—has been endowed ... and it's been funny, because it's been endowed under this rubric of decentralization when more and more it is command and control." When I asked what this tells him about decision making within indymedia, Caruso replied, "This was never the intention of anyone who talked in setting it up in the first place. It was intended to be a communications medium to help build relationships—not to make decisions."[13]

Caruso articulates the vision of a network of autonomous unions that share an idea about democratizing the media but do not share a governance structure or have any strict organizational ties. This is akin to an all-channel network, which only shares information and has no governance ties. This position reduces indymedia to, as one member called it, a "branding." It also converges with a popular saying within the network that indymedia is "a tactic," not an organization.

Ultimately, this conceptualization of indymedia does not allow for a structure that binds the network together through accountability and shared governance. When decisions about the global network or the role of the global body arise, democratic governance and network-wide accountability are put in direct tension with local autonomy of the collectives and the ethos of decentralization, which is central to network organizational forms.

Caruso elaborates this conception of indymedia democracy as he argues that indymedia has "been endowed under this rubric of decentralization, when more and more [it has been dictated by] command and control." This is interesting phraseology because the notion of "command and control" is linked to military-style governance and implies the most hierarchical and centralized form of governance. In this case, indymedia's attempt at a direct democracy and, importantly, sovereignty is equated with hierarchical governance. This articulation illustrates an interesting theoretical tension, as indymedia, like most new social movements from the World Social Forum to People's Global Action, espouse the twin principles of decentralization and direct democracy as complementary goals. However, one ideology, which puts forth a radical and at times isolated localism and individualism, is actually in tension with the other, which puts forth a collective and engaged democratic project.

Speaking to this tension, a member of indymedia Belgium responded to the Ford Foundation situation by accusing IMC-Argentina of having a lack of respect for local decision making and trying to force a centralized process on the network. She wrote:

> I'm pissed off because i read mails that show a TOTAL lack of RESPECT and CONFIDENCE. Some people are always there to talk about "grassroot democracy," "autonomy and decentralization," etc., but as soon as they don't agree with the decision made, this all become "undemocratic." . . . IMCs have different experiences and are working in different situations. Some talk to mainstream medias, others refuse, some accept to work with activists or political groups, others don't, some get money from funds, other refuse it, etc. . . . They choose their own way, because ONLY THEY can judge the situation, see what can be positive for them and what could endanger their practice.[14]

In this passage, the author confirms the tension between a structure of decision making and the autonomy and right to make decisions based on local needs. This is one of the central tensions of a network form, especially a weak network such as indymedia, which is bound as much through distrust of centralization of power as it is by any foundational doctrine.

Another email quickly followed, from an indymedia activist from the United States, capturing the dilemma: "But if it's EITHER respect for local autonomy OR democratic structures i don't understand what democratic structures are, i'm afraid. Could [you] take a little moment to explain what you mean?"[15] Again, what is articulated and ultimately counterposed by members of indymedia is the relationship between a network-wide, democratic or consensus-based decision-making process where collective sovereignty is established, and the autonomy of local collectives.

Following the initial emails, a series of messages from local collectives around the world took different positions on the crisis. The majority of these posts emphasized the necessity of the network to exercise collective sovereignty and make a democratic decision, articulating a position that stood out against Caruso's logic that the network should favor autonomy over democratic praxis. The main position enunciated was that although a local collective under the direction of a specific working group was applying for the Ford Foundation grant, the grant would affect the entire indymedia network; for this reason, a network-wide decision must be made on this matter. This was best exemplified by the San Francisco IMC, which wrote a lengthy collective response weighing in on the proposal to accept Ford money. Members of San Francisco indymedia claimed that the Ford money should be rejected on two grounds: (1) the process involved in accepting the money was problematic, and (2) the source of the money was a problem. With respect to the former, they wrote:

> SFIMC is concerned that UCIMC and individuals are acting on behalf of the global IMC network and multiple IMCs—without the knowledge of, or accountability to, global working groups and affected local IMCs.
>
> The majority of individuals and local IMCs heard about this grant proposal to the Ford Foundation only a few days before the deadline for the grant. SF Indymedia believes that, though technically an "autonomous affinity group" of Indymedia volunteers has "affiliated" with the Urbana-Champaign IMC to apply for the grant, the issue is one that directly affects all local IMCs and should therefore have been proposed/discussed on imc-finance instead of the encuentros list. We recognize there is a difference between UCIMC raising funds, to donate to one particular IMC, like IMC-Nigeria or IMC-Argentina, as a completely distinct set of processes and goals compared with raising funds to facilitate regional IMC gatherings. . . . We do not think building trust between individuals and IMCs in the network can be done successfully when a small group claims autonomy and seeks funding for the entire Indymedia network, on behalf of the entire Indymedia network. It seems clear that the Ford Foundation had every intention of granting money for *regional gatherings*, which intrinsically involved and impact *all* IMCs, not just UCIMC.[16]

San Francisco IMC articulates a different logic than that of autonomy and decentralization put forth by members of the encuentro working group. The basis of their response was that the network is a shared structural body, especially regarding a decision that "impact[s] all IMCs, not just UCIMC." Consequently, the individual nodes or collectives are *not completely autonomous* but instead have a responsibility to the body or network as a whole, especially if a decision is being made that affects the entire network. Consequently, any decision, such as accepting a grant for all of indymedia, must be decided upon through a global decision-making process and not fall back on a decentralized, autonomous ethos wherein the individual collective (UC-IMC) or the appropriate working group makes the decision without accountability to the network. Whereas Caruso and others deny the existence of a structural body with collective sovereignty over the network, the SF IMC presumes that there is a structure to the network and a sovereign, the global decision-making body, which is responsible to all of indymedia.

Ultimately, in the case of the Ford Foundation money, the belief in the power of a sovereign over the network and the logic of accountability through a shared decision-making process prevailed, and most collectives agreed to affirm the network and "stand in solidarity with IMC-Argentina" in rejecting the money. However, while indymedia ultimately did not accept the money, members from the original encuentro group that solicited the grant from Ford developed a different organization, the Tactical Media Fund, which accepted the funds to be used to the same ends. While this may make the decision by the global indymedia structure to reject the Ford grant seem like a pyrrhic victory, rejecting the funds was not an empty expression. Through a collective and difficult democratic process, and ultimately the action of a sovereign network, IMC-Argentina was able to force a decision and in this temporary moment compel global indymedia to employ sovereign power over the movement. Consequently, the Argentine collective was not directly linked to the Ford Foundation and the "dirty war" in Argentina.

On a more substantive or precedent-setting level, in a clash between two central indymedia ideologies, local autonomy and direct democracy, in this case autonomy and decentralization were overcome. As I discuss later, however, this was an exception, and in most cases indymedia has not been able to make collective democratic decisions and instead has fallen back on local autonomy. In this regard, the Ford decision forces some serious questions regarding networked organizational structures: In balancing the network structure and its tendency toward decentralization, how do these networks deal with shared governance? Can networks effectively govern across the autonomous nodes? And what would effective governance across a global network look like? Is the indymedia movement dependent on spontaneity and the hope that particular nodes or collectives act in concert, or is there a form of strategic organizational power that can flow from the network to allow it to govern and be proactive?

The case of the Ford Foundation grant is instrumental in showing some of the central tensions in democratic governance within the network. Another incident is also useful in understanding democracy in global social movements: the attempted disaffiliation of one of the first local Independent Media Centers, the Belgian IMC. The long, tortuous decision-making process regarding the Belgian IMC complements the Ford case, as it highlights the difficulty of making democratic decisions about a particular locale across a transnational movement, while again emphasizing the suspicion indymedia activists have regarding democratic decision making as a concrete step toward the centralized authority structures that Lenin has come to represent.

Local Autonomy and the Case of Belgian Disaffiliation

Established in the summer of 2000, the Brussels-based IMC-Belgium, was one of the first Independent Media Centers in Europe, second only to IMC-UK. IMC-Belgium started with almost thirty volunteers and a great deal of excitement, as activists were inspired by the birth of the Seattle IMC and the growing power of the antiglobalization movement. The founders of Belgium indymedia saw the IMC as a vehicle for building bridges across the many social divides and the diverse communities in the country, and thus one of their first decisions was to institute a dual-language media project, in French and Flemish. Of this, the Belgian collective claimed, "Belgium.indymedia. org is one of the only media outlets in Belgium where the different language communities are confronted with each other on the website and other media productions. . . . It is for sure about the only media outlet where French- and Dutch-speaking people work together daily on the same media project." This multilingual outlook was met with exuberance and made the new Belgian IMC a popular project across the country.

Over the course of the first few years of its existence, however, there was a great deal of infighting within the IMC collective, particularly regarding the relationship of IMC-Belgium to political parties, specifically the Workers Party of Belgium (PVDA/PTB). Some of the founders of indymedia complained that members of the Workers Party of Belgium commandeered the national IMC, not allowing for an open democratic process around decision making or the promotion of media. In a letter documenting the conflict, they wrote, "Members of PTB started then to merge to form a hard core . . . which pushed people one by one to leave. . . . Subsequently the decisions by consensus were not respected . . . and the small group could dictate its law."[17] By 2005, many of the original founders of indymedia Belgium had left the collective and started IMCs across Belgium in the cities of Liege, Antwerp, and East and West Vlaanderen.

In the early stages of the IMC-Belgium conflict, there was a great deal of discussion on the global IMC-Communication listserv.[18] In the early stages, however, indymedia activists were averse to getting involved with the situation in Belgium. Articulating a discomfort with centralized decision-making power and a desire for local intervention, one indymedia activist from Portland, Oregon, exclaimed: "I also do not want to be put into the position of being police or judge. I am uncomfortable to be asking questions and having both 'sides' responding to me, as if I have power over your lives. I have thought much about this situation in the past few days. It highlights feelings I have about Indymedia in general."[19] This rejection of a responsibility to intervene in the Belgian conflict was shared by most of the activists on the communications listserv. Most IMCistas resisted getting involved, asserting that they did not want to become part of a centralized or bureaucratic authority that determined the situation. In fact, this anti-authoritarian ethos is enshrined in the first decree of the Principles of Unity of the indymedia network: "The Independent Media Center Network (IMCN) is based upon principles of equality, decentralization, and local autonomy. The IMCN is not derived from a centralized bureaucratic process but from the self-organization of autonomous collectives that recognize the importance of developing a union of networks."[20]

In this case, the belief that decisions should not be made by a central authority was enhanced by a convergent belief that although technology lets people connect across space—enabling global decisions—new technologies like the Internet and email listservs are not good for thick, important, long-distance decisions about a particular locale. In this sense, many indymedia activists pushed back against the Internet as a mediator of space. One activist explained that instead of the global indymedia body making a decision, perhaps IMC-Europe, as a regional body, should make this decision because they had a more local view of the issue:

> Maybe this would be an issue best approached in the context of imc-europe? (please forgive me if imc-europe has already made a statement and I have missed it.) I would imagine people around IMCs in Europe would have a better idea of the personalities involved, the political nuances and all the issues that don't come across in an e-mail. I don't know how active the imc-europe

list is, or if there's any kind of way IMCs in Europe could come to some kind of consensus about what to do, but I'd certainly feel better if this kind of deep disagreement were dealt with on as much of a face-to-face level as possible.[21]

A Portland IMC activist ("Ronaldo") articulated a similar belief that the Internet is a bad medium for making this sort of important decision about local dynamics:

> It is not my business to overlook what people are doing in Belgium. It is for the people there to work out whatever issues exist. They are the ones who can do that. I believe it is not possible for me to be of any help even if I were to spend a lot of time reading all about the situation as expressed in emails. That would be a waste and distraction of time. . . .
>
> The globe spanning email lists are mostly useless for this sort of thing. It would be a good thing to refrain from using them for any sort of conflict resolution. *Face to face is where life happens. It is real. Virtual life has little power. It is empty.*[22]

I highlight the last sentences of this statement because the comment by Ronaldo captures a convergence between the anti-authoritarian discourse of indymedia, which prioritizes and even fetishizes the local component of the indymedia network, and a belief that the global, instantaneous capacities of digital media do not have the social and contextual richness to facilitate real, thick decisions, and therefore those decisions must be made face-to-face in the "real" world. This belief about the thinness of digital media as a venue for dialogue converges with the "reduced social cues" model for understanding computer-mediated communications.

The belief that the Internet is a deficient space for dialogue was an argument that indymedia activists made throughout my research. Jay Sand explained in an interview that while technology is a core component of the network, it does not allow for the consistency and rigor that some decisions require. Jay, along with a few other activists, recognized this problem and attempted to create a Decision Making Working Group (DMWG) for the network. From 2000 until 2003, the DMWG put forward a host of ideas and processes for decision making, from a weekly spokes-council meeting to the use of video conferencing, in an effort to enable real network-wide decisions. However, none of these ideas were formally accepted, and the DMWG ultimately folded because of a lack of engagement across indymedia.[23]

Because of this inability of the global indymedia decision-making structure to create a viable decision-making process, indymedia activists were hesitant to become involved with the internecine struggle in Belgium, and thus the problems between the different indymedia activists and local collectives across the country went on for three years. While indymedia members consistently discussed the situation on the global lists, no one put forward a proposal, and the global body took no action to solve the situation. Throughout the episode, indymedia activists on the global lists lamented the fact that there was nothing they could do without a proposal for action.

Finally, in April 2005, after a series of public conflicts between the two groups, members of IMC-Liege sent an email to IMC-Process in which they called for the disaffiliation of IMC-Belgium from the indymedia network. In dramatic fashion, they wrote, "We ask to the network to put an end for once to the lingering death of www.indymedia.be, before it carries with its fall the other local collectives and the neighbors."[24] The basis for their argument was that the Brussels-based IMC broke the core principles of the indymedia network as enshrined in the Principles of Unity, and consequently it should be kicked out of the network:

Today, we concluded that:
- A collective which is composed by a big majority of members from the same political party and which pushes the other opinions to leave is not a condition for a diversity.
- A collective where the independent media center is based in a building which belongs to this same political party is not a proof of independency.
- A collective which profits off of the image of indymedia and which uses it during election as a cover for the propaganda of its political party is a not a free alternative media.
- A collective which is financed by the state funds through some ghost organisations can't claim to be honest and non-lucrative.
- A collective which spends its time by spamming, insulting, and spreading false rumors to sabotage other indymedias is not worthy of the network.
- A collective which censures the other Belgian indymedias, including [during] the FBI crisis, can't say it's based on the solidarity.
- A collective with only 4 or 5 people really active is not able to represent the diversity of a country while at same time [there] exist 5 other local indymedias (with one under construction).
- A collective which is built like a real professional redaction and where 3/4 of the visible contributions are coming from this team of drafting can't say it applies the [principles of] open publishing.
- A collective which shares the list and website access only to a restricted group and which refuses to share it with the others is against the principles of non-hierarchy and [egalitarianism].

- A collective which is boycotted by the local activist community is not able to say that it's the mirror of the no-global movement.
- A collective which has a very little respect for the POU [Principles of Unity] by applying only 2 points of it is not able to say it still adheres to the principles of indymedia.

Consequently, members of IMC Liege called for IMC Belgium to be kicked out of the indymedia network, and if it was not disaffiliated, at least the Web address of IMC-Belgium (www.belgium.indymedia.org) should be reappropriated as an address for all IMCs in the country, and the IMC currently in Brussels should relinquish its national identity and take on a local identity as IMC Brussels. This, they argued, would allow all the local collectives within Belgium to come together to develop a national collective at the Web address currently held by IMC-Belgium. They closed out the proposal by stating, "We ask officially to the network the disaffiliation of www.indymedia.be. . . . [W]e ask [for] a deadline of 3 weeks so each collective will have time to debate."[25]

Once IMC-Liege made this proposal, seven local IMC collectives around Europe and within Belgium supported the proposal to disaffiliate the Brussels-based IMC-Belgium: IMC-Nantes (France), IMC-Switzerland, IMC-Marseille (France), IMC-Netherlands, IMC-OVL (Belgium), IMC-WVL (Belgium), and IMC-Sweden. Just as quickly, however, a group of IMCs challenged the proposal, including IMC-Cleveland, IMC-Canarias (Canary Islands), IMC-São Paulo (Brazil), IMC-Goiâna (Brazil), IMC-Florianopolis (Brazil), and IMC-Campinas (Brazil). Thus, while the proposal put forward by IMC-Liege got a great deal of attention, the members of the Cleveland IMC were the first to collectively reject the proposal, claiming there was not enough evidence offered by IMC-Liege that the Brussels-based IMC-Belgium was in noncompliance with the Principles of Unity. More importantly, they argued that the three-week timeline for making a decision was too short and did not afford the opportunity to thoroughly examine the situation: "We fear such a relaxed standard for disaffiliation without the knowledge of many imcs would leave the indymedia network vulnerable, jeopardizing our existence. We thus BLOCK THE PROPOSAL of Liege imc to disaffiliate indymedia Belgium."[26]

Following this failed proposal, there was renewed effort on the IMC-Process listserv to solve the problem in Belgium. Eventually, IMC-Germany put forth a new proposal, which had three core components:

1. The url *http://belgium.indymedia.org* becomes a static page linking to all Belgian IMCs equally.

2. The current belgium.indymedia.org collective rename themselves using either a locality or topic or [something] similar. This new name is used for a new indymedia subdomain and treated equally to the other collectives.

3. The current belgium.indymedia.org collective stops presenting themselves as "Indymedia Belgium" as they do not represent all of Belgium.[27]

In an interesting turn of events, while eight local collectives accepted the proposal by Germany, the Brussels-based IMC-Belgium attempted to block this proposal using the rules of consensus to forestall Germany's proposal. The members of the global decision-making body of indymedia, however, vetoed this block by Belgium indymedia, stating that the affected party in this case did not have a right to block the proposal. This was an important move because if it had not happened, as one member of global indymedia stated, "the global collective would never be able to make a decision which adversely affected a local site as that local collective would always have the recourse to block said decision."

Consequently, the network accepted the German proposal, which was a moderate solution to the problem. The Brussels IMC was compelled by indymedia global to change their Web address and identity. Belgium IMC identified as "indymedia.be." In the meantime, another informal IMC-Brussels collective began calling itself the "CEMAB.be," or the Center of Alternative Media of Brussels.

Getting to a Decision

Through a host of indymedia listservs, in different chatrooms, and through phone calls, indymedia activists worked to build an engaged democratic decision across the network regarding the conflict in Belgium. On the IMC-Communications listserv alone there were over five hundred messages from different activists. In the initial stages, the majority of the discussion was dominated by activists who held the opinion that global indymedia should not get involved in the local dispute in Belgium. In this period, most activists saw the global network as playing the role of mediator, facilitating a discussion between the central actors at the local level, not as a sovereign body with a right and responsibility to act in the name of the shared network. Ultimately, however, because of the seriousness of the problem in Belgium and the inability of local actors to come to a solution, the global indymedia network was forced, against the will of many indymedia activists, to get involved and find a consensus-based resolution on the issue.

The actions of the global indymedia network and the eventual resolution of the Belgian conflict help to clarify the processes for decision making across the indymedia network. There was a great deal of hesitance by members of the global decision-making body to get involved with the Belgium situation. Activists across the network believed that this was a local problem that needed to be handled locally without intervention from the global indymedia body. Accordingly, the desire for local autonomy converged with a belief that although technology connects people across space, new information and communication technologies are not an appropriate medium for people to make real decisions because the virtual is not a substitute for face-to-face interaction.

This dynamic highlights the difficulty faced by the indymedia movement and all networked social movements in making network-wide decisions across space through the Internet. These realities of the governance structure of indymedia form the basis of its ability to act as a shared organization. While indymedia has developed a participatory democratic governance system that is dynamic and creates egalitarian social relations, it often does so at the expense of developing a sovereign authority that can act and make the movement a powerful, sustained effort. In this sense, I argue that indymedia and other global, relatively weak social-movement networks can only make decisions when faced with the mortality of the network. This in itself is not a problem; however, the indymedia network as a whole has never made a proactive decision to work on a particular project, utilize a particular strategy, or reach out to a particular community. In this sense, with the prioritization of decentralization over democracy, indymedia and other comparable networks tend to thrive in reaction to the external environment and are not able to create proactive strategies and collective decisions.

At the same time, while the Belgian situation illustrates a problem of global decision making for networked social movements, it also offers a window onto the actual process. While indymedia has had significant trouble creating an infrastructure for shared decisions at the global level, in certain circumstances IMCistas have been able to forge global, consensus-based decisions. In the cases discussed in this chapter, two conditions were critical. The first condition was crisis: the threat of a serious situation forced networked actors to act and build consensus. This inability leads to weak networks, in the long term, that are unable to establish a shared strategy for movement building. Second, in order to build this consensus, there had to be an infrastructure and capacity to share massive amounts of information so people and collectives could be fully informed and come to a resolution. These baseline attributes were the same in the Ford incident and the Belgian conflict.

Turtles and Democracy All the Way Down

Toward the conclusion of *Multitude: War and Democracy in the Age of Empire* (2004), Michael Hardt and Antonio Negri offer a vision for a world of equality and freedom based on the democratic impulse of the multitude. Taking inspiration from the open-source software movement, Hardt and Negri contend:

> One approach to understanding the democracy of the multitude, then, is as an open source society, that is, a society whose source code is revealed so that we can work collaboratively to solve bugs and create new, better social programs. The creation of the multitude, its innovation in networks, and its decision-making ability in common makes democracy possible for the first time today. Political sovereignty and the rule of one which has always undermined any real notion of democracy, tends to appear not only unnecessary, but absolutely impossible.... The autonomy of the multitude and its capacities for economic, political, and social self-organization take away any role for sovereignty.... When the multitude is finally able to rule itself, democracy becomes possible. (340)

In Hardt and Negri's vision of a new world order, "democracy" acts as a transcendental signifier. At one level, democracy is the end goal of a just society; at another, it is a revolutionary tool to remake that society; and at yet another, it is everyday practice that allows for innovation and new forms of collective power. Much like turtles, then, in this worldview it is democracy "all the way down."

This complex and at times contradictory logic of democracy characterizes the logic of resistance within the Cyber Left. Democracy stands in for a diversity of ideals and practices, including the development of open systems that anyone can join (from media platforms to decision-making arrangements), the preference for horizontal organizational structures with no power differentials, and the belief that activists must develop, or prefigure, the structures and processes within the movement that they aim to achieve in the world. Within this broad understanding of democracy is the embrace of the twin concepts of decentralization and participatory democracy, two underlying principles of nonhierarchical networks. The belief is that each of these concepts is part and parcel of a broader worldview where the vertical power structures championed by Lenin and others are replaced by open, horizontal processes.

However, as this chapter illustrates, these dual aspects of the network age are often in tension with each other as they presuppose differing notions of the nature of a network structure and differing theories of power. Decentralization assumes complete autonomy and therefore no formal decision-making relationship among the separate nodes, while participatory democracy assumes shared decision making across the nodes in an attempt to create strategic unity or a sovereign network. These differing notions of where power lies within networks have profound effects on the vision and capacity of social-movement-based democratic organizational structures. Thus, while decentralization and radical democracy are often seen to work in concert, decentralized networks cultivate a radical, at times isolated localism that is in tension with democratic decision making. This reality brings to the fore the complex tensions of local autonomy and networked authority as competing theories in the contemporary age. Moreover, these episodes bring to light the inability of decentralized networks to build proactive power, highlighting the conservative and often reactive nature of contemporary social movements, which leads to disordered, ineffectual networked social-movement structures. This cultural logic of resistance within indymedia actually disorganizes and debilitates the network.

6

Strategy: Communications and the Switchboard of Struggle

The intelligence of the swarm is based fundamentally on
communication.
—Michael Hardt and Antonio Negri

In *Hegemony and a Socialist Strategy* (1985), Ernesto Laclau and Chantal Mouffe contend that left-based political strategy is at a crossroads. Challenging a long history of Marxist theory, they argue that socialism is "in crisis" and no longer the counter-imaginary to capitalism. More importantly, they argue that the working class is no longer the historical agent of change. Building on a series of philosophical and theoretical turns toward discourse and language, the initial aim of their intervention is the overthrow of the materialist view of history, which claims that people's identity and interests are tied to their economic location vis-à-vis the social structure. Laclau and Mouffe argue that this "economistic" concept is reductionist, as identity is constructed discursively first and foremost, and is not necessarily tied to material experience. Thus the Marxist fiction of a historical agent, the proletariat, that springs forth from the bowels of industrial capitalism, shovel in hand, with the mission of bringing socialism to humanity, is not foreordained and is inherently flawed.

Laclau and Mouffe's belief in the failure of the socialist project leads them to propose a new strategy of social change, "radical and plural democracy," which expands classic notions of democracy by embracing difference and dissent. This "democratic revolution" is constituted not by the singular struggle of the working class but instead by a multiplicity of antagonisms and the resistance to all forms of power and domination. Without a privileged agent or a particular political program, this new vision of radical democratic society valorizes decentralized political action and "the autonomization of the spheres of struggle and the multiplication of political spaces" (178). However, recognizing the danger of this model's tendency toward fragmented social struggle that is likely "condemned to marginality" (189), Laclau and Mouffe argue that the many autonomous struggles must develop a shared vision in order to organize into a hegemonic bloc. This logic of nonhierarchical struggle, where multiple nodes or collectives attack an enemy but there is no center that dictates orders, has been called swarming or "swarm intelligence"[1] and has been hailed as the new democratic form of resistance (Hardt and Negri 2004).

While many scholars have challenged *Hegemony and a Socialist Strategy* for (1) misunderstanding Marx's conception of political economy, (2) essentializing a small part of the Marxist tradition, (3) returning to a call for liberal pluralism, and (4) lacking historical specificity,[2] Laclau and Mouffe's political vision has become a predominant element of the cultural logic of resistance for social-movement scholars and actors. This is exemplified in the work of political theorists from Michael Hardt and Antonio Negri (2000; 2004) to John Holloway (2005) and in the praxis of new social-movement actors and organizations, which no longer privilege the working class and aim to build a society based on the vision of democracy and dissent.

As I discuss in Part I, the Zapatistas and their catchphrase, "One No, Many Yeses," bring this strategy to life. The No/Yes equation of the slogan illustrates the two principles of this political strategy: (1) the many autonomous movements of the Left share a common resistance to all forms of power and domination (one no); (2) despite a history of movement building that prioritized the working class, there is no central actor or political protagonist in twenty-first-century struggle—instead, indigenous movements, environmental movements, and labor movements are all vital (many yeses).

Following the EZLN, this theory of social change became the clarion call for the antiglobalization movement and was made actionable for media activists after the Zapatista declaration that we must "make a network of communication among all of our struggles and resistances." Building on this vision, the indymedia global-communications network aims to cohere a global social movement out of many singular fronts of resistance. In practice, indymedia activists harnessed the local, national, and global communications infrastructure to link people and struggles, becoming a connective tissue across space and theme, which I call the "switchboard of struggle." As a switchboard, indymedia ideally conducts stories of shared struggle across a diverse web of actors, nodes, and institutions on local, national, regional, and global levels, thereby becoming a vehicle for the coming together of multiple singular points of resistance.

In this chapter, I document how indymedia uses communications to help congeal these otherwise isolated and dispersed points of insurgency, conducting stories of shared struggle across space at multiple scales, from the hyper-local (within cities and neighborhoods) to the regional, national, and global. Specifically, I look at how indymedia links movements and people in three distinct ways: (1) across local spaces, linking different communities together to build a stronger localized movement; (2) across geographic spaces, on a particular theme such as labor or immigrant rights; and (3) across space and theme, in an attempt to forge a global social movement. I also show the shortcomings of this new strategy and political mode of action, which eschews leadership and therefore can't build long-term political power. I first focus on the way the network operated as a connective tissue in the case of farmers in South Central Los Angeles to offer a rubric for this strategy of action. I then look at different ways that this connective strategy operates at the local, national, and global levels, on- and offline.

South Central Farm and the Switchboard of Struggle

In the early morning of June 2006, the Los Angeles Police Department raided an urban farm at 41st and Alameda Streets in an industrial zone of South Central Los Angeles. In the course of a few hours, the LAPD arrested dozens of people, while city bulldozers steamrolled dozens of small gardens that were overflowing with cilantro, beets, corn, and other fruits and vegetables. The South Central Farm, as it was known, was used by over 350 working-class Latino families to cultivate their own produce in an area of densely concentrated poverty and, correspondingly, little access to healthy food.[3]

The storied life of this fourteen-acre plot of land began in the 1980s, when the City of Los Angeles seized the parcel, claiming eminent domain. At the time, city leaders intended to place a trash-to-energy incinerator at the site. However, in the face of massive neighborhood opposition, the city abandoned the plan and turned the land over to the Los Angeles Regional Food Bank (Chawkins 2008). In turn, the food bank agreed to lend the plot to community residents to establish an urban garden.

In 2002, however, one of the original owners of the plot sued the city to reclaim the land. The parcel was subject to a lengthy legal process, and during that time the farmers formed South Central Farmers Feeding Families and began organizing to keep the garden. Ultimately, the property owner negotiated with the municipality, purchased the land for five million dollars, and then issued a notice for the termination of the garden in 2004.[4] The farmers countersued, but they lost the suit, and on May 23, 2006, the Los Angeles County Sheriff's Department declared that they would execute an order to evict the South Central Farmers.

The following day, the L.A. indymedia editorial collective published the feature "RED ALERT!! Encampment and Tree Sit to Resist Eviction and Save South Central Farm."[5] The article was posted by "FYI" in the name of the South Central Farmers, and it called on readers to converge on the farm to create an encampment and resist the eviction: "Encampment and tree sit to resist the eviction and save the South Central Farm has begun! . . . The Farm and farmers need your help now!! . . . The greater the numbers encamped increases our chances of success."

In the days that followed, hundreds of people flocked to the garden and established an encampment of over one hundred tents. Indymedia journalists and activists who became journalists for the occasion documented the struggle with written word, video, and photography and posted their stories on the L.A. indymedia Web site. The indymedia site became a central space for up-to-date news, pictures, and videos, as well as discussion and organizing around the situation at the Los Angeles garden.

Three weeks after the first "red alert," at 5:00 A.M. on June 13, 150 riot cops surrounded the farm and began forcible eviction. Shortly thereafter, another urgent message appeared on L.A. indymedia: "Emergency Alert: Police Evicting South Central Farmers—Take Action." The alert included a message from the South Central Farmers: "At this moment, the South Central Farm is under siege. If you live in LA or in the surrounding area, we urge you to come to the farm to keep the protesters and farmers safe from LA County Sheriffs and the LAPD."[6] While hundreds converged on the farm, the L.A. indymedia story broke across the United States and could be found on twenty to thirty local indymedia sites, from Pittsburgh to Seattle.[7] On the same day, the Los Angeles IMC coverage of the South Central Farm became the central story on the IMC-US site,[8] and then it quickly became the central feature on the global indymedia site.[9] Ultimately, the indymedia network took the story to over one million people in localities as far afield as Germany, the Philippines, the Netherlands, Malta, Barcelona, and Israel. The global indymedia site gave audiences up-to-the-minute details of the events taking place on this fourteen-acre plot of land.

Leslie Radford, a freelance journalist and adjunct professor of communications who wrote multiple stories about the situation for L.A. indymedia, explained the role of the news site during the standoff and struggle:

Los Angeles Indymedia was chiefly responsible for taking the story of the Farm west of the 110, the freeway in Los Angeles that divides the predominantly affluent and white Westside from the generally poorer and Black and Brown Eastside. Much of the engagement was, I suspect, because of the pictures that so many of us (most better photographers than I) posted. The wonder of such a magical garden in the most industrialized warehouse district of this City of Quartz was conveyed in the images, and the story was relatively easy to tell after that. What it [LA Indymedia] inspire[d] was individual actions that evolved into financial and political support from influential Westside individuals and groups, a significant contingent of young people joined the Farmers' actions and encampment, and perhaps thousands of people who would otherwise have never crossed the 110 made their way to the Farm itself to support the effort there.[10]

As Radford explains, L.A. IMC's coverage of the struggle over this relatively small plot of land first resonated across class lines within the city, building a larger base of support for the farmers. However, in time, the story reverberated across the complex circuits of the indymedia infrastructure, reaching a worldwide activist community.

The ability of indymedia activists to circulate this struggle across the Web inspired people from Los Angeles and Boston to Venezuela and South Africa to take action offline. Money came to the urban farmers through indymedia appeals and fund-raising events, while the Annenberg Foundation promised the farmers ten million dollars. Correspondingly, while hundreds flooded the farm in an attempt to resist eviction, activists across the country from Boston to Portland held solidarity protests. During the standoff, public messages of support came in from Ralph Nader and U.S. Representative Maxine Waters,[11] and the protest had a celebrity slant as Daryl Hannah, Leonardo DiCaprio, Willie Nelson, Joan Baez, Danny Glover, and Charlie Sheen, among others, visited the farm during the siege. Meanwhile, social-movement organizations focused on land rights, such as the Philippine Peasant Support Network (Pesante-USA)[12] and the Zapatistas, put out messages of solidarity. In a communiqué, members of the EZLN explained: "We know that there are many more injustices in the world, like that suffered by our compañeras farmers of South Central Farm in Los Angeles, who were evicted from their land where they lived and worked collectively. We have to support these brothers and sisters."[13]

Indymedia coverage and circulation of the struggle created a physical, digital, and financial convergence around the South Central Farm, ultimately playing an important role in the money and attention the farmers received.

Following the lead of indymedia, more institutionalized elements of the left press, such as KPFK 90.7 in Los Angeles and *Democracy Now!*,[14] as well as the Web-based news sites *CounterPunch* (Radford and Santos 2006) and the *Huffington Post* (Hannah 2006), picked up the story, taking it to a far wider audience of concerned left-leaning spectators.

This moment offers a window onto how indymedia operates, in its ideal, as a switchboard, facilitating multi-issue, multiscalar collective action that reverberates at a much wider scale than previously possible. Local indymedia journalists simultaneously swarmed on the farm during the standoff, while reporting on the Los Angeles local digital hub or node of the vast indymedia network. The story of the seizure of the South Central Farm began as a local story, but in time it echoed across the world as a tale of injustice pitting urban migrants against a large corporation,[15] aided and abetted by the state, seizing the land of the poor. Epitomizing the asymmetry of contemporary society, the story went viral, becoming prominent at the national and global levels and having a "boomerang effect,"[16] where national and global audiences attempted to use different forms of leverage to impact a local issue.

Specifically, the IMC network was helpful in building connections and a network of support for the South Central Farmers across three interrelated scales. First, it broadcast the story connecting and mobilizing people across the urban terrain of Los Angeles, building a local community of people who were aware of the struggle and were able to physically converge on the farm during the standoff in support of the urban farmers. Second, the indymedia communications network built issue-based support across a network of groups fighting over land-use and property rights—connecting the South Central Farmers to Pesante-USA and the Zapatistas, groups involved with similar battles. Third, through broadcasting the story, the indymedia network helped raise money and rallied support across a broad, diverse transnational activist network.

At the same time, the loss of the farm points to some of the limits of this mode of action. While indymedia broadcast the story and effectively reached thousands of supporters who swarmed on the farm, the plot was ultimately seized by the LAPD. Further, while the farm continued in another location, many of the networks of support it generated were not sustained or able to take proactive political action. Along these lines, the seizure of the farm points to the limited power and capacity of contemporary collective action that operate without leadership and depends on multiple points of insurgency in a network to operate in an independent but coordinated fashion.

Circuits of Communication:
The Indymedia Platform

In a "how-to" indymedia toolkit, *Hands On: Creating an Independent Media Center in Your Community*, a few of the founding members of indymedia described the nuts-and-bolts process for creating a local IMC. Detailing a wide array of issues, the toolkit walked potential IMCistas through the various steps for running a successful community media center. Writing a year after the Seattle IMC went live, the authors used the introduction of the handbook to discuss the innovative nature of the indymedia movement and the rationale for its exponential growth over its first year of operations.

> This movement for an alternative media, with its flexible open structure, its democratic rendering of the use-value of new technologies, and its continual involvement in interconnecting people in a transnational movement, provides an example of the evolution of a radical opposition, from the spontaneous appearance of individual creative practice, to the collective gatherings of small collectives, and to the growth of national and international collectives whose identities increasingly cluster around the negation of capital. . . . In this way, a spontaneously developing collective evolves into a community of resistance.[17]

Forecasting the expansion of indymedia, the authors marked the role of "new information sharing" in knitting together a global movement. They highlighted the connective force of communications technologies, which consolidate small, fragmented collectives working in isolation into a coherent, transnational "community of resistance." The implicit argument is that a shared communications network will create circuits or pathways across fragmented communities to build a stronger shared movement.

The indymedia Web sites are the central space where this strategic outlook is brought to life. At the height of the movement, almost all indymedia sites were designed with the same simple three-column architecture. On the left side was a geographical list and hyperlink to all of the different local IMC collectives. The center column contained editorial features, which focused on stories of strategic importance. The right column housed the indymedia open-publishing newswire, where people were able to share their stories. The uniform architecture of indymedia sites was specifically designed to enable the greatest amount of communication across the indymedia network and between the different autonomous social movements that use the network. Before expanding on details about each column, it is important to reiterate that this architecture was developed at a time when the Web was not generally interactive,

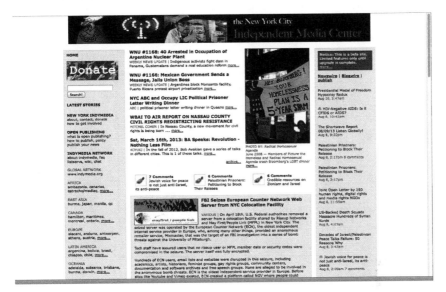

Screen Shot 1: the New York City Independent Media Center homepage exemplifies three-column architecture.

and many of the social technologies that indymedia activists and technologists pioneered became the forerunners to the social-media revolution today, from blogs to Facebook, Twitter, and community journalism.

ENVISIONING A GLOBAL MOVEMENT:
THE LEFT-HAND COLUMN OF THE INDYMEDIA PLATFORM

The left side of virtually all indymedia Web sites is structured as a hyperlink directory of all the other indymedia sites in the world, grouped by continent and country. This hyperlink directory offers a list of the network and enables links between different local collectives as well as connections to larger national and global hubs. Indymedia activists named this the "city list," and its role was to offer a visual representation of a global social movement, a map of the different nodes of the network. In this sense, while the indymedia movement is locally constituted, and most indymedia activists, journalists, and audiences are based in a local IMC collective, the city list offers a broader picture of the interconnections across the transnational movement.

If a reader on a particular U.S. local Web site wants information on local news in Jakarta, Bolivia, Toronto, or Istanbul, this information is a click away. If there is a story on a Belgian site that refers to a related event or situation in Ecuador, audiences can follow a hyperlink to the Ecuador indymedia site, tracking the particular struggle or issue from Belgium to Ecuador. Jeff Perlstein (2001) discussed this Web-based strategy when he argued that the aim of the communications network was to "affirm local struggles while simultaneously inviting an exploration of larger networks of struggle" (336).

An example of affirming "local struggles" while offering people the capacity to explore "larger networks" came during the Massive Immigration General Strike, or "Gran Paro Americano 2006." On May 1, 2006, U.S.-based immigrants and their allies, seeking to make their presence and work visible in U.S. society, walked off their jobs in dozens of cities and states. An indymedia Web site in San Francisco, www.indybay.org, coordinated coverage of the Gran Paro from around the country.[18] Indybay focused on reporting across northern and central California, including dozens of written reports, hundreds of pictures, and hours of video and audio of events from Humboldt and San Jose to Bakersfield (see Screen Shot 2, below).

Once indybay journalists established the local and regional aspect of the general strike, the Web site linked to national reports, looking at actions in Washington, D.C., Oregon, Colorado, Chicago, New York, and Miami, each of which carried photographs, audio recording, and video footage of the events in their locales. This reporting of the May Day protests illustrates the way the communications infrastructure invites local exploration of an issue and then

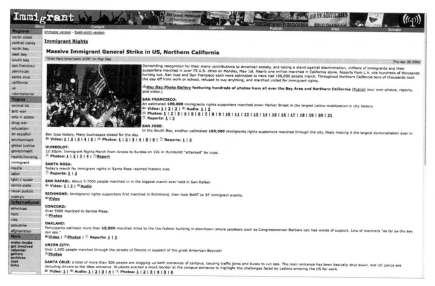

Screen Shot 2: Indybay regional coverage of the Immigration General Strike of 2006.

pulls the audience out into the larger network of the struggle. This operation, as indymedia founders like Perlstein claim, is the basis of indymedia's attempt to break isolation by creating linkages and showing audiences that they are part of a worldwide community. Through this new media practice, activists work to cultivate a broader movement by offering reporting as well as an infrastructure that operates as a connective tissue to build concerted action against shared targets.[19]

STRATEGIZING THE USE OF SPACE:
THE CENTER COLUMN OF THE INDYMEDIA PLATFORM

The center column of each indymedia Web site—the "feature column"—is a vital communicative space where each local collective prioritizes local, national, or global stories. This section of the site is usually the largest, often taking up half of the usable space. The editorial board of each local IMC decides how to best use this space.

In the Philadelphia-based IMC, the center column is a space where activists draw links between different local struggles, creating connective communicative practices. As one member of the Philly editorial team explained, "We have to choose our stories strategically so that we can link different communities together."[20] In a Philly IMC strategic-content memo, a longtime Philly indymedia activist, Marisa, explained this tactic in detail:

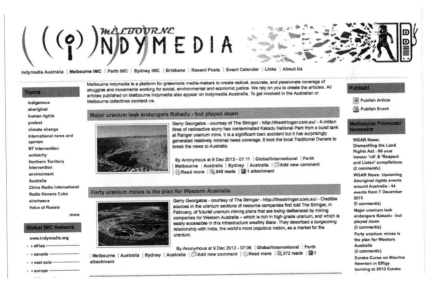

Screen Shot 3: Feature column of Melbourne IMC.

The mainstream news defines their editorial positions by asking, what sort of combination of writing do we want our end product to contain? I think we should do the same. I would like to see us claim the center column as a strategic zone, and make collective decisions about how to fill it based on strategic priorities. I would like to see us take some time to think, what should be in the center column in order to accomplish our strategic goals[?] . . . This is more importantly about us thinking of our writing (and photography and audio or video documentation) as being about organizing and movement-building. . . . As recruiters, we have to be able to be practicing the micro-level of movement building, which is supporting each other—and in this day and age supporting MANY each others. This means we must have policies and practices that explicitly encourage us to practice responsiveness regularly and vigilantly.[21]

This memo highlights the intended practice of using communication, specifically on the feature column, as a space for movement building. As Marisa details, the center column is a strategic space that must be utilized for the "micro-level practices" of movement building. In a strategy meeting where she presented this document, Marisa elaborated on this point, explaining that "micro practices" refers to the expectation that there should be organizing between indymedia activists and members of social movements. Practically, she noted that this means encouraging members of movements to write stories, while training members of these movements in media making.[22]

The memo goes on to articulate that indymedia communication practices are done with the intent of building across the "many each others" that comprise the regionally based social movement, pointing to the autonomous struggles that can be aligned through communication. This is a practice that Philly IMC has repeatedly focused on in their work and offers a window into the broad strategy of indymedia Web sites and, more broadly, communications tools working as switchboards that connect across individuals, organizations, social struggles, and space. In a Philly IMC "outreach memo," drafters explain the strategy of connecting the "many each others." The authors argue for a joint outreach and educational program in an effort to "create strong links with the various communities and activist groups that comprise Philadelphia, developing a truly grassroots indymedia movement that highlights the stories of Philadelphians with an eye towards building solidarity throughout the city."[23]

While these memos lay out the strategy for a coherent connective-communications practice, it is less clear how Philly IMC organizers believe that different groups will link together. Sheethl, one of the members of the Philly

IMC as well as a community-based organizer, specified that for her the primary focus of Philly IMC is to support the organizing of poor people and the labor movement, the two classes, in her view, "most exploited by globalization and left out of mainstream media."[24] Along these lines, Philly IMC also prioritized engagement on immigrant workers and housing. Indymedia activists wrote and promoted stories on groups such as the Kensington Welfare Rights Union, a poor-led social movement; Project HOME, a nonprofit organization committed to ending homelessness; Juntos, a community-based organization focused on immigrant rights; and the Taxi Workers Alliance of Pennsylvania, a coalition of cab drivers organizing for a more just taxi industry in the city and state.

OPEN PUBLISHING: THE RIGHT-HAND COLUMN

Next to the feature column, on the right side of the Web site, is the open-publishing newswire, where people can post stories, editorials, and up-to-the-minute news. Arguably the most important innovation of the network sociopolitically and technologically, this part of the site is meant to offer an open, democratic space for the public to speak. The most important aspect of the open wire is that it offers transparency. When an individual posts a story to the open-publishing wire of any IMC, that post instantly goes up on the front page of the Web site, offering a sense of immediacy and direct control over the site. IMC-Scotland's explanation of open publishing captures the democratic essence of the newswire: "The online newswire is designed to empower individuals to become independent journalists by providing a direct forum for presenting media, including text articles, audio and video recordings, and photographs, to the public via the Internet. . . . The Indymedia Scotland website operates on a system of 'open publishing,' i.e. anyone can upload a written report, image or audio clip directly to the site through an openly accessible web interface, given the guidelines detailed."[25] The purpose of the open wire is to allow all citizens of a local community to freely publish stories, messages, first-person accounts, editorials, and press releases. This is done, as the IMC-Scotland activists explain, with an eye toward building unity across the progressive movement.

As Matt Arnison, one of the programmers who developed indymedia Web software, explained, the tools and practices developed by indymedia "revolutionized the way media works," as the indymedia site was one of the first Web experiments where hundreds of users were actually generating content, as opposed to merely receiving and/or retrieving content. Arnison continued:

"The flow of information was stood on its head. Instead of corporate media moguls telling people what was important, information was created from everyday people and it bubbled up, in effect giving people new tools to express themselves and more importantly, to impact political life."[26]

While the claim is bold, others have corroborated[27] the fact that indymedia Web technology and social use of that technology was a central factor leading to the famed Web 2.0 revolution. Consequently, while the open-publishing newswire and the interactive Web innovation of the indymedia network seems commonplace today, with many bloggers using the same basic configuration, these developments were critical building blocks for new social technologies that catalyzed the citizen-journalism movement.[28]

Since the inauguration of the IMC, the open-publishing wire has become the cornerstone of the movement, capturing the belief in openness and the logic of many points of resistance. As many have pointed out, open publishing maximizes the capacity for everyday people and activists to communicate. Whether through front-page articles or feature-column comments, the open-publishing wire allows readers to become authors, authors to become advocates, and advocates to become organizers, and ultimately lays the foundation for people in fragmented movements to build connections. While each of the three aspects (open publishing, city list, feature column) of the Web site is important, it is the totality of the environment that makes IMC Web sites a platform for movement building.

The Total Web Environment

When Raymond Williams (1974) famously analyzed television in Britain, he argued that it is not a singular message or show that captures the nature of TV's impact on human consciousness, but rather the flow of images and ideas: "In all these ways and in their essential combination, this is the flow of meanings and values of a specific culture" (120–21). Though Williams is describing TV, this idea also translates to the indymedia Web sites and the flow of ideas and meanings that the indymedia technologists and activists attempt to create through the Web platform. Each of the three central components of the site— the map of the network, the central-column feature, and the open-publishing newswire—is important for thinking through the different strategies of creating nonhierarchical communication platforms across space and struggles.

The central function of indymedia is to act as a communications network, facilitating the development of a broader movement through building strong lines of communication. This is meant to occur at the local level, offering stories to build connections across the local and regional community (embodied in the center column and open wire) while also building connections to regional, national, and global concerns (embodied in the left column linking to other sites). In this sense, indymedia sites work to forge unity on three levels: (1) across local spaces, linking different movements together to build a stronger localized movement; (2) across spaces on a particular theme, such as labor or immigrant rights; and (3) across space and theme in an attempt to forge a global social movement.

Philadelphia: The Local Switchboard

While the indymedia logic of resistance is typified by the online spaces IM-Cistas have created, some activists have attempted to bring this logic of resistance offline by creating physical spaces and "real-world" campaigns. In Philadelphia, indymedia activists, along with other activists in the community, collaborated to purchase a building in West Philadelphia, the Lancaster Avenue Autonomous Zone (LAVA). The purpose of the center was to create a "public space . . . that would connect to a diverse group of communities throughout Philadelphia" in an effort to "build a broader movement for social justice."[29] At the time of my fieldwork, LAVA was used and occupied by approximately eleven different groups. These groups exemplified the wide spectrum of Philadelphia's progressive activist community, from worker- and prisoner-rights organizations to an HIV/AIDS direct-action group. In addition to Philly IMC, five other organizations held office space in LAVA: the Philadelphia chapter of the Green Party, the Taxi Workers Alliance of Pennsylvania, the Human Rights Coalition, ACT-UP,[30] and the local newspaper *The Defenestrator*.[31] LAVA's shared space was used for a diverse range of activities. Music and performance collectives held practices and shows there, and other affiliated groups used the rooms for meetings, lectures, and parties. The projects associated with LAVA all coalesced around the idea of creating an "empowering and welcoming physical space where diverse communities converge to build connections and break down barriers, blending media-making, artistic expression and hearty nuts-and-bolts organizing in order to advance movements for justice."[32]

LAVA became a critical space for Philly IMC campaigns. In 2005, the Philadelphia IMC began a campaign challenging Wal-Mart business practices as part of a new outreach strategy that combined "independent media making" and "political organizing" to build a broader-based movement focused on labor issues. According to an internal Philly IMC document, the intent of the campaign was as follows: "To initiate new ways to share stories, organizing people around issues of local, national, and global importance.

. . . Correspondingly, Philly IMC's foundational commitment is to create strong links with the various communities and activist groups that comprise Philadelphia, developing a grassroots indymedia movement that highlights the stories of Philadelphians with an eye towards building solidarity."[33] According to Sheethl they chose Wal-Mart as their first campaign because it was "the perfect enemy." Focusing on Wal-Mart helped coalesce many different forces across the city, including "unions, working poor, consumer rights activists, environmental groups, immigrant's rights leaders." Sheethl thought this was important because it offered the possibility of creating convergence across the many different movements in the city.[34] The Philly IMC Web site as well as LAVA became a grounding for this movement, offering spaces both virtual and real for differently situated local movements to congregate and ultimately join forces on the Wal-Mart campaign.

The Philadelphia campaign was spearheaded by Philly IMC and Philly Jobs with Justice (JWJ), and it was part of a nationwide week of action organized by unions and social-justice organizations that coincided with the release of a prominent documentary by the filmmaker Robert Greenwald, *Wal-Mart: The High Cost of Low Prices*. Philly IMC organizers worked with JWJ organizers to develop a campaign to make media and organize around Wal-Mart issues in the month leading up to the screening of the documentary.

Philly indymedia organizers aimed to use Wal-Mart's corporate irresponsibility as the common ground for discussion, education, media training, and protest. The hope was that these different tactics would be the basis for a broader coalition of groups in the city. In this campaign, as Sheethl explained, Philly IMC used "interactive media and organizing practices enabled by new media to inspire the formation of networks or coalitions that work toward movement building." Tanya Jameson, an organizer involved with the campaign, said that the idea was to experiment with a model of political organizing as media making, taking the concept of a switchboard of struggle offline.[35]

The explicit strategy was to call new constituencies into the media-making and organizing process. In the first stage, members of Philly IMC offered community-journalism training with civic leaders and rank-and-file union members. The four-hour training sessions, which took place three times over the course of the one-month campaign, focused on podcasting, interviewing, and investigative journalism. In the second stage, three Philly IMC members led these new journalists on trips to Wal-Mart outlets across Philadelphia, where they could interview Wal-Mart employees about working conditions (they paid ten dollars per interview). The new journalists captured interviews with over twenty workers, focused on working conditions, pay, union busting, and upward mobility within the company. As the campaign progressed, Philly IMC members held a few media-making sessions where the rank-and-file union members, independent journalists, and students came together for political-education and media-production sessions. During these meetings, members listened to interviews and watched media about Wal-Mart. As Fischer explained, the aim was to create a pedagogical space. After watching the media, the new journalists broke into groups and created their own media, creating a series of short public-service announcements (PSAs) from the worker interviews. With news and editorials, commercials on Wal-Mart, and longer documentary-style features and podcasts, the group made the Philly IMC Web site into a repository of local journalism and of information on Wal-Mart for protestors nationwide.

The media-production and organizing process culminated in the documentary screening, which was held on November 14, 2005. Three hundred people in Philadelphia came out to preview the new documentary, but the evening program began with the locally produced PSAs about Wal-Mart. The executive director of the Philly JWJ claimed that this was the biggest event across the country and the most exciting because of the innovative use of media-making as an organizing tool.

Out of this campaign grew two different local efforts. The first was spearheaded by Jobs with Justice, and Philly IMC led the second. The first effort was to establish a workers'-rights collective, so Wal-Mart employees could find out their rights and organize in the workplace. However, this collective would work with Philly IMC and also become a media collective, working to document organizing campaigns throughout the city. The second effort that grew out of this campaign was cross-movement dialogues. Led by Philly IMC, these dialogues aimed to bring together leaders of different movements to talk about how their interests were aligned in an effort to build a broader social movement across Philadelphia.

Philly IMC's use of media as a switchboard moved offline when UNITE HERE Local 274, which represents hotel and food service workers, was fighting with a local branch of the Embassy Suites hotel chain. Members of the Philly IMC editorial team learned about the fight and contacted a UNITE HERE organizer to make sure that struggle was being reported on, either by members of UNITE HERE or, alternatively, by Philly IMC journalists. In this case, members of UNITE HERE and indymedia worked together to ensure coverage of the events. Philly IMC journalists wrote a story on the protest and worker lockout, and a UNITE HERE member created a short video.

Indymedia activists placed the article and video online on the Philly IMC site as well as other local Web sites. Philly IMC activists also used a listserv to circulate the story to three thousand people and multiple organizations. Pete, the UNITE HERE member who made the video, works as a waiter in a local hotel. He said that working with indymedia supported the goals of workers and union leadership to make a plan to speak for themselves and document their work. After this collaboration, leaders of the local UNITE HERE union, including Pete, began using the Web site to make sure that Philly IMC readers were aware of other labor actions across the city.

Following this first contact, Philly IMC organizers began working with UNITE HERE hospitality workers, training them in basic video production and investigative reporting. UNITE HERE leadership then purchased a video camera, and workers used it to film protests around workers' struggles and to conduct interviews with union and nonunion hotel workers about high rates of injury in the workplace.

Philly IMC's strategy of focusing on particular types of struggles and communities means that there is less "openness" in Philly IMC than in some other local indymedia collectives. Philly IMC members prioritize disenfranchised voices instead of creating an open platform and allowing for different voices to emerge. By intentionally focusing on disenfranchised communities, Philly IMC organizers sacrifice the purely democratic, decentralized structure, and ethos that many IMC collectives hold sacred, and they do it on purpose. While members of Philly IMC value "openness," they feel that it is more critical to create, and sometimes reserve, space for particular issues and voices. As Sheethl explained, absolute openness leads to the domination of an upper-middle-class white voice. The problem with openness in indymedia, she continued, "is that communities that don't have Internet access or the time to learn how to use the indymedia platform, are often left out."[36] Members of Philly IMC believed that if there was not some targeted action to get disenfranchised voices onto the Philly IMC site, then the site would de facto highlight certain communities, and consequently prioritize openness over justice and democracy over equality.

We can contrast Philly IMC's efforts to the editorial collective of Portland IMC. The explicit objective of Portland IMC is not to produce media, but rather to produce an "open space" or platform for members of the Portland community to use. Practically, this means that Portland IMC activists do a great deal of public education about the existence of the Web site. They have a very active open-publishing newswire on the right-hand column of the site, which gets twenty to thirty posts per day, as opposed to ten per day in Philadelphia. Portland IMC activists choose which stories from the newswire to promote as the center feature column.

In Portland IMC's "About Us" section, the drafters explain this perspective: "Indymedia activism can take many forms, but is rooted in the indymedia Principles of Unity, which profess that the open exchange of and open access to information is the prerequisite of a more free and just society. . . . The articles that are featured in the center column are taken right from the newswire, thus highlighting original content and reporting. This system empowers anyone to become the media."[37] Theoretically, the Portland model is empowering because it becomes an open space where citizen reporting is highly respected and promoted to the center of the site. At the same time, it is arguably less strategic than the Philly IMC practice because there is a less explicit impulse among Portland IMC activists to get certain stories, groups, or ideas represented on the site. Consequently, the Portland IMC Web site accentuates certain voices in Portland because those people or communities utilize the platform the most, whereas in Philadelphia, certain voices are accentuated because the Philadelphia collective determined that those voices are socially and politically disenfranchised. While the tactics are different, it is clear that in each strategy the editorial collective plays a mediating role, deciding which philosophy of media justice should be prioritized.

This difference between Philly IMC and Portland IMC also illustrates a broader ideological tension that exists across the network. Some members of Philly IMC are self-consciously guided by an ethic of economic justice and organize around issues of social and economic displacement. In general terms, the Portland collective is focused on ideas of openness, horizontality, and decentralization, which are priorities more closely aligned with the radical democratic vision of Laclau and Mouffe. The political tensions that exist across indymedia are an important aspect of the network; however, the Portland ethic of openness and horizontality is dominant within the indymedia network and more closely approximates the Cyber Left logic of resistance.

The process of strengthening offline struggle through digital media in Philadelphia offers a window onto the broader strategy of movement building that some IMCs undertake, which I argue is the tendency of the Cyber Left. Members of the Philly IMC teamed with other local organizations, training members in basic media production, offering a communications platform, and building social relationships in an effort to build a linked social movement. This exemplifies the logic of radical democracy, where multiple points of struggle challenge power, and it brings forth the goal of indymedia to use communications to ally multiple, distinct movements for justice, harnessing them in a common challenge.

The organizing that Philly IMC activists attempted was focused on building a bigger shared movement across Philadelphia, using targets like Wal-Mart because of symbolic value. This goal of using media to build long-term power across the many points of struggle in Philadelphia, however, was not necessarily the norm within indymedia or in the Cyber Left more generally. In most instances, indymedia activists were only able to accentuate particular struggles; they were not able to build links across these struggles that facilitated shared struggle or a shared vision. In fact, the only consistent form of political action I witnessed across indymedia was what scholars have called "swarming."

Political Action of the Cyber Left: Swarming

The critical question indymedia activists and other Cyber Left actors face is how to create concerted collective action from the multiple autonomous fronts of struggle. Laclau and Mouffe recognized this problem, arguing that distinct spheres of struggle must create a shared political vision. While a shared vision has not emerged across indymedia, the ability of multiple collectives or fronts of struggle to attack an issue or enemy in a swarming manner has been the predominant form of collective action. Scholars have called this "swarm intelligence." Ronfeldt and Arquilla (1996) define swarming as a moment when a myriad of small units (which could be organizations, collectives, or other social formations) that are normally dispersed converge on a target from all directions, conduct an attack, and then redisperse to prepare for the next operation. This form of political action was exemplified during the standoff between the Mexican government and the EZLN in 1994.

After the EZLN's uprising, the Mexican government sent twelve thousand troops to Chiapas to retain control. A battle ensued, and overmatched by the Mexican military, the EZLN retreated into the mountains. The Mexican government planned to pursue the EZLN using air strikes and superior military power. At this point, however, a massive network of citizens and human-rights activists swarmed on Mexico City, Chiapas, and Mexican consulates throughout the world to stop the conflict. The network of people and organizations were linked through an already established communications infrastructure of Web sites and listservs used for international NGOs.

Once the situation in southern Mexico escalated, these groups and organizations shared information about the conflict in Chiapas and swarmed the capital, demanding that peace be restored. The diverse delegation held marches, demonstrations, and caravans, pressuring the Mexican government to agree to an armistice. They were successful, and a ceasefire was signed, which led to a peace accord.

As the economist Harry Cleaver (1998b) documents, this massive action took shape without any centralized coordination or system of hierarchical accountability. Instead, the swarming action was born through a decentralized communication infrastructure of faxes, cell phones, and the Internet. Cleaver argues that the swarming was facilitated as information was passed quickly and effectively across networks of actors and enabled individuals and organizations to use this information and the newly developed forums of communication (mostly in the form of listservs) to create a shared challenge to the Mexican state. The digital and physical convergence around the EZLN illustrates the quintessential mode of action of the Cyber Left, which has no central point of leadership or political program. Without a substantial preexisting infrastructure or coordinated call, a decentralized and diverse network rapidly developed, first online and then offline, in Mexico and globally, forcing the Mexican government to offer an armistice.

As a switchboard of struggle, indymedia supports swarming by offering an open venue so multiple actors can produce massive amounts of information on a particular situation and then uses communication spaces, like Web sites, for these decentralized actors to interact and set strategy. Along these lines, local, national, or global indymedia Web sites act as repositories of reporting and documentation. Through in-depth documentation, indymedia sites have the capacity to highlight the intensity and scale of actions that take place across geographic territories, as illustrated by the U.S. indymedia reports on the 2006 antiwar march, or the global coverage of the February 15, 2003, protest against the war with Iraq.[38]

At the same time, indymedia Web sites also have the ability to capture the magnitude of specific localized events during short but intense periods of time, as exemplified by global indymedia coverage of the WTO protests in Hong Kong in 2005 (Screen Shots 4 and 5). During the WTO meetings in Hong Kong, known as the Doha Round, indymedia journalists created a massive amount of information on the Hong Kong protest.[39] The purpose of this rich content was to build communication links across space and/or issue, maximizing the amount of on-the-ground coverage and shared information and communication about the WTO meetings. To cover the protests in Hong Kong, indymedia activists established a media-convergence center, which became a central hub and critical communication center during the protests. This practice of creating convergence centers is common across indymedia and exemplifies the logic of indymedia activists to use media as the basis for swarming political action.

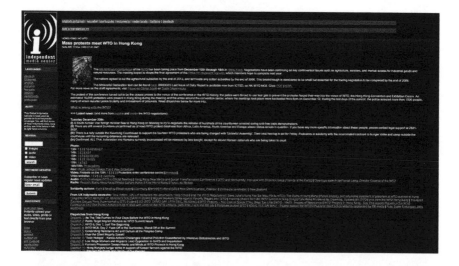

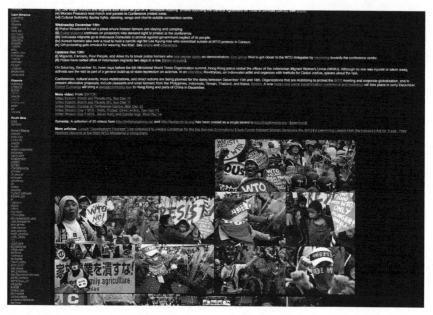

Screen Shots 4 and 5: Global indymedia coverage of WTO protests in Hong Kong, December 2005. The screen shots illustrate the massive amount of information and imagery that was collected, curated, and shared.

7.10 Convergence Centers and Offline Swarming

To strengthen information sharing during large-scale political protests, in-dymedia activists set up media-convergence centers, temporary public sites for independent reporting. Activists first established Seattle IMC as a media-convergence center during the WTO meetings in 1999, and Philly IMC was established during the Republican National Convention in 2000. Following this pattern, activists established many IMCs during protests as media-convergence centers, and once the protests ended, local activists transformed them into long-term community media centers.

During the summer of 2005, I attended political protests that targeted the Group of Eight (G8) meetings in Scotland. I worked for five days at the media-convergence center established in Edinburgh. The protests against the 2005 G8 meetings were particularly large, as they coincided with a series of global concerts (Live 8) and a massive march to end poverty, two events that were used to pressure members of the G8 to forgive global debt. In preparation for the massive political protest, indymedia activists established three different media-convergence centers across Scotland, in Gleneagles (the town where the G8 meetings were held), Glasgow, and Edinburgh. The Edinburgh Convergence Center, which activists constructed in the weeks leading up to the 2005 G8 meetings, was located above a cafe in the city's downtown center. The convergence center consisted of approximately sixty computers, a specialized video center to upload and edit video footage, a dispatch center with phones and computers, an FM radio station, and a still-photography uploading station.

The Edinburgh center was frantic, with hundreds of people in the room at any one time. One of the organizers of the center told me that over the four days of action, over 2,500 people entered the convergence center. Like in Hong Kong, over the course of the 2005 G8 meetings, citizen journalists produced massive amounts of information in the form of written reports, video, photographs, and audio programming. According to one internal in-dymedia report, "over 2,300 photographs and hundreds of written reports were published on the open newswire . . . creating an in-depth record"[40] of the events.

While the production and creation of information for a broader public was a central goal of the convergence center, the leaders of the center also said that the role of the space was to help collect and dispense information to activists leading the protests. During the weeklong event, I worked the dispatch desk. I answered phone calls that came into the Scotland IMC, and I relayed this information to a list of different indymedia journalists and activists. The people on the list were trusted indymedia journalists or people who were attempting to coordinate road blockages, protests, and other forms of action. Often the calls included information about where the police were amassed and which intersections were susceptible to sabotage. In this sense, the convergence center acted as a central command for protestors, collecting and relaying information across the network of protestors and journalists.

Indymedia convergence centers and other physical spaces, like LAVA in Philadelphia, bring to the fore the importance of the corporeal in the age of digital media and despatialized organizing. While important work can be done online, powerful organizing often has a critical material component. In my research on indymedia it became quite clear that while the methods of political action that activists forged were inherently digital—from building a switchboard of struggle to using a swarming style of political praxis—they were more successful and powerful when there was an offline component or a physical space that grounded the activism and organizing. This was visibly on display in Tahrir Square and Zuccotti Park during the most recent cycle of resistance, as both struggles prioritized the fight over physical public space.

Conclusion

The strategy of indymedia activists, at the local, national, and global levels, is to use new communication technologies and other practices to circulate stories of struggle across fragmented points of resistance so they can begin to come together in a shared movement. In this sense, it is a switchboard of struggle. This logic of resistance implicitly builds on the vision of radical democracy developed by Laclau and Mouffe, and more explicitly emerges out of the praxis of the EZLN. However, indymedia activists brought this vision to life by creating and deploying a transnational, networked, communications infrastructure.

The indymedia Web site and the events around the South Central Farmers illustrate how the indymedia switchboard of struggle worked to link movements and people: (1) across local spaces, linking different communities together to build a stronger localized movement; (2) across geographic spaces on a particular theme, such as labor or immigrant rights; and (3) across space and theme in an attempt to forge a global social movement. At the local level, however, as illustrated by Philly IMC, the switchboard effect is based on the synthesis of online and offline activities using pedagogy, alliance building, and media practices to create a spokes-council of social movements in the city. While these outcomes are positive, one of the problems with the switch-board effect is the inability to create sustained campaigns.

Swarming, online and offline, is a significant form of action whereby the indymedia network and other network formations are able to impact the world. This mode of political action is well suited to short-term events such as protests or convergences, but it is not as useful for sustained struggle and organizing. In this sense, the strength of the network, a decentralized structure, is also its weakness, as without a centralized body, it is difficult to coordinate over a long period of time. This was exemplified over the course of my research, as coordinated organizing was never successful, primarily because the structure and decision making of the indymedia network did not allow for proactive collective decisions, only reactive decisions, as I discuss in the conclusion.

Conclusion

Social Movement Logics—
Past, Present, and Future

Part of an accurate estimate of the social problems we face involves power relationships. In the National Union of the Homeless we coined the slogan, "Power grows from organization. . . . Freedom is never given. It must be taken. And therefore you only get what you are organized to take!" All of history—U.S. and world history—confirms this statement. Are you able to generate a critical mass of power to counter the existing power relationships to make change? . . . The only thing that the oppressed classes have at their disposal is their numbers. They only enter in the scale of power struggle if those numbers are organized and are led by knowledge or an understanding of what they're up against.

—Willie Baptist, *It's Not Enough to Be Angry*

It started with an image—the arresting image of a ballerina elegantly, and perhaps defiantly, poised atop the iconic Wall Street Bull, the symbol of free-market capitalism. In the backdrop, just beyond the bull and ballerina, stands a throng of riot cops or protestors obscured by the haze of tear gas, foreshadowing the struggle to come. The ad hails the reader, "What Is Our One Demand?"

Published online on July 13, 2011, in the Canadian magazine *Adbusters,*[1] the prophetic image called on people to "#OccupyWallStreet" on "September 17th." Just below the ad, the drafters asked, "Are you ready for a Tahrir moment?" The advertisement continued:

A worldwide shift in revolutionary tactics is underway right now that bodes well for the future. . . . The beauty of this new formula, and what makes this novel tactic exciting, is its pragmatic simplicity: we talk to each other in various physical gatherings and virtual people's assemblies . . . we zero in on what our demand will be, a demand that awakens the imagination and,

if achieved, would propel us towards the radical democracy of the future . . .
and then we go out and seize a square of singular symbolic significance and
put our asses on the line to make it happen. The time has come to deploy this
emerging stratagem, against the greatest corrupter of our democracy: Wall
Street, the financial Gomorrah of America. On September 17, we want to see
20,000 people flood into lower Manhattan, set up tents, kitchens, peaceful
barricades and occupy Wall Street for a few months.[2]

Reminiscent of the Situationist-inspired street art of May '68, the *Adbuster*
provocation reverberated across the Web, and the vision of a radical democratic future—where people occupy, deliberate, and act—caught on, capturing the zeitgeist of a generation.

In the months to follow, activists planned the initial stages of Occupy Wall
Street, launched the Tumblr page "We are the 99%," and, on September 17, began the encampment at Zuccotti Park in lower Manhattan. While OWS grew
slowly, garnering modest media coverage, two events brought the encampment into the public gaze. First, police sprayed mace on two young women
connected to the protests, and the incident was caught on video and quickly
went viral. Shortly thereafter, on October 1, over seven hundred OWS activists
were arrested during a march across the Brooklyn Bridge. These two events
were widely broadcast by the mass media, and—like Birmingham, Alabama, or
Kent State—the media attention incited rapid growth of Occupy Wall Street. As
OWS grew, so did the real and symbolic power of the uprising, and the newly
minted model of struggle proliferated. Within weeks there were hundreds of
Occupy encampments and thousands of Occupiers across the United States,
and then the world, calling to life the Occupy Movement.

Since its meteoric rise, Occupy has become one of the most important and
creative social movements in recent U.S. history. Responding to the conditions in Zuccotti Park, in particular New York City's prohibition on the use
of microphones, organizers and activists developed innovative repertoires of
social-movement action like the human mic,[3] while redefining old repertoires
like the seizure of public space and the use of general assemblies. Moreover,
having been surrounded with digital technologies all their lives, many of the
young OWS activists imaginatively deployed social media and cutting-edge
digital tools like live streaming to bring attention to the encampments, while
simultaneously developing new social-movement frames that transformed
the narrative around the economic crisis, including the meme "We are the
99 percent." Most notably, the Occupy movement cultivated the physical
and mental terrain to reimagine what resistance could look and feel like in a

moment when there seemed to be no alternative to the dominant neoliberal capitalist paradigm.

While these are important attributes, the brilliant, seemingly spontaneous explosion of the Occupy Movement in many respects blinds scholars and activists to the fact that this new wave of protests is rooted in a long history of left-based movement building. OWS did not emerge sui generis but rather is part and parcel of a broader logic of resistance that connects it to indymedia and the Global Social Justice Movement, while also linking it to a deeper history of social struggle in the United States and beyond. In fact, this bond between the current cycle of protest and the Global Social Justice Movement is highlighted in the original *Adbusters* appeal, as the editors quoted the Spanish organizer and scholar Raimundo Viejo: "*The anti-globalization movement was the first step on the road.* Back then our model was to attack the system like a pack of wolves. There was an alpha male, a wolf, that led the pack, and those who followed behind. Now the model has evolved. Today we are one big swarm of people."[4]

Though Viejo claims that a hierarchical logic dominated the Global Social Justice Movement, a point this and other research refutes,[5] the quotation is interesting as, in its inception, OWS was understood as a direct extension of the antiglobalization movements that emerged between 1994 and 2006. However, while drawing the historical and political connection between OWS and the Global Social Justice Movement is important, Viejo's contention that the earlier movement was "the first step on the road" is inaccurate. In point of fact, an excavation of political struggle would show that OWS is deeply tied to a long history of struggle across the twentieth century.

For instance, the idea of physical occupations of space, the foundational tactic of Occupy, has a long and powerful history in the United States. Take, for example, the Bonus Army of 1932. In the wake of the Great Depression, thousands of World War I veterans converged on Washington, D.C. The vets named themselves the Bonus Expeditionary Force, and their central demand was for immediate payment of a bonus (thus their name) that they had been promised by the U.S. government for their military service. The government pledged to pay the vets or their families, but not until 1945, some twelve years down the road. However, in the dark times of the Depression, when many families were unable to scrape together the money for their next meal—and breadlines, soup kitchens, and shantytowns dotted the landscape—the vets and their families demanded the money immediately. The U.S. Congress denied their request for payment, and members of the Bonus Army set up encampment in Anacostia Flats in Washington with the intention of occupying the capitol until their demands were met. On July 28, a few months after the occupation commenced, President Hoover ordered an army regiment, led by General Douglas MacArthur, into the capitol to wipe out the resistance. MacArthur raided the encampment with infantry, cavalry, and tanks, routing the Bonus Army and burning the shantytown to the ground, calling an end to the first domestic occupation of Washington, D.C.

Thirty-six years later, in 1968, inspired by the Bonus Army, Martin Luther King Jr. and members of the Southern Christian Leadership Conference announced the launch of the Poor People's Campaign. In a series of lectures in Canada in late 1967, King made the case for the necessity of this movement when he argued, "There are millions of poor people in this country who have very little, or even nothing to lose. If they can be helped to take action together they will do so with a freedom and a power that will be a new and unsettling force in our complacent national life."[6] Building on this vision, the goal of the Poor People's Campaign was to secure an economic bill of rights that would focus legislation on joblessness, income inequality, and poverty. The campaign included thousands of poor people from across racial lines, marching in mule trains (a symbol of their poverty) from different parts of the country and converging on Washington, D.C. The marchers then set up a shantytown on the National Mall called "Resurrection City." Tragically, King did not make it to Resurrection City, as he was assassinated in Memphis about a month before the occupation began. In the wake of King's death, the Poor People's Campaign did proceed; however, with a vacuum of leadership, the struggle for economic justice had trouble building traction. After six weeks, police forcibly drove inhabitants out of Resurrection City, the National Mall, and the city, thus ending the second major occupation of Washington, D.C.

These two occupations, and their subtle and perhaps unrecognized relationship to the Occupy Movement, bring to light the historical dynamics of the American left. In this book I argue that it is these relationships that we must unearth if we are to understand the logic of social movements and generations of left-based activism. In his study of the historical conjuncture of the Old and New Left, the historian Maurice Isserman (1987) captures this perspective:

> The more I looked into the history of radical movements in the 1950s, the more it became apparent that I was laboring under the misconception about both the death of the Old Left and the birth of the New Left. I gradually came to understand that the early New Left had emerged from the Old Left in ways that made it difficult to perceive exactly where the one ended and the other began. Not only were the "dark ages" of the 1950s less dark and static than I

had supposed, but the "renaissance" of the 1960s (I use the term advisedly) was also "less bright and less sudden" than I had previously assumed. The recent history of American radicalism began to seem less spasmodic, and more of a continual process of unfolding. (xii–xiii)[7]

Isserman's reminder that the history of the American left is best seen as a continual process of unfolding offers a window through which we can more clearly apprehend the movements of yesterday, today, and tomorrow. In particular, his quote brings forth three points of import with respect to the concept of the Cyber Left. First, different periods of left-based movement building (Old, New, and Cyber Left) are interlinked and informed by one another. Second, the U.S. left and social movements that fall within a particular period are not homogenous but have diverse strategies and approaches to social change. Finally, while different periods of struggle are linked, and each period is diversified, in each era of struggle there is what Fredric Jameson (1991) has called a cultural dominant: a hegemonic set of tactics, strategies, and visions of social change that govern and define a particular period.

Along these lines, in understanding the history of the contemporary left it is critical to see how it is at once historically rooted and diverse while also exemplary of a particular logic. In this light, it is not hard to see in the horizontal general assemblies, or the clever use of media, or the narrative of "99 percent" the same logic and strategy of resistance that drives indymedia and many of the institutions of the Global Social Justice Movement. The activists in these movements are often part of a singular generation, and thus they share a common understanding of the historical problem and a similar strategy of political action.

This brings us back to one of the central propositions of this book. Building on social-movement theorists who have attempted to historicize social movement logics and practices (Tilly 1986; Tarrow 1998), I argue that to understand a specific period of resistance, it is vital to look at historical antecedents as well as the current socioeconomic environment. Through this trilateral interaction between social-movement actors, the history of struggle, and the contemporary socioeconomic environs, we are able to more thoroughly map and understand a particular logic of resistance. This reality forms the backdrop of this study, which aims to be an initial step in understanding the shared strategy for action and common problems of contemporary movements for social change.

A second goal of this book was to illustrate the cultural dominant or core logic of the Cyber Left. To that end, I argue that there are three characteristics of indymedia that set it and other contemporary global movements apart from early movements for social change. Those characteristics are the multi-scalar network structure, the global application of participatory democracy, and the strategy of using media and communications to bind across autonomous movements. Together, these characteristics form the countenance of a new social formation that is at once local and global, online and offline, and decentralized and democratic.

To briefly recount each of these dynamics: The strategy of indymedia and Cyber Left movements is to create platforms and processes where different fragmented struggles can be networked together, not in an effort to become one singular struggle but to become stronger together as a complex of struggles. Said differently, Cyber Left actors and institutions presume that there are multiple irreducible fronts of struggle that must exist independently and cannot be subsumed under one banner, framework, or organizational structure. Indymedia takes up this strategy, utilizing the local, national, and global communications infrastructure to link people and struggles across space and theme, becoming a platform for this diversity of struggle.

Second, indymedia and other Cyber Left institutions tend to be structured as global, decentralized networks. In the specific case of indymedia, this means that the network is composed of a collection of local Independent Media Centers, usually based in urban settings across the world. The local IMCs are part of one loosely shared network, but they have almost complete autonomy. This structure is in contradistinction to the past, where social-movement organizations were structured as political parties, unions, or organizations.

Third, the internal governance of indymedia is a form of direct democracy, enacted through a complex, consensus decision-making process at the local, national, and global scale. As a governing doctrine, this means that each member of indymedia has a right to equal participation in any decision affecting the organization. Accordingly, indymedia has no formally expressed hierarchy, there are no elections, and there is no president or executive director of the network. Everyone is considered a leader.

The three core dynamics of the Cyber Left—strategy, structure, and governance—form a discernable pattern of action, captured by the desire to build a new world order without hierarchy or entrenched forms of power. As a way to focus on this broader political praxis, I have used the concept of the Cyber Left's "logic of resistance." The Cyber Left logic of resistance is defined by a desire to build a movement, and ideally a world without hierarchy. Theorists have described this as a preference for flat or horizontal structures. This logic of horizontality is clearly present in the strategy, structure, and governance of the Cyber Left, as each of these aspects of contemporary movements is marked by an aspiration to create open, flat, nonhierarchical arrangements, a tendency we also see in Occupy Wall Street.

As we step back and look at the contemporary logic of resistance at this broad level, it becomes clear that while it emerged out of the history of the U.S. left, the Cyber Left is reacting to and arguably rejecting the tools, strategies, and social horizon of the Old Left that emerged in the first half of the twentieth century. In fact, the better part of the last seven decades have seen social movements in the United States arise in response to what they perceive to be the rigid orthodoxies, sectarian struggles, and incongruous hierarchies of the Old Left. This rejection of the Old Left, arguably the only left formation with political victories and defeats on the world stage, in many ways defined the development of the New Left, and I contend that the rejection of that period of struggle is still one of the defining elements of the Cyber Left today. In this sense, the logic of horizontalism is best understood as a challenge to the hierarchical structures of capitalism and the state, but also the perceived hierarchy of communist and socialist movements that flowered in the first part of the twentieth century.

The other defining influence on the Cyber Left is the social and material present, which in this case is keyed to the imperatives of informational capitalism. Thus, the overriding logic within the Cyber Left toward the irreducible nature of different struggles and individual identities, along with the desire for flat-networked forms, maps onto the imperatives of flexible postindustrial production with its individuated form of consumption and global-networked forms that trumpet liberty and choice, but which some theorists see as a fantasy of democracy in the era of neoliberalism (Dean 2009). By looking at the tactics and strategies of the Cyber Left through the lens of history and the materialist present, we can begin to see how the logic of horizontality was overdetermined by the relationship Cyber Left actors and organizations have to the history of resistance as well as the underlying imperatives of a neoliberal, informational form of capitalism. This logic, while important, has its problems and limits.

The Slow Fade of Indymedia: "When Things Return to Normal"

In October 2012, the IMC-London collective circulated a letter to the broader indymedia movement announcing that they had closed their doors—or, more appropriately, shut down the open-publishing wire. Members of IMC-London explained,

> The Indymedia London has taken the decision to close. . . . When Indymedia started it broke new ground, technically, socially, and politically. . . . This model of "open publishing" or "direct media" allowed everyone to add their voice to the collaborative creation of news, challenging the narrative of single narrative news journalism. . . . We are not going away defeated, we are moving on to more exciting projects that we feel are needed, and which we cannot do whilst maintaining a site that we no longer see as strategically or tactically essential. The vision remains the same, as do many of the challenges—we'll see you in the streets![8]

And with that message, the oldest Europe-based IMC, which had been operating for twelve years, went dark. A few months after London IMC closed, the global indymedia Web site, which is the centerpiece of the global communications network, crashed and stayed dark for months. At the time of this writing, the global indymedia site is back online, but the last published story was backdated more than six months, to December 2012. I highlight these two moments as they mark the effective, if not the actual, end of the indymedia experiment. I say this with the caveat that specific local IMCs are still important in their communities, such as the Greek IMCs, which were very active during the 2012–13 struggles against austerity. All the same, the Zapatista vision of a network of communication that connects across "all of our struggles," the vision that drove the development of a global network of communications, is effectively dead. So while local IMCs are still operating, the dream of a bigger project no longer exists, and with it one of the last remaining institutions of the Global Social Justice Movement has faltered.[9]

While every cycle of protest comes to an end, it is important to mark the breakthroughs and the problems with indymedia and the larger Cyber Left's logic of resistance organized around horizontality. The core logic and strategy of the Cyber Left played a significant role in the inability of the Global Social Justice Movement to build long-term power. I will point to four interrelated, core problems: (1) a retreat from class and capitalism as analytic and political categories, (2) a tendency toward technological determinism, (3) an anti-institutional bias, (4) no emphasis on political education and leadership development.

The first problem is that contemporary social-movement theorists and activists of the Cyber Left tend to downplay capitalism and class as central analytic categories. This tendency developed because of the perceived problems with the praxis of Marxism as it operated in actually existing communist nations and communist and socialist movements. This disenchantment with Marxism and socialism led to a few converging analytic trends among radical scholars, challenging what C. Wright Mills (1960) once called "the labor metaphysic," or the long-standing commitment to the working class.

This shift away from capitalism and class happened in the academy and in activist communities. Within the academy, the disenchantment came from a host of analytic trends. The first of these trends was the attempted sociological transcendence of capital and class in social-movement theory. Building on the seers of postindustrial society like Daniel Bell (1973), New Social Movement theorists, from Alain Touraine (1971) to Alberto Melucci (1996) and most recently Manuel Castells (1996), argued that with new technologies, the antagonism between capital and labor would no longer be the central concern in postindustrial or informational society. These scholars argued that as capitalism produced an abundance, class antagonism would recede, and people would struggle over identity and "ways of life," pushing class struggle and material concerns to the background. Alongside this sociological model, the second trend emerged in the political theory of Ernesto Laclau and Chantal Mouffe (1985), as discussed in chapter 6, who together developed the theory of radical democracy. The goal of their political theory was to detach politics and ideology from social and economic relations, refocusing on discourse, and consequently depriviledging the working class as a historical subject, in an effort to elevate all forms of antagonism. The final tendency comes from autonomist Marxists, who have focused on the changing nature of contemporary capitalism, arguing that the relations of production have escaped the factory floor, oppressing an ever-increasing swath of the population and therefore demanding a newly historicized concept of class and capitalism. While there are divergent theories of class among autonomist Marxists,[10] the most well-known theory of class is Michael Hardt and Antonio Negri's concept of the multitude. Hardt and Negri (2004) argue that under contemporary capitalism everyone is part of the social factory, and thus we need to broaden the definition of class. By opening up this theory of class, Hardt and Negri de-link class from production, arguing that the multitude is a plurality of classes, while not attempting to understand the interrelationship among this plurality, ultimately evacuating class of analytic power. While these three analytic trends are different—with Hardt and Negri historicizing capitalism and class, while New Social Movement theorists offer a sociological model that sees class antagonism as withering away, and Laclau and Mouffe argue that oppression is experienced and acted out through discourse, not material conditions—the culmination is what Ellen Meiksins Wood (1986) refers to as a "retreat from class."

The scholarly retreat from class has similarly led to a retreat from class and capitalism as analytic categories among activists, which has created practical problems in organizing. For instance, without recognizing the structuring power of capitalism and the consequent social exclusions, which lead to a varied class formation along material lines, scholars and activists are forced to offer ad hoc rationales for the development and coherence of the Global Social Justice Movement. The consequence is that scholars argue that the basis of this transnational social formation lies in unattenuated ideas of affinity and solidarity, blanket challenges to all power structures, or idealized notions of the plane of freedom. This analytic position for the development of a mass movement for true change is much thinner than a notion that there is a national or transnational working class (employed and unemployed), made up of women, racial minorities, and indigenous populations, among others, that holds a new and particular set of relations to the globalizing mode of production. Consequently, through a set of shared experiences as well as through class struggle, this local, national, regional, and transnational working class develops a common understanding of its sundry but singular class interests, and therefore begins to transform from a class in itself to a class for itself.

Along similar lines, because there is a lack of attention to the material social relations that develop out of capitalism, along with an underlying tendency toward openness and horizontality, the Global Social Justice Movement focuses on creating institutions and spaces that all can join, without privileging any particular community. The consequence is that these spaces (in the case of the social forum) or communications platforms and collectives (in the case of indymedia) tend to be dominated by upper-middle-class white communities, or what Marcuse referred to as "the discontented." This happens as Cyber Left organizations like indymedia do not prioritize reaching out to those most disenfranchised by capitalism, as collectively this is not a part of the analysis of the network as reflected in the Principles of Unity. The consequence is that individuals with higher levels of cultural capital and expendable time come to dominate the movement in practice and ideological doctrine. This reality is lamented by members of the indymedia movement. Every conference or convening of the network focuses on the topic of reaching out and developing more diversity; however, because of the lack of a collective analysis of capitalism's real material exclusions, which would lead to clear strategic directives, the network is unable to account for this problem. While this is captured saliently in indymedia, it was evident in many organizations and networks of the Global Social Justice Movement, and more recently this has become a common criticism of Occupy Wall Street.

Building on the retreat from class and capitalism, a second problem is the overreliance on technology and the belief that technological tools are the basis of the movement. This problem, as we have seen throughout this book, has led indymedia activists to prioritize technology over organizing and social relationships. While this outlook has enabled the movement to build an amazing technological infrastructure, and in many ways defined the cutting edge of participatory media from 1999 to 2004, it has not allowed for indymedia to build a long-term, organized, powerful institution nor connect with local struggles and local communities on a consistent basis. One of the founders of the first IMC in Seattle, Dan Merkle, emphasized this point. When looking back at the problems with the indymedia movement and, in particular, the problem with activists that depend heavily on the media and technology, he explained, "They're not doing the hard work building the relationships with potential allies to create their stable set of relationships. They're expecting the network to do it for them."[11] Merkle is making the point that new-media technology became more important than the relationships and organizing that was meant to undergird it, and this is one of the reasons indymedia has not continued to grow or become more integrated into communities.

A third problem exists at the organizational level and has developed because of the logic of horizontalism and the antibureaucratic bias of Cyber Left actors, which results in the elevation of organizational or process-based questions to the highest order. Cyber Left organizations do not ask, what do we want to achieve, and therefore what is the correct organizational form? Instead they begin with the organizational form, with the intent that through building the "correct" social structures and social relations, society will change—otherwise known as "prefigurative politics." The consequence is that most contemporary movement-based organizations have weak organizational structures with little collective power because centralized power of any sort is dismissed outright. In the case of indymedia, this weak network structure compels the movement to prioritize decentralization over democracy, not allowing for proactive decision making.

To look at this in greater detail, while indymedia is a network, for the network organizational form to cohere across space without a centralized institutional structure, it is necessary to have a strong, shared doctrine. This doctrine acts as a coagulant that holds the decentralized, deconstructed network together. In the case of indymedia, however, there is no shared doctrine or political philosophy. Consequently, the foundational principle of indymedia is to build a movement devoted to the creation of an independent, grassroots media infrastructure. In fact, members within indymedia range in their politics from libertarian and anarchist to progressive and Marxist, and the central fissures within and across the network come from strategic and tactical deviations that are based on these underlying ideological differences. Consequently, the shared doctrine of indymedia does not create the type of shared collectivity that a national, religious, or ideological identity would create.

These realities of the governance structure of indymedia form the basis of its ability to act as a shared organization. While indymedia has developed a participatory governance system that structures egalitarian social relations, it often does this at the expense of developing a collective power, which could proactively take action, creating a sustained effort. This is illustrated in the central mode of indymedia's political power, swarming. While this is an effective short-term strategy, swarming does not facilitate long-term movement building because by nature it is a temporary reaction to an external sociopolitical situation.

Finally, indymedia has not emphasized the political education and leadership development of its members. The lack of focus on leadership development grows out of the ideology of leaderless movements, but it has hampered indymedia as it has not allowed members and activists to learn skills and develop collective strategy. Moreover, without a focused leadership-development plan, the different nodes of indymedia favored individuals with more social and cultural capital, and thus the leadership of poor and working people, people of color, immigrants and women, were often minimized. While this pushed indymedia to emerge with a dominant ideological focus, emerging out of the social location of white middle-class activists, it was also one of the critical obstacles for creating a mass indymedia network that linked to the poor and working classes.

Each of the problems enumerated above is connected to the broader logic of horizontalism that is the driving ideological engine of the Cyber Left. Thus, while the majority of scholars and activists have celebrated the logic of horizontalism, recently some scholars and activists have challenged this logic. Paolo Gerbaudo (2012) convincingly argues that the recent movements from Occupy Wall Street to the Arab Spring were not actually as leaderless and flat as the ideology claims. He uses the concept of choreography to argue that there is a form of soft leadership that takes place in these new, networked structures. Extending this argument and following Jo Freeman's (1972–73) famous essay of the feminist movement, "The Tyranny of Structurelessness," a critical problem of soft leadership is that it is not visible nor accountable.

Jodi Dean (2009) offers a stronger argument against the logic of horizontalism, making the claim that it is actually an outgrowth of neoliberal capitalism and the consequent capture of new information and communication technologies. Thus the prioritization of horizontal forms plays into the hands of those with power. More recently, Slavoj Žižek asked a simple question of horizontal organizational forms and the correspondent logic of resistance: "I think the greatest, most dangerous dream of the left was precisely this idea of some type of immediate self-transparent direct democracy where finally people will get rid of all alienated forms and so on, and directly self organize themselves. Show me one, only one example where it worked for more than two, three months. . . . I want the left to author an alternative for the daily life when the enthusiasm is over. Give me one example where it worked . . . when things returned to normal."[12]

Žižek's harsh rejoinder to the short-term temporary nature of Occupy Wall Street and the Global Social Justice Movement does bring up critical questions: Is the logic of the left across the twentieth and twenty-first centuries teleological? Do we see progressive growth in the unfolding strategy of the American left, in its trajectory from the Old and New Left to the Cyber Left? While these are questions for each generation to answer anew, from my perspective as a scholar and activist, I believe the evidence weighs against the new logic of activism. While there are some important breakthroughs, particularly in the vision of the role of media and communications in building collective identity and the desire for democratic structures, in the medium term there is little in the strategies of contemporary resistance that makes it more humane, efficient, or likely to produce social change. In fact, if pushed, I would say that the balance of the evidence leads one to the opposite conclusion. The logic of resistance and therefore the strategies, practices, and organizations that have emerged in the last two to three decades might not have the facility to build power and create real-world change, at the scale of the Old Left, which was instrumental in building the labor movement, the Communist Party of the USA, and the infrastructure of the welfare state—all significant victories. Since the Old Left, however, there has been a consistent move away from building institutional power, developing leaders through political education, creating clear, consistent strategy, forging a united front, and embedding struggles in the mass of humanity that seeks (or has an interest in seeking) social change. And this is not an academic discussion, as these problems emerge not only in looking at indymedia or the other organizations of the Global Social Justice Movement, but also in the forms and strategies of Occupy Wall Street. While Occupy offered a new vision of struggle, forced a national discussion on class and economic inequality, and became the breeding ground of new activists and organizers, since the camps were raided and the working groups stopped functioning, the Occupy movement has disbanded. There are many reasons Occupy did not transform from a largely spontaneous uprising into a long-term mass movement, and some of the reasons parallel the problems of the Global Social Justice Movement—from a distrust of institution building to a lack of leadership development and political education, and an inability to create encampments where the mass of the working class felt welcomed. These are important questions, and scholars analyzing the OWS phenomenon must not merely celebrate this moment but look to understand the strengths and weaknesses of this emergent model of struggle.

The aim to describe and analyze contemporary social movements, and perhaps offer immanent critique, is vital to social movements. And while this task certainly is the job of activists and organizers, it is also the job of scholars, particularly social-movement scholars who are embedded in and believe in the mission and goal of the left to build a more humane world and ease the mass of human suffering while fighting for social, economic, and political equality. Unfortunately, while our role is to offer critique, the overriding tendency, perhaps because of our distance, is celebration, or what the anthropologist Lila Abu-Lughod (1990) once called the "romance of resistance." While this romance is understandable in the face of the desert of the real, it is not sufficient. Only through description and analysis that is rooted in the history of resistance and the political and socioeconomic present can we create scholarship that is symbiotic and rooted in the spirit of social justice.

Notes

Introduction

1. Scholarship on cycles of protest began with the groundbreaking work of Charles Tilly in *The Contentious French* (1986) and was extended in the work of Sidney Tarrow in *Power in Movement: Social Movements and Contentious Politics* (1998).

2. Scholars like Craig Calhoun (1993) have pointed to the problems of using periodization of social movements, but as I discuss later in this introduction, carefully applying periodization to social movements offers a great deal to understanding the prevailing patterns in a particular historical conjuncture.

3. For further discussion of this dialogue between the Old and New Left, see Maurice Isserman, *If I Had a Hammer: The Death of the Old Left and the Birth of the New Left* (1987) and John Patrick Diggins, *The Rise and Fall of the American Left* (1992).

4. Here I am influenced by the work of the philosopher of technology Andrew Feenberg and his work *Critical Theory of Technology* (1991).

5. For a thorough discussion of the role of the left in American history, see Diggins (1992).

6. For historical examinations of the Old Left, see Irving Howe (1957), Theodore Draper (1957), Maurice Isserman (1987), Michael Dennings (1998), Robin D. G. Kelley (1990), and John Patrick Diggins (1992). Diggins actually disaggregates the Old Left into two periods—the Lyrical Left, from the turn of the century through World War I, and the Old Left from World War I through the McCarthy period—but recognizes a set of shared concerns and strategies in the Lyrical and Old Left.

7. Members of the Old Left had not been exposed to Marx's earlier writing and primarily engaged with *Capital* and the economically focused writings of members of the Second International.

8. This stage is not meant to designate that this was the only way social protest was articulated, as of course the early twentieth century was marked by the suffragette

movement among others, but rather to argue that there was a historical tendency to social movements of the time that included the IWW, AFL, and the birth and growth of the Socialist Party (Diggins 1992).

9. Historians note that the civil rights movement in many ways acted as a bridge between these two stages, with roots in the Old Left while inspiring many of the leaders of the New Left. For more on the civil-rights origins in the Old Left, see Robin D. G. Kelley (1990) and Glenda Elizabeth Gilmore (2008); and for discussion of the link between the civil rights movement and the New Left, see Barbara Epstein (1991).

10. For a historical and sociological discussion of the New Left, see John Patrick Diggins (1992) Greg Calvert (1971), George Vickers (1975), Winni Breines (1989), Barbara Epstein (1991), and Max Elbaum (2002).

11. For more on the connection between the New Left and environmental movements, see Mark Dowie (1996) and Robert Gottlieb (2005).

12. For more on the connection between the New Left and the gay-rights movement, see Barry D. Adam, Jan Willem Duyvendak, and Andre Krouwel (1998).

13. For more on the connection between the New Left and later stages of the feminist movement, see Sara Evans (1980).

14. Some of the best analysis of the shifts in capitalism over the course of the last forty years comes from David Harvey (1991, 2005), Gary Teeple (2000), William I. Robinson (2004), and more recently Leo Panitch and Sam Gindin (2012).

15. While the concept of the "is" and the "ought" has a long history, in this case Diggins is referencing Herbert Marcuse's *One Dimensional Man*. Reading Hegel, Marcuse argues of dialectical thinking that the "is" contains an implicit reference to an "ought" it has failed to some degree to achieve. This "ought" is its potential, which is intrinsic to the "is" and not merely projected by human wishes or desires (1991, 133–34).

16. Here I use Cornelius Castoriadis's concept of the imaginary, which comes from *The Imaginary Institution of Society* (1998), in which the imaginary is understood as a horizon of possible meanings and actions within the political.

17. Romantic socialism was epitomized by Pierre-Joseph Proudhoun's *System of Economical Contradictions or The Philosophy of Poverty* (2011), which was first published in 1847. In the same year, Karl Marx responded with his work *The Poverty of Philosophy* (1992).

18. Jeffrey Juris (2008) has an interesting article based on the 2007 U.S. Social Forum that looks at the process of establishing intentional spaces that emphasize race and class over the default strategy within the social-forum process to create open, horizontal spaces.

Part I. Origins

1. A slightly altered version of this video can still be found online at the following address: https://www.youtube.com/watch?v=dxlwcfldxIw (accessed April 14, 2014).

2. See Nancy Davies (2007).

3. See http://www.indymedia.org/or/static/about.shtml.

4. The Global Social Justice Movement has been given a few names, including the Anti-Globalization Movement. That said, activists within this movement are not against globalization per se, as the movements themselves are global formations. Instead, they aim to challenge neoliberal globalization. Thus I will use "Global Social Justice Movement" to characterize the different threads of movements and organizations that have risen up to challenge neoliberal capitalism.

5. "Last Communique from NYC Indymedia Journalist Brad Will," October 27, 2006, accessed October 15, 2011, http://nyc.indymedia.org/en/2006/10/77760.html.

6. Brad died wearing an indymedia t-shirt, and some within the indymedia movement speculate that the bullet hole went right through the movement's iconic logo: (((i))). See NYC indymedia activist Joshua Breitbart's blog for this discussion, October 26, 2006; accessed March 18, 2014, http://breitbart.wordpress.com/2006/10/27/indymedia-journalist-murdered-by-government-paramilitaries-in-oaxaca-marcos-calls-on-alternative-media-to-demand-justice/.

7. Brad capturing his own death on camera in Oaxaca is an echo of Patricio Guzman's film *Battle of Chile* (1975), where the Argentinian cameraman Leonard Hendrickson is targeted and killed during the Chilean coup of 1973. Hendrickson, like Brad, captures his own shooting on camera.

8. Throughout this research I use pseudonyms to protect the identity of my subjects when possible; however, some informants have public profiles or opted to have their real names used, in which case I do not change their names.

9. This is exemplified by a picture of Brad that adorns the standard banner of the New York City IMC Web site and was on many sites throughout the network for a period after his death.

10. "Brad Will, Loisaida," November 13, 2006, accessed April 14, 2014, https://www.youtube.com/watch?v=ob-k5sPb5U4.

11. For examples, see Terrence Turner's (1992) and Faye Ginsburg's (1993) work on Kayapo and Aboriginal media, respectively.

12. Laura Stengrim (2005) focuses on this aspect of indymedia, arguing that corporate mergers and media consolidation are the cause for the development of the indymedia movement.

13. For example, see the work of Robert W. McChesney (1999) and Eric Klinenberg (2007).

14. This is not the first time that people have organized around the mass media, as historical studies by Robert W. McChesney (1993), and Victor Pickard (2014) detail.

15. See, for example, the work of Christina Dunbar-Hester, "Soldering Toward Media Democracy: Technical Practice as Symbolic Value in Radio Activism" (2012) and her forthcoming book, *Low Power to the People* (2014). The media reform movement is led by a diverse coalition of mostly Washington, D.C.–based groups that include policy organizations like the Media and Democracy Coalition, Prometheus Radio Project, Free Press, Consumers Union, Media Access Project, New America Foundation's Open Technology Initiative, and Public Knowledge.

16. See this video of Malkia Cyril explaining media justice: https://www.youtube.com/watch?v=WftYx1vKmbE (accessed April 10, 2014).

17. The skepticism of corporate media's coverage of the WTO protests was corroborated by the left-leaning media watchdog Fairness and Accuracy in Reporting (FAIR), which released the report "Prattle in Seattle: WTO Coverage Misrepresented Issues, Protests" (1999).

18. Interview with Jeff Perlstein by Miguel Bocanegra, University of Washington Center for Labor Studies, October 15, 2000, accessed March 22, 2014, http://www.indybay.org/uploads/2007/05/06/perlstein.pdf.

19. Many of the activists involved in the first IMC in Seattle testify that mainstream journalists scouted out these bright green press passes because they knew that if they found a cluster of people with these passes, they were sure to find the story.

20. For instance, John Downing (2003) focused on indymedia's adoption of the social-anarchist traditions of direct action and prefigurative politics; Graham Meikle (2002) argued that punk culture was central to indymedia's development; Douglas Morris (2005) situated indymedia's roots in the Free Open Source Software movements; and Anna Nogueria (2001) focused on the ideological connections between indymedia and the Zapatistas.

21. See Scott Uzelman (2001); DeeDee Halleck (2002); Christopher A. Shumway (2003); Graham Meikle (2002); Lisa Brooten (2004); Jeffrey Juris (2005); Victor Pickard (2006a); and Todd Wolfson (2013).

22. Dmitra Milioni (2009); Richard Templin (2009).

23. Andy Opel and Rich Templin (2005); Laura Stengrim (2005).

24. See Dorothy Kidd (2003b).

25. See Kate Milberry (2003).

26. See Nick Dyer-Witheford (1999); Michael Hardt and Antonio Negri (2004); Mario Diani and Doug McAdam (2003); Richard J. F. Day (2005); Boaventura de Sousas Santos (2006); Jeffrey Juris (2008); Alex Khashnabish (2008); Peter Funke (2012); Arturo Escobar (2009); Paolo Gerbuado (2012); Manuel Castells (2012); Joss Hands (2011); and Paul Mason (2012).

27. This is exemplified by Jeffrey Juris's (2008) ethnographic study of activists in Barcelona connected to People's Global Action, in which he argues that the "the rise of new digital technologies has profoundly altered the social movement landscape" (9). Likewise, Arturo Escobar (2009) examines Afro-Colombian movements, and building on Manuel de Landa (2006), argues that nonhierarchical, nonbinary networks, or what he calls "flat alternatives," rewrite not only social movements but social theory more generally. Finally, Peter Funke's (2012) critical work on the World Social Forum and associated social-forum processes focuses on the emergence of what he calls the "Rhizomatic Left," which emphasizes transnationality, diversity, multiconnectivity, and communication.

28. The sociologist John Holloway encapsulates the celebratory mood with the recent title of his book, *Change the World without Taking Power* (2005).

Chapter 1. The EZLN and Indymedia

1. The Zapatistas take their name from the early twentieth-century Mexican revolutionary Emiliano Zapata.

2. For a discussion of the EZLN's use of this strategy, see John Ross (1995) and David Ronfeldt and John Arquilla.(1998). For a full discussion of this military strategy, see Robert Taber (2002).

3. See David Ronfeldt and John Arquilla (1998) on this stage in the struggle.

4. For research on the contradictions of Chiapas, see George Collier (1999) and Ana Esther Cecena and Andres Barreda (1998).

5. The Lacandon jungle is less then 1 percent of the land area of the country and constitutes 20 percent of the country's biological diversity (Cecena and Bereda 1998).

6. On the ejidos, see John Gledhill (1997).

7. By most reports, the FLN developed as a response to the Mexican government's massacre of students in Tlatelolco in 1968 (Ronfeldtand Arquilla 1998, 31).

8. The FMLN was an umbrella group for left-wing guerilla organizations in El Salvador during the civil war in the 1980s. The FMLN became a legal political party after a ceasefire in 1992, and in 2009, Mauricio Fuenes of the FMLN was elected president of El Salvador.

9. Please see a review of *Zapatista Chronicles,* http://www.hopedance.org/book-reviews ?start=235 (accessed April 19, 2014).

10. See Maria Elena Martinez-Torres (2001), which details the development of the Peacenet and Usenet Internet-based communications webs.

11. See Alex Khasnabish's account of the role of the EZLN in influencing North American social movements (2008).

12. Greg Ruggiero, interview by the author, New York City, 2005.

13. Ibid.

14. Interview with Jeff Perlstein by Miguel Bocanegra, University of Washington Center for Labor Studies, October 15, 2000, accessed March 22, 2014, http://www .indybay.org/uploads/2007/05/06/perlstein.pdf.

15. This is a partial history of the founding of indymedia, specifically focused on the intersection with the EZLN and the Freeing the Media Teach-In. This is not meant to be an exhaustive history, and it does not touch on many of the important activists who helped found the organization.

16. On the role of the EZLN in building across national boundaries, see Kara Zugman (2008) and Alex Khasnabish (2008).

17. The aim is not to argue that the EZLN is the only influence on the birth and growth of indymedia. For instance, the social-anarchist tradition (Downing 2003), the Free Open Source Software movement (Morris 2003), HIV/AIDS activism, and other movements have played key roles in the development of indymedia.

18. The original name for these communities was "Aguascalientes" (autonomous municipalities), but the name was changed in 2003 to coincide with a larger change in the way the Zapatistas worked with the broader solidarity movement.

19. Peacenet was an early online network that focused on conflict. A part of the early Internet at the time the Web was more fragmented, it was a series of nets run by the Institute for Global Communications to provide low-cost entry points to the Internet.

20. See Ronfeldt and Arquilla (1996 and 1998).

21. See Isaac Deutscher (1963) and Tony Cliff (1976).

22. As I discuss in chapter 5, prefigurative politics means that you prefigure in your movements the type of world and change you aim to make. In this sense, to the extent that movements in the 1960s were focused on democracy and cooperation, the structures of the movements aimed to incorporate these values.

23. See Francesca Poletta (2001).

24. For a review of command-obeying and walking while asking as democratic principles of the EZLN, see Patricia King and Francisco Javier Villanueva (1998) and Luis Lorenzano (1998).

Chapter 2. Activist Laboratories

1. Znet, "Z Media Institute," accessed May 6, 2014, http://zcomm.org/z-media -institute/.

2. The backbone of the Internet, Web servers act as digital libraries, storing information (sometimes in the form of Web sites) and making that information accessible online.

3. Chris Burnett, telephone interview by the author, November 9, 2008.

4. The BURN! Web site can be accessed via the Way Back Machine, http://web.archive .org/web/*/burn.ucsd.edu (accessed April 19, 2014).

5. Please see "The BURN! Project and Primary Source Media" on the BURN! Web site, accessed April 19, 2014, http://web.archive.org/web/20030216230910/http://burn .ucsd.edu/about.html.

6. Michael Dartnell, "Insurgency Online," November 7, 1999, accessed September 11, 2012, http://web2.uwindsor.ca/courses/ps/dartnell/mrta.html.

7. Elizabeth Frantz, "The Real Revolution: Net Guerrillas," *Time-Warner Pathfinder,* July 21, 1997, accessed May 6, 2014, http://www.hartford-hwp.com/archives/29/019.html.

8. BURN! did host 915E Community space in San Diego, but the general pattern was to prioritize global and transnational struggle.

9. Burnett interview.

10. Michael Albert, interview by the author, phone and email, November 23, 2005.

11. Ibid.

12. Znet, "Z Media Institute," accessed May 6, 2014, http://zcomm.org/z-media -institute/.

13. Jay Sand, interview by the author, Philadelphia, March 4, 2005.

14. Jeff Perlstein, interview by the author, November 2011.

15. Sand interview.

16. Albert interview.

17. Sand interview.

18. Albert interview.

19. "Alternative Coverage of the '96 Democratic National Convention," Counter-Media, 1996, accessed April 20, 2014, http://www.cpsr.cs.uchicago.edu/countermedia/.

20. Greg Willerer, "Countermedia," July 22, 1996, accessed March 22, 2014, http://archives.econ.utah.edu/archives/aut-op-sy/1996-07-22.163/msg00043.html.

21. "Alternative Coverage of the '96 Democratic Convention."

22. Perlstein interview.

23. Please see "Off the Record" on Deep Dish TV: Fearless Grassroots Video, accessed April 19, 2014: http://www.deepdishtv.org/programs/3458.

24. Sand interview.

25. Ibid.

Chapter 3. The Battle of Seattle and the Birth of Indymedia

1. Jonathan Lawson, "Indymedia Turns 10," *Reclaim the Media*, 2009, accessed April 19, 2014, http://www.reclaimthemedia.org/grassroots_media/indymedia_turns_102348.

2. Direct Action Network, "Action Packet," p. 2, *The WTO History Project*, 1999, accessed March 22, 2014, http://content.lib.washington.edu/cdm4/document.php?CISOROOT=/wto&CISOPTR=498&REC=1.

3. Ibid., p. 3.

4. King County Labor Council, "Labor's Voice: Labor News for King County's Working Families," *The WTO History Project*, 1999; accessed March 22, 2014, http://content.lib.washington.edu/cdm4/item_viewer.php?CISOROOT=/wto&CISOPTR=222&CISOBOX=1&REC=2.

5. Interview with Jeff Perlstein by Miguel Bocanegra, University of Washington Center for Labor Studies, October 15, 2000, accessed March 22, 2014, http://www.indybay.org/uploads/2007/05/06/perlstein.pdf.

6. Ibid.

7. Ibid.

8. Ibid.

9. The micro-radio movement is a low-power radio movement where people set up unlicensed "pirate" radio stations that broadcast community news and music in areas where there are little or no community voices on the public airwaves.

10. The term "zine" comes from the word "fanzine" and is most commonly associated with noncommercial, self-published material or the appropriation of material for a publication.

11. See DeeDee Halleck (2002).

12. See Biella Coleman (2005).

13. Jeff Perlstein, interview by Todd Wolfson by phone, November 2011.

14. See DeeDee Halleck (2000), Dorothy Kidd (2003b), and Jeff Perlstein (2001).

15. Dan Merkle, telephone interview by the author, October 22, 2005.

16. Sheri Herndon, panel presentation to "Our Media," Barranquilla, Colombia, May 2003.

17. Michael Eisenmenger, interview by the author, New York City, November 21, 2005.

18. See Christopher A. Shumway (2001).

19. Matthew Arnison, telephone interview by the author, September 8, 2005.

20. J18 Web site, accessed July 12, 2011, http://bak.spc.org/j18/site/bulletin2.html.

21. Arnison interview.

22. Active was based on the programming work of the CAT collective in Australia, previously written for the global Reclaim the Streets festivals and protests in the summer of 1999.

23. Arnison interview.

24. According to a Web counter, alexa.com, CNN.com is one of the highest-rated news Web sites in the world. Accessed April 19, 2014, http://www.alexa.com/siteinfo/www.cnn.com.

25. Eisenmenger interview.

26. Eric Galatas, special report to the director of Free Speech TV, 2000.

27. Interview with Jeff Perlstein.

28. Ibid.

29. "Showdown in Seattle: Five Days that Shook the WTO," accessed May 7, 2014, https://www.youtube.com/watch?v=EEfk1ZtrtGc.

30. Ibid.

31. Jay Sand, interview by the author, Philadelphia, March 4, 2005.

32. Arnison interview.

33. Ibid.

34. See C.W. Anderson (2003) on the role of IMC in the birth of blogs and the citizen-journalism movement.

35. Perlstein interview.

36. Perlstein interview.

37. Merkle interview.

Part II. The Logic of Resistance

1. See their correspondence in Theodor Adorno and Walter Benjamin (1999), and a discussion of this debate by Susan Buck-Morris (1977).

2. Forty years later, Raymond Williams (1974) made a similar argument against Marshall McLuhan regarding the revolutionary role he was according technology in his "medium is the message" thesis.

3. See Thomas Andrae (1979).

4. Of course, the Luddites themselves were fully aware of the dialectical relationship between technology and society and were not opposed to technology per se, but rather the domination of humanity, or more accurately the working class, through

technology. In his history of the Luddites, Kirpatrick Sale (1996) captures this outlook: "it was not all machinery that the Luddites opposed, but 'all machinery hurtful to commonality'" (261).

5. For examples, see David Harvey (1991), Saskia Sassen (2001), and Arjun Appadurai (1996).

6. See Karl Marx (1978) and Antonio Negri (1989).

7. For example, see Giorgio Agamben (2001).

8. See Max Horkheimer and Theodor Adorno (1972), Edward S. Herman and Noam Chomsky (1988), Nicholas Garnham (1990), and Herbert Schiller (1976).

9. See Katie Hafner and Mathew Lyon (1996), Manuel Castells (1996a), and Paul Virilio (2006).

10. Here I use Castoriadis's concept of the imaginary, which comes from *The Imaginary Institution of Society* (1998) in which the imaginary is understood as a horizon of possible meanings and actions within the political.

Chapter 4. Structure: Networks and Nervous Systems

1. See Funke (2010); S. Walgrave and J. Verhulst (2006); and "The Day the World Said No to War," *Socialist Worker Online*, February 22, 2003, accessed March 23, 2014, http://socialistworker.co.uk/art/3244/The+day+the+world+said+no+to+war+on+Iraq.

2. "To All Citizens of Europe: Together We Can Stop This War!" Globalise Resistance Web site, November 14, 2001, accessed March 23, 2014, http://www.resist.org.uk/global/social-forums/esf-florence-2002/to-all-citizens-of-europe-together-we-can-stop-this-war/.

3. "Call for F15 Features Contributions," Indymedia archives, February 14, 2003, accessed March 24, 2014, http://archives.lists.indymedia.org/imc-portugal/2003-February/000441.html.

4. For Indymedia Global Reporting on F15, see Feature Archive (all accessed March 24, 2014), http://www.indymedia.org/en/feature/archive35.shtml; "Melbourne Kicks off F15," February 15, 2003, http://www.indymedia.org/en/2003/02/107341.shtml; "Millions March Worldwide to Denounce Bush's War Plan," February 15, 2003, http://www.indymedia.org/en/2003/02/107355.shtml; "F15 Demonstrations in Eastern Europe," February 16, 2003, http://www.indymedia.org/en/2003/02/107372.shtml; "F15 Demonstrations in Oceana," February 16, 2003, http://www.indymedia.org/en/2003/02/107377.shtml; "F15 Demonstrations in Western Europe—Part One," February 16, 2003, http://www.indymedia.org/en/2003/02/107379.shtml; "F15 Demonstrations in Western Europe—Part Two," February 18, 2003, http://www.indymedia.org/en/2003/02/107397.shtml; "F15 Demonstrations in North America," February 18, 2003, http://www.indymedia.org/en/2003/02/107403.shtml; F15 Demonstrations in South America," February 18, 2003, http://www.indymedia.org/en/2003/02/107406.shtml; F15 Demonstrations in Tel Aviv and Beirut," February 19, 2003, http://www.indymedia.org/en/2003/02/107408.shtml; "F15: The World Said No," February 20, 2003, http://www.indymedia.org/en/2003/02/107433.shtml.

5. See Kevin Danaher and Jason Mark (2003).

6. For a good review of the work on the politics of scale, see Neil Brenner (2001).

7. In chart 1, you begin to see how the indymedia network exemplifies a fractal structure made up of self-dividing collectives at each level.

8. Indymedia Documentation Project, "IMC US Mission," October 29, 2004, accessed March 24, 2014, https://docs.indymedia.org/view/Local/ImcUsMission.

9. This national network no longer exists in Great Britain, but it did exist for multiple years and offered a window onto a how a strongly centralized national IMC network works.

10. UK Indymedia, "From Indymedia UK to the United Kollektives," December 16, 2004, accessed March 24, 2014, http://www.indymedia.org.uk/en/2004/12/302894 .html (emphasis added).

11. IMC-Process Listserv, April 23, 2005, accessed March 26, 2014, http://lists.indy media.org/pipermail/imc-process/2005-April/0425-h7.html.

12. Indymedia Documentation Project, "Welcome to the Wiki for the ATX Indyme- dia Conference," January 21, 2006, accessed March 26, 2014, http://docs.indymedia .org/view/Local/IndyConference.

13. Indymedia Documentation Project, "IRC: How to Use Indymedia Chat," De- cember 9, 2007, accessed March 26, 2014, http://docs.indymedia.org/view/Sysadmin/ IrcHowTo.

14. Christopher Palgrave, interview by the author, Philadelphia, July 10, 2004.

15. IMC-Communication Listserv, "Important: Invitation to IMC Communica- tion IRC Meeting J13," January 12, 2001, accessed March 26, 2014, http://archives.lists .indymedia.org/imc-communication/2001-January/000312.html.

16. IMC-Communication, "Proposal: New Principle of Unity for IMC—What Do We Mean by Principle?" October 25, 2005, accessed April 19, 2014, http://lists.indy media.org/pipermail/imc-communication/2005-October/1025-3c.html.

17. IMC-Editorial, "Toward an IMC Encuentro," October 8, 2000, accessed April 19, 2014, http://archives.lists.indymedia.org/imc-editorial/2000-October/000651 .html.

18. Chris Burnett, telephone interview by the author, November 9, 2008.

19. Chris Burnett, "Proposed Charter of the Confederated Network of Indepen- dent Media Centers," Draft Version 0.1, 2001.

20. The Independent Media Center Network (IMCN) is based upon principles of equality, decentralization, and local autonomy. The IMCN is not derived from a centralized bureaucratic process, but from the self-organization of autonomous collectives that recognize the importance in developing a union of networks.

All IMCs consider open exchange of and open access to information a prereq- uisite to the building of a more free and just society.

All IMCs respect the right of activists who choose not to be photographed or filmed.

All IMCs, based upon the trust of their contributors and readers, shall use open web-based publishing, allowing individuals, groups, and organizations to express their views, anonymously if desired.

The IMC Network and all local IMC collectives shall be not-for-profit.

All IMCs recognize the importance of process to social change and are committed to the development of non-hierarchical and anti-authoritarian relationships, from interpersonal relationships to group dynamics. Therefore, shall organize themselves collectively and be committed to the principle of consensus decision making and the development of a direct, participatory democratic process that is transparent to its membership.

All IMCs recognize that a prerequisite for participation in the decision-making process of each local group is the contribution of an individual's labor to the group.

All IMCs are committed to caring for one another and our respective communities both collectively and as individuals and will promote the sharing of resources including knowledge, skills, and equipment.

All IMCs shall be committed to the use of free source code, whenever possible, in order to develop the digital infrastructure, and to increase the independence of the network by not relying on proprietary software.

All IMCs shall be committed to the principle of human equality, and shall not discriminate, including discrimination based upon race, gender, age, class, or sexual orientation. Recognizing the vast cultural traditions within the network, we are committed to building [diversity] within our localities. Indymedia Documentation Project, Principles of Unity, accessed April 19, 2014, http://docs.indymedia.org/view/Global/PrinciplesOfUnity.

Chapter 5. Governance: Democracy All the Way Down

1. Recent research (Lih 2008; Harding 2009) has challenged the assertion that Lenin was calling for a party to emerge outside the working class. Instead, scholars like Lars Lih argue that Lenin's entire political career was devoted to creating the conditions for Russians to have political and basic liberal freedoms.

2. While this aspect of democracy will not be taken up in this study, it is interesting to note that Bolshevik democracy was keyed to the Fordist industrial apparatus, whereas the contemporary decentralized democratic praxis is keyed to the post-Fordist economic system.

3. See discussion of Cornelius Castoriadis and Claude Lefort challenging Marxism in Dick Howard's *The Specter of Democracy* (2002).

4. See the book Daniel Cohn-Bendit coauthored with his brother, Gabriel Cohn-Bendit, *Obsolete Communism: The Left-Wing Alternative* (2001), or Dick Howard's *The Specter of Democracy* (2002).

5. IMC activists refer to themselves as "IMCistas," using the same suffix as Zapatistas in deference to that movement.

6. Jeff Perlstein, telephone interview by the author, December 12, 2005.

7. Indymedia Documentation Project, Principles of Unity, accessed April 19, 2014, http://docs.indymedia.org/view/Global/PrinciplesOfUnity.

8. Indymedia Documentation Project, "A Quick Guide to 'Decision Making by Consensus,'"October 21, 2002, accessed March 26, 2014, http://docs.indymedia.org/view/Global/DecisionMakingGuide.

9. IMC-Finance listserv, September 15, 2002.

10. IMC-Process listserv, September 13, 2002.

11. Ibid.

12. IMC-Process listserv, September 15, 2002 (italics added).

13. David Caruso, telephone interview by the author, November 13, 2005.

14. IMC-Process listserv, September 15, 2002.

15. Ibid.

16. IMC-Finance listserv, September 25, 2002.

17. Indymedia Documentation Project, "Who Is Behind 'www.indymedia.be,'" accessed March 26, 2014, http://docs.indymedia.org/view/Local/BelgiumSituationEn.

18. The IMC-Communication listserv took over from the IMC-Process listserv as the main space for internal communication across the network. The Process listserv was then reserved for urgent decision-making processes and not for communication traffic.

19. IMC-Communication listserv, April 30, 2005.

20. Indymedia Documentation Project, Principles of Unity, accessed March 26, 2014, https://docs.indymedia.org/view/Global/PrinciplesOfUnity.

21. IMC-Communication listserv, April 21, 2005.

22. IMC-Communication listserv, March 16, 2005 (italics added).

23. Jay Sand, interview by the author, Philadelphia, March 4, 2005.

24. IMC-Process, "Indymedia.be Disaffiliation," April 7, 2005, accessed March 26, 2014, http://lists.indymedia.org/pipermail/imc-process/2005-April/0407-05.html.

25. Indymedia Documentation Project, "Who Is Behind www.indymedia.be."

26. IMC-Process listserv, April 27, 2005.

27. IMC-Process listserv, May 6, 2005.

Chapter 6. Strategy: Communications and the Switchboard of Struggle

1. See Ronfeldt and Arquilla (1996) and Hardt and Negri (2004).

2. Some of the strongest critiques of Laclau and Mouffe's *Hegemony and a Socialist Strategy* come from Ellen Meiksins-Wood (1986), Stanley Aronowitz (1986–87), and Norman Geras (1988).

3. See Samina Raja, Changxing Ma, and Pavan Yadav (2008); Anne Short, Julie Guthman, and Samuel Raskin (2007); and Neil Wrigley, Daniel Warm, Barrie Margetts, and Amanda Whelan (2002). Also see Tracie McMillan (2008).

4. This amount is well below the land valuation, which the L.A. City Council estimated at minimum was $6.6 million.

5. "RED ALERT!! Encampment and Tree Sit to Resist the Eviction and Save the South Central Farm," May 25, 2006, accessed March 27, 2014, http://la.indymedia.org/news/2006/05/159857_comment.php#159945.

6. "Emergency Alert: Police Evicting South Central Farmers—Take Action," June 14, 2006, accessed March 27, 2014, http://la.indymedia.org/news/2006/06/163977.php.

7. See, for example, http://www.indybay.org/newsitems/2006/05/24/18251311.phpl; http://pittsburgh.indymedia.org/news/2007/06/27623.php; http://nyc.indymedia.org/en/2006/06/71535.shtml; http://boston.indymedia.org/feature/display/77831/index.php; http://publish.portland.indymedia.org/en/2006/07/342161.shtml; and http://www.phillyimc.org/en/node/49710.

8. "South Central Farmers Forcibly Evicted," June 13, 2006, accessed March 27, 2014, http://indymedia.us/en/2006/06/17234.shtml.

9. "Los Angeles Police Forcibly Evict and Bulldoze the South Central Farm," June 15, 2006, accessed March 27, 2014, http://www.indymedia.org/en/2006/06/840859.shtml.

10. Leslie Radford, interview by the author, email, September 23, 2012.

11. See Leslie Radford and Juan Santos (2006).

12. While Pesante-USA did write a letter in support of the South Central Farmers, the Web site where the letter of support was archived is no longer maintained, and consequently the letter is gone.

13. To see the message from the EZLN, see El Kilombo Intergalactico, "Communiqué from the EZLN Intergalactic Commission," accessed April 19, 2014, http://www.elkilombointergalactico.blogspot.com/2006_07_01_archive.html.

14. "Activists, Celebs Stage Encampment for South Central Farm," *Democracy Now!* June 5, 2006, accessed March 27, 2014, http://www.democracynow.org/2006/6/5/activists_celebs_stage_encampment_for_south.

15. Many reports held that the warehouse Horowitz planned to build on the land would be used by Wal-Mart. For example, see this L.A. Indymedia report: John McIntosh, "Save the South Central Farm—Photo Essay," May 13, 2006, accessed March 27, 2014, http://la.indymedia.org/news/2006/05/157152_comment.php.

16. For Keck and Sikkink (1998), the boomerang effect works when a local group has trouble effectively pressuring their government. Instead, they push the issue to the national or global level through "transnational advocacy networks," which are knitted together through the Internet and other communication technologies. The advocacy networks then put pressure on the government in question through different means.

17. "Hands On!!! Creating an Independent Media Center in Your Community," accessed March 27, 2014, http://www.hybridvideotracks.org/2001/archiv/IMC.pdf.

18. "Massive Immigrant General Strike in U.S., Northern California," April 20, 2006, accessed March 27, 2014, http://www.indybay.org/newsitems/2006/04/20/45172.php.

19. Interview with Jeff Perlstein by Miguel Bocenegra, University of Washington Center for Labor Studies, October 15, 2000, accessed March 22, 2014, http://www .indybay.org/uploads/2007/05/06/perlstein.pdf.

20. Christopher Palgrave, interview by the author, Philadelphia, July 10, 2004.

21. Indymedia Documentation Project, "Strategic Content Production and 'Coverage Teams' or 'Beats,'" accessed April 19, 2014, http://docs.indymedia.org/view/Local/PhillyIMCwebedteams.

22. Fieldnotes, LAVA Center, Philadelphia, March 17, 2005.

23. Indymedia Documentation Project, Philly IMC Outreach, September 12, 2005, accessed April 19, 2014, https://docs.indymedia.org/Local/PhillyIMCOutreach. (The author was one of the indymedia activists involved with creating the Philly IMC outreach memo.)

24. Sheethl Fischer, interview by the author, Philadelphia, March 5, 2005.

25. See Indymedia Scotland Editorial Guidelines, accessed April 19, 2014, http://www.indymedia.org.uk/en/regions/scotland/static/editorial.html.

26. Matthew Arnison, telephone interview by the author, August 12, 2005.

27. See, for example, the Columbia journalism graduate student Anderson's discussion of the role of indymedia on social-networking platforms: "'Actually Existing' Citizen Journalism Projects and Typologies: Part 1," July 31, 2006, accessed March 27, 2014, http://indypendent.typepad.com/academese/2006/07/actually_existi.html.

28. Particularly see C. W. Anderson's work (2003) on the role of IMC in the birth of blogs and the citizen-journalism movement.

29. Jay Sand, interview by the author, Philadelphia, March 4, 2005.

30. ACT-UP (the AIDS Coalition to Unleash Power) is a coalition of diverse groups committed to direct action to end the AIDS crisis.

31. See http://www.defenestrator.org/info.

32. Lancaster Avenue Autonomous Space, accessed March 27, 2014, http://www .lavazone.org/.

33. Strategy paper on Philly IMC and Jobs with Justice Wal-Mart campaign, October 8, 2005.

34. Sheethl Fischer, interview by the author, Philadelphia, March 3, 2005.

35. Tanya Jameson, interview by the author, Philadelphia, November 19, 2006.

36. Fischer interview.

37. "About Portland Indymedia," accessed March 27, 2014, http://portland.indymedia .org/en/static/about.shtml.

38. A typical example is found on the indymedia U.S. site: "Weekend Demonstrations Draw Thousands as Bush's Approval Ratings Hit All-Time Low," March 20, 2006, accessed March 27, 2014, http://indymedia.us/en/2006/03/15115.shtml.

39. A typical example is found on the global indymedia site: "Mass Protests Meet WTO in Hong Kong," December 12, 2005, accessed March 27, 2014, http://www .indymedia.org/en/2005/12/829714.shtml.

40. Annie and Sam, "Alternative Media Handbook," accessed March 27, 2014, https://docs.indymedia.org/view/Local/ImcUkWritingAltMedHandbookDraft.

Conclusion

1. As Todd Gitlin (2012) and Manuel Castells (2012) both observe, *Adbusters* was not the only progenitor of Occupy Wall Street. There was another group, A99, that was calling for an occupation of Wall Street as part of Operation Empire State Rebellion.

2. Adbusters #OccupyWallStreet, July 13, 2011, accessed March 27, 2014, https://www.adbusters.org/blogs/adbusters-blog/occupywallstreet.html.

3. Chris Garces has an interesting discussion of the political meaning of the human mic in *Cultural Anthropology*'s special online Hot Spot, Occupy Anthropology (2012), accessed April 19, 2014, http://www.culanth.org/fieldsights/65-people-s-mic-and-leaderful-charisma.

4. Adbusters #OccupyWallStreet (emphasis added).

5. For discussions of the nonhierarchical nature of the Global Social Justice Movement, see David Graeber (2009) and Jeffrey Juris (2008).

6. Thanks to the Poverty Initiative at Union Theological Seminary, who use this quote, and King's legacy, to argue that it is time to build a new Poor People's Campaign. For more on the continuing relevance of this quote and vision, see Willie Baptist (2010).

7. A similar argument was made by Craig Calhoun (1991) in his analysis of the New Left.

8. London Indymedia, "Time to Move On: IMC London Signing Off," October 13, 2012, accessed March 28, 2014, http://london.indymedia.org/articles/13128.

9. I say this with the recognition that some specific IMCs still exist and are doing good work, such as Urbana-Champaign IMC; however, the broader vision of an indymedia network is gone.

10. For instance, Nick Dyer-Witheford (1999) discusses the idea of the "socialized worker."

11. Dan Merkle, telephone interview by the author, October 22, 2005.

12. Alex Tspiras and Slavoj Žižek, "The Role of the European Left," May 15, 2013, accessed April 19, 2014, https://www.youtube.com/watch?v=aUh96oXYt18.

Bibliography

Abu-Luhgod, Lila (2004). *Dramas of Nationhood: The Politics of Television in Egypt.* Chicago, University of Chicago Press.

———(1990). "Romance of Resistance: Tracing Transformations of Power through Bedouin Women." *American Ethnologist* 17.1: 41–55.

Adam, Barry D., Jan Willem Duyvendak, and Andre Krouwel (1998). *The Global Emergence of Gay and Lesbian Politics: National Imprints of a Worldwide Movement.* Philadelphia: Temple University Press.

Adorno, Theodor (1991). *The Culture Industry: Selected Essays on Mass Culture.* London: Routledge.

Adorno, Theodor, Walter Benjamin, Ernst Bloch, Bertolt Brecht, and Georg Lukacs (1999). *Aesthetics and Politics: The Key Texts of the Classical Debate within German Marxism.* Ed. Fredric Jameson. London: Verso.

Agamben, Giorgio (2001). "On Security and Terror." Frankfurter Allgemeine Zeitung. September 20, 2001, accessed April, 19, 2014, http://www.egs.edu/faculty/giorgio-agamben/articles/on-security-and-terror/.

Albert, Michael (2006). "Their Mass Media and Ours." *Z Magazine.* Accessed April 19, 2014. http://web.archive.org/web/20070624214214/http://zena.secureforum.com/Znet/zmag/articles/oldalbert6.htm.

Althusser, Louis (2001). *Lenin and Philosophy and Other Essays.* New York: Monthly Review Press.

Anderson, Benedict (1983). *Imagined Communities: Reflections on the Origin and Spread of Nationalism.* London: Verso.

Anderson, C. W. (2003). "The Role of Indymedia in the Blogosphere: Thoughts on Indymedia in the Age of Blogging." Cleveland Indy Media Center. September 12. Accessed April 19, 2014. http://cleveland.indymedia.org/news/2003/09/6350.php.

Andrae, Thomas (1979). "Adorno on Film and Mass Culture: the Culture Industry Reconsidered." *Jump Cut: A Review of Contemporary Media*, 20: 34–37

Ang, Ien (1985). *Watching Dallas: Soap Opera and the Melodramatic Imagination.* London: Methuen.

Appadurai, Arjun (2002). "Deep Democracy: Urban Governmentality and the Horizon of Politics." *Public Culture* 14.1: 21–47.

——(1996). *Modernity at Large: Cultural Dimensions of Globalization.* Minneapolis: University of Minnesota Press.

Aronowitz, Stanley. *How Class Works: Power and Social Movement.* New Haven, Conn.: Yale University Press.

Arrighi, Giovanni, Terrence Hopkins, and Immanuel Wallerstein (1989). *Antisystemic Social Movements.* New York: Verso.

——. (1986–87). "Theory and Socialist Strategy." *Social Text* 16: 1–16.

Atkinson, Joshua (2010). *Alternative Media and the Politics of Resistance: A Communication Perspective.* New York: Routledge.

Bagidkian, Ben (2000). *The Media Monopoly.* Boston: Beacon Press.

Baptist, Willie (2009). "Willie Baptist: It's Not Enough to be Angry." Organizing Upgrade. November 10. Accessed April 28, 2014. http://www.mediamobilizing. org/updates/willie-baptist-its-not-enough-be-angry.

——(2010). "A New and Unsettling Force: The Strategic Relevance of Rev. Dr. Martin Luther King's Poor People's Campaign." *Interface* 2.1 (May): 262–70.

Bell, Daniel (1973). *The Coming of Post-Industrial Society: A Venture in Social Forecasting.* New York: Basic Books.

——(1967). *Marxian Socialism in the United States.* Princeton, N.J.: Princeton University Press.

Benjamin, Walter (1969). "The Work of Art in the Age of Mechanical Reproduction." In *Illuminations: Essays and Reflections.* New York: Schocken Books. 217–52.

Bennett, W. Lance, Christian Breunig, and Terri Givens (2008). "Communication and Political Mobilization: Digital Media and the Organization of the Anti-Iraq War Demonstrations in the U.S." *Political Communication* 25: 269–89.

Bourdieu, Pierre (1977). *Outline of a Theory of Practice.* Cambridge: Cambridge University Press.

Breines, Winni (1989). *Community and Organization in the New Left.* New Brunswick, N.J.: Rutgers University Press.

Breitbart, Joshua, Mike Burke, and NYC IMC (2003). "Eye on the Street: World Unites for Peace." *Clamor* (May/June 2003) 20: 34–36.

Brenner, Neil (2001). "The Limits to Scale: Methodological Reflections on Scalar Structuration." *Progress in Human Geography* 25.4 (December): 591–614.

——(2004). *New State Spaces: Urban Governance and the Rescaling of Statehood.* Oxford: Oxford University Press.

Brezinski, Zbigniew (1970). *Between Two Ages: America's Role in the Technetronic Era.* New York: Viking Press.

Brooten, Lisa (2004). "Digital Deconstruction: The Independent Media Center as a Process of Collective Critique." In *Global Media Goes to War: Role of News and Entertainment Media during the 2003 Iraq War*. Ed. Ralph D. Berenger. Spokane, Wash.: Marquette Books.

Buck-Morriss, Susan (1977). *The Origin of Negative Dialectics: Theodor W. Adorno, Walter Benjamin, and the Frankfurt Institute*. New York: Free Press.

Burbach, Roger (2001). *Globalization and Postmodern Politics*. London: Pluto Press.

———(1996). "For a Zapatista Style Postmodernist Perspective." *Monthly Review* 47 (March): 39.

Calhoun, Craig (1991). *Question of Class Struggle: The Social Foundation of Popular Radicalism during the Industrial Revolution*. Chicago: University of Chicago Press.

———(1993). "'New Social Movements' of the Early Nineteenth Century." *Social Science History* 17.3 (Autumn): 385–427.

Calvert, Greg, and Carol Nieman (1971). *A Disrupted History: The New Left and the New Capitalism*. New York: Random House.

Carr, C. (2000). "Get Me Download! Reporting the Real Philadelphia Story." *Village Voice*, August 1, 2000. Accessed April 19, 2014. http://www.villagevoice.com/2000-08-01/news/get-me-download/.

Castells, Manuel (1996a). *The Rise of the Network Society*. Oxford: Blackwell Publishers.

———(1996b). *Information Society: The Power of Identity*. Oxford: Blackwell Publishers.

———(2012). *Networks of Outrage and Hope: Social Movements in the Internet Age*. Malden, Mass.: Polity Press.

Castoriadis, Cornelius (1998). *The Imaginary Institution of Society*. Cambridge: Massachusetts Institute of Technology Press.

Cecena, Ana Esther, and Andres Barreda (1998). "Chiapas and the Global Restructuring of Capital." In *Zapatista! Reinventing Revolution in Mexico*. Ed. John Holloway and Eloína Peláez. London: Pluto Press. 39–63.

Chawkins, Steve (2008). "A New Setting for their Plots." *Los Angeles Times*, April 28. Accessed March 27, 2014. http://www.latimes.com/news/local/la-me-buttonwillow28apr28,1,4825943,full.story.

Childers, Peter, and Paul Delany (1994). "Wired World, Virtual Campus: Universities and the Political Economy of Cyberspace." *Works and Days* 12.2: 61–73.

Cleaver, Harry (1995). "The Chiapas Uprising and the Future of Class Struggle in the New World Order." Spunk.org. Accessed April 19, 2014. http://www.spunk.org/texts/places/mexico/sp000651.txt.

———(1998a). "The Zapatista Effect: The Internet and the Rise of an Alternative Fabric of Struggle." *Journal of International Affairs* 51.2 (Spring): 621–40.

———(1998b). "The Zapatista and the Electronic Fabric of Struggle." In *Zapatista! Reinventing Revolution in Mexico*. Ed. John Holloway and Eloína Peláez. London: Pluto Press. 81–103.

Clecak, Peter (1973). *Radical Paradoxes: Dilemmas of the American Left, 1945–1970*. New York: Harper and Row.

Cliff, Tony (1976). *Lenin: All Power to the Soviets*. London: Pluto Press.

Cohn-Bendit, Daniel, and Gabriel Cohn-Bendit (2001). *Obsolete Communism: The Left-Wing Alternative*. Oakland: AK Press.

Coleman, Biella (2005). "Indymedia's Independence: From Activist Media to Free Software." *Multitudes* 21 (May): 41–48.

Collier, George (1999). *Basta! Land and the Zapatista Rebellion in Chiapas*. Oakland: Food First Books.

Danaher, Kevin, and Jason Mark (2003). *Insurrection: Citizen Challenges to Corporate Power*. New York: Routledge.

Day, Richard J. F (2005). *Gramsci Is Dead: Anarchist Currents in the Newest Social Movements*. London: Pluto Press.

Dean, Jodi (2010). *Blog Theory: Feedback and Capture in the Circuits of Drive*. London: Polity Press.

De Certeau, Michel. *The Practice of Everyday Life*. Berkeley: University of California Press.

De Landa, Manuel (2006). *A New Philosophy of Society: Assemblage Theory and Social Complexity*. New York: Continuum Books.

———(2009). *Democracy and Other Neoliberal Fantasies: Communicative Capitalism and Left Politics*. Durham, N.C.: Duke University Press.

Della Porta, Donatella, and Hanspeter Kriese, eds. (1999). *Social Movements in a Globalizing World*. New York: Palgrave.

Della Porta, Donatella, and Sydney Tarrow, eds. (2005). *Transnational Protest and Political Activism*. Lanham, Md.: Rowan and Littlefield.

Dennings, Michael (1998). *The Cultural Front: The Laboring of American Culture in the Twentieth Century*. New York: Verso.

De Sousas Santos, Boaventura (2006). *The Rise of the Global Left: The World Social Forum and Beyond*. London: Zed Books.

Deutscher, Issac (1963). *The Prophet Armed: Trotsky, 1879–1921*. London: Verso.

Dewey, John (1988). "Creative Democracy: The Task Before Us." In *The Later Works of John Dewey*. Vol. 14. Carbondale: Southern Illinois University Press. 224–30.

Diani, Mario, and Doug McAdam (2003). *Social Movements and Networks: Relational Approaches to Collective Action*. Oxford: Oxford University Press.

Diggins, John Patrick (1973). *The American Left in the Twentieth Century*. New York: Harcourt Brace Jovanovich.

——— (1992). *The Rise and Fall of the American Left*. New York: W. W. Norton and Co.

Dowie, Mark. (1996). *Losing Ground: American Environmentalism at the Close of the Twentieth Century*. Cambridge, Massachusetts: MIT Press.

Downing, John (2003). "The Independent Media Center Movement and the Anarchist Socialist Tradition." In *Contesting Media Power: Alternative Media in a Networked World*. Ed. Nick Couldry and James Curran. Lanham, Md.: Rowan and Littlefield. 243–57.

——— (1999). *Radical Media: Rebellious Communications and Social Movements*. Thousand Oaks, Calif.: Sage Publications.

Draper, Theodore (1957). *The Roots of American Communism*. New York: Viking Press.

Dunbar-Hester, Christina (2012). "Soldering toward Media Democracy: Technical Practice as Symbolic Value in Radio Activism." *Journal of Communication Inquiry* 36 (April): 149–69.

——— (2014). *Low Power to the People: Pirates, Protest, and Politics in FM Radio Activism*. Cambridge: MIT Press.

Dyer-Witheford, Nick (1999). *Cyber-Marx: Cycles and Circuits of Struggle in High Technology Capitalism*. Urbana: University of Illinois Press.

Edelman, Marc (1999). *Peasants against Globalization: Rural Social Movements in Costa Rica*. Stanford, Calif.: Stanford University Press.

——— (2001). "Social Movements: Changing Paradigms and Forms of Politics." *Annual Review of Anthropology* 30: 285–317.

Elbaum, Max (2002). *Revolution in the Air: 6os Radicals Turn to Lenin, Mao and Che*. New York: Verso Press.

Elliot, Larry (2001). "Clock Turning Back for World's Poor." *The Guardian* online, n.d. Accessed May 6, 2014. http://www.theguardian.com/guardianweekly/story/0,12674,999337,00.html.

Epstein, Barbara (1991). *Political Protest and the Cultural Revolution: Nonviolent Direct Action in the 1970s and 1980s*. Berkeley: University of California Press.

Escobar, Arturo (2009). *Territories of Difference: Place, Movements, Life, Redes*. Durham, N.C.: Duke University Press.

Escobar, Arturo, Sonia Alvarez, and Evelina Dagnino (1998). *Culture of Politics, Politics of Culture: Revisioning Latin American Social Movements*. Boulder, Colo.: Westview Press.

Evan, William M. (1972). "An Organization-Set Model of Interorganizational Relations." In *Interorganizational Decision Making*. Ed. Matthew Tuite, Roger Chisolm, and Michael Radnor. Chicago: Aldine Publishing Co. 181–200.

Evans, Sara (1980). *Personal Politics: The Roots of Women's Liberation in the Civil Rights Movement*. New York: Vintage Books.

Fairbanks, Robert (2009). *"How It Works.": Post-Welfare Politics in the Kensington Recovery House Movement*. Chicago: University of Chicago Press.

Fanon, Frantz (1965). *Studies in a Dying Colonialism*. New York: Monthly Review Press.

Feenberg, Andrew (1991). *Critical Theory of Technology*. New York: Oxford University Press.

Fontes, Carlos (2010). "The Global Turn of the Alternative Media Movement." In *Understanding Community Media*. Ed. Kevin Howley. Thousand Oaks, Calif.: Sage Publications. 381–90.

Freeman, Jo (1972–73). "Tyranny of Structurelessness." *Berkeley Journal of Sociology* 17: 151–65.

Fuentes, Carlos (1994). "Chiapas: Latin America's First Post-Communist Rebellion." *New Perspectives Quarterly* 11.2 (Spring): 54–58.

——— (1992). *Return to Mexico: Journeys beyond the Mask*. London: Norton Company.

Funke, Peter (2008). "The World Social Forum: Social Forums as Resistance Relays." *New Political Science: A Journal of Politics and Culture* 30.4 (December): 449–74.

——(2010). "Late Capitalism and the World Social Forum: Social Movement Based Resistance in the Twenty-first Century." Ph.D. dissertation, University of Pennsylvania.

——(2012). "The Rhizomatic Left, Neoliberal Capital and Class: Theoretical Interventions on Contemporary Global Social movements in the North." *International Critical Thought* 2.1 (March): 30–41.

Galloway, Alexander, and Eugene Thacker (2007). *The Exploit: A Theory of Networks.* Minneapolis: University of Minnesota Press.

Ganz, Marshall (2009). *Why David Sometimes Wins: Leadership, Organization and Strategy in the California Farm Worker Movement.* Oxford: Oxford University Press.

Garnham, Nicholas (1990). *Capitalism and Communication: Global Culture and the Economic of Information.* New York: SAGE Publications.

Geras, Norman (1988). "Ex-Marxism without Substance: Being a Real Reply to Laclau and Mouffe." *New Left Review* 169 (May–June): 34–61.

Gerbaudo, Paolo (2012). *Tweets and the Streets: Social Media and Contemporary Activism.* London: Pluto Press.

Gerlach, Luther P. (2001). "The Structure of Social Movements: Environmental Activism and Its Opponents." In *Networks and Netwar: The Future of Terror Crime and Militancy.* Ed. John Arquilla and David Ronfeldt. Santa Monica, Calif.: Rand Corporation. 289–310.

Giddens, Anthony (1991). *The Consequences of Modernity.* Cambridge: Polity Press.

——(1984). *The Constitution of Society: Outline of the Theory of Structuration.* Berkeley: University of California Press.

Gilmore, Glenda Elizabeth (2008). *Defying Dixie: The Radical Roots of Civil Rights, 1919–1950.* New York: W. W. Norton and Co.

Ginsburg, Faye (1993). "Aboriginal Media and the Australian Imaginary." *Public Culture* 5.3: 557–78.

Gitlin, Todd (2012). *Occupy Nation: The Roots, the Spirit, and the Promise of Occupy Wall Street.* New York: IT Books.

——(1993). *The Sixties: Years of Hope, Days of Rage.* New York: Bantam Books.

Gladwell, Malcolm (2010). "Small Change: Why the Revolution Will Not Be Tweeted." *New Yorker,* October 4. Accessed April 19, 2014. http://www.newyorker.com/reporting/2010/10/04/101004fa_fact_gladwell?currentPage=all.

Gledhill, John (1997). "Fantasy and Reality in Restructuring Mexico's Land Reform." Paper presented at the "Modern Mexico" session of the Society for Latin American Studies. St. Andrews, Scotland. April 6.

Goffman, Ervin (1974). *Frame Analysis: An Essay on the Organization of Experience.* Cambridge, Mass.: Harvard University Press.

Gottlieb, Robert (2005). *Forcing the Spring: The Transformation of the American Environmental Movement.* Washington, D.C.: Island Press.

Graeber, David (2009). *Direct Action: An Ethnography.* Oakland: AK Press.

———(2004). *Fragments of an Anarchist Anthropology.* Chicago: Prickly Press Paradigm.

Gray, Matthew (1995). "Measuring the Growth of the Web." Accessed April 19, 2014. http://www.mit.edu/people/mkgray/growth/.

Grossman, Lev (2006). "You—Yes, You—Are TIME's Person of the Year." *TIME,* December 25. Accessed March 27, 2014. http://content.time.com/time/magazine/article/0,9171,1570810,00.html.

Guattari, Felix (2000). *The Three Ecologies.* Trans. Ian Pindar and Paul Sutton. London: Athlone Press.

Habermas, Jürgen (1981). "New Social Movements." *Telos* 49: 33–37.

Hafner, Katie, and Mathew Lyon (1996). *Where Wizards Stay Up Late: The Origins of the Internet.* New York: Simon and Schuster.

Hale, Charles (1997). "Cultural Politics of Identity in Latin America." *Annual Review of Anthropology* 26: 567–90.

Hall, Kathleen (2002). *Lives in Translation: Sikh Youth as British Citizens.* Philadelphia: University of Pennsylvania Press.

Hall, Stuart (1974). "Encoding and Decoding in the Television Discourse." *Culture and Education* 25: 8–14.

———(1979). "The Great Moving Right Show." *Marxism Today* (January): 14–20.

Halleck, DeeDee (2002). *Hand Held Visions: The Impossible Possibilities of Community Media.* New York: Fordham University Press.

———(2003). "The Censoring of BURN!" In *The Politics of Information: The Electronic Mediation of Social Change.* Ed. Marc Bousquet and Katherine Wills. Stanford, Calif.: Alt X Press. 18–44.

Halleck, DeeDee, and Joel Kovel (2000). *Indymedia Center Handbook: Hands On!!! Creating an Independent Media Center in Your Community.* Accessed April 19, 2014. http://archief.debalie.nl/artikel.jsp;jsessionid=544DDF742DA1444241D62D69494E8F61?dossierid=7165&subdossierid=0&articleid=9034.

Hands, Joss (2011). *@ is for Activism: Dissent, Resistance, and Rebellion in the Digital Age.* London: Pluto Press.

Hannah, Daryl (2006). "Saving the South Central Farm." *Huffington Post,* June 3. Accessed March 27, 2014. http://www.huffingtonpost.com/daryl-hannah/saving-the-south-central-_b_22129.html.

Haraway, Donna (1991). *Simians, Cyborgs, and Women: The Reinvention of Nature.* New York: Routledge.

Harding, Neil (2009). *Lenin's Political Thought: Theory and Practice in the Democratic and Socialist Revolutions.* Chicago: Haymarket Press.

Hardt, Michael, and Antonio Negri (2000). *Empire.* Cambridge, Mass.: Harvard University Press.

———(2004). *Multitude: War and Democracy in the Age of Empire.* New York: Penguin Press.

Hartnett, Tim (2011). *Consensus-Oriented Decision-Making: The CDOM Model for Facilitating Groups to Widespread Agreement.* Gabriola Island, Can.: New Society Publishers.

Harvey, David (2005). *A Brief History of Neoliberalism*. New York: Oxford University Press.

——— (1991). *The Condition of Postmodernity: An Enquiry into the Origin of Cultural Change*. New York: Wiley Blackwell.

——— (1999). *The Limits to Capital*. London: Verso.

Hayden, Tom, ed. (2002). *The Zapatista Reader*. New York: Thunder's Mouth Press/National Books.

Herman, Edward S. (1999). *The Myth of the Liberal Media: An Edward Herman Reader*. New York: P. Lang.

Herman, Edward S., and Noam Chomsky (1988). *Manufacturing Consent: The Political Economy of Mass Media*. New York: Pantheon Books.

Holloway, John (2008). *Change the World without Taking Power*. London: Pluto.

Holloway, John, and Eloína Peláez (1998). "Introduction: Reinventing Revolution." In *Zapatista! Reinventing Revolution in Mexico*. Ed. John Holloway and Eloína Peláez. London: Pluto Press. 1–18.

Horkheimer, Max and Theodor Adorno (1972). *The Dialectic of Enlightenment*. New York: Seabury Press.

Howard, Dick (2002). *The Specter of Democracy*. New York: Columbia University Press.

Howe, Irving (1957). *The American Communist Party: A Critical History*. Boston: Beacon Press.

Huebner, Jeff (1996). "Active Cultures: Covering the Other Convention." *Chicago Reader*, August 22. Accessed March 22, 2014. http://m.chicagoreader.com/chicago/active-cultures-covering-the-other-convention/Content?oid=891323.

Huntington, Samuel P. (1991). *The Third Wave: Democratization in the Late Twentieth Century*. Norman: University of Oklahoma Press.

Independent Media Center (1999). *Strategic Funding Document*. Seattle: Independent Media Center.

Isserman, Maurice (1987). *If I Had a Hammer: The Death of the Old Left and the Birth of the New Left*. New York: Basic Book Publishers.

Jameson, Fredric (1991). *Postmodernism, or the Cultural Logic of Late Capitalism*. Durham, N.C.: Duke University Press.

Juris, Jeffrey (2008). *Networking Futures: The Movements against Corporate Globalization*. Durham, N.C.: Duke University Press.

——— (2005). "The New Digital Media and Activist Networking within Anti–Corporate Globalization Movements." *Annals of the American Academy of Political and Social Science* 597: 189–208.

——— (2008). "Spaces of Intentionality: Race, Class, and Horizontality at the United States Social Forum." *Mobilization: An International Journal* 13.4: 353–71.

Katzenberger, Elizabeth (1995). *First World Ha Ha Ha! The Zapatista Challenge*. San Francisco: City Lights Books.

Kearny, Michael (1996). *Reconceptualizing the Peasantry: Anthropology in Global Perspective.* Boulder, Colo.: Westview Press.

Keck, Margaret, and Kathryn Sikkink (1998). *Activists beyond Borders: Advocacy Networks in International Politics.* Ithaca, N.Y.: Cornell University Press.

Kelley, Robin D. G. (1990). *Hammer and Hoe: Alabama Communists during the Great Depression.* Chapel Hill: University of North Carolina Press.

Khasnabish, Alex (2008). *Zapatismo beyond Borders: New Imaginations of Political Possibility.* Toronto: University of Toronto Press.

Kidd, Dorothy (2003a). "Become the Media: The Global IMC Network." In *Representing Resistance: Media, Civil Disobedience, and the Global Justice Movement.* Ed. Andrew Opel and Donelyn Pompper. Westport, Conn.: Praeger Publishers. 224–40.

——(2003b). "Indymedia.org: A New Communications Commons." In *Cyberactivism: Online Activism in Theory and Practice.* Ed. Martha McCaughy and Michael D. Myers. New York: Routledge. 47–69.

——(2003c). "The Independent Media Center: A New Model." In *Indymedia.Global. Brochure.* Accessed April 19, 2014. https://docs.indymedia.org/pub/Global/PDFs OfIndymediaGuide/brochurepages.pdf.

——(2004). "Carnival to Commons." In *Confronting Capitalism: Dispatches from a Global Movement.* Ed. Eddie Yuen, Daniel Burton Rose, and George Katsiaficas. New York: Soft Skull Press. 328–38.

Kiesler, S. L., J. Siegel, and T. W. McGuire (1984). "Social Psychological Aspects of Computer Mediated Communication." *American Psychologist* 39.10: 1123–34.

King, Patricia, and Francisco Javier Villanueva (1998). "Breaking the Blockade: The Move from Jungle to City." In *Zapatista! Reinventing Revolution in Mexico.* Ed. John Holloway and Eloína Peláez. London: Pluto Press. 104–25.

Klinenberg, Eric (2007). *Fighting for Air: The Battle to Control America's Media.* New York: Henry Holt and Co.

Laclau, Ernesto, and Chantal Mouffe (1986). *Hegemony and Socialist Strategy: Towards a Radical Democratic Politics.* London: Verso.

Lawson, Jonathan (2009). "Indymedia Turns 10." Reclaim the Media. Accessed April 19, 2014. http://www.reclaimthemedia.org/grassroots_media/indymedia_turns_102348.

Lefort, Claude (1988). *Democracy and Political Theory.* Cambridge: Polity Press.

Lenin, Vladimir (1975). "Left-Wing Communism—An Infantile Disorder." In *The Lenin Anthology.* Ed. Robert Tucker. New York: Norton. 550–618.

——(2005). "*What is to be Done? Burning Questions of Our Movement.*" In *Lenin Rediscovered: What Is to Be Done? In Context.* Ed. Lars Lih. Chicago: Haymarket Books. 671–840.

Lexer, James (1998). *The Undeclared War: Class Conflict in the Age of Cyber Capitalism.* Toronto: Penguin Group.

Lih, Lars (2008). *Lenin Rediscovered: What Is to Be Done?* Chicago: Haymarket Books.

Lorenzano, Luis (1998). "Zapatismo." In *Zapatista! Reinventing Revolution in Mexico.* Ed. John Holloway and Eloína Peláez. London: Pluto Press. 126–58.

Mantovani, G. (1994). "Is Computer Mediated Communication Apt to Enhance Democracy in Organizations." *Human Relations* 47.1: 45–62.

Marcos, Subcomandante (2001). *Our Word Is Our Weapon: Selected Writings of Subcomandante Insurgente Marcos.* Ed. Juana Ponce de León. New York: Seven Stories Press.

—— (2003). *¡Ya Basta! Ten Years of the Zapatista Uprising: Writings of Subcomandante Insurgente Marcos.* Ed Ziga Vodovnik. Oakland: AK Press.

Marcus, George (1996). Introduction to *Connected: Engagements with the Media.* Ed. George Marcus. Chicago: University of Chicago Press. 1–18.

Marcuse, Herbert (1991). *One Dimensional Man: Studies of Ideology in Advanced Industrial Society.* Boston: Beacon Press.

Marcuse, Peter (2009). "From Critical Urban Theory to the Right to the City." *City* 13.2–3: 190.

Martinez-Torres, Maria Elena (2001). "Civil Society, the Internet and the Zapatistas." *Peace Studies* 13.3: 347–55.

Marx, Karl (1978). "Contribution to a Critique of Philosophy of Right." In *Marx-Engels Reader.* Ed. Robert Tucker. New York: Norton. 16–25.

—— (1978). "The Eighteenth Brumaire of Louis Bonaparte." In *Marx-Engels Reader.* Ed. Robert Tucker, New York: Norton. 594–617.

—— (1992). *The Poverty of Philosophy.* New York: International Publishers.

Mason, Paul (2012). *Why It's Kicking Off Everywhere: The New Global Revolutions.* London: Verso Press.

Mayer, Robert (1999). "Lenin and the Practice of Dialectical Thinking." *Science and Society* 63.1 (Spring): 40–62.

Mazzarella, William (2003). *Shoveling Smoke: Advertising and Globalization in Contemporary India.* Durham, N.C.: Duke University Press.

McAdam, Doug, Sidney Tarrow, and Charles Tilly (1997). "Toward an Integrated Perspective on Social Movements and Revolution." In *Comparative Politics: Rationality, Culture, and Structure.* Ed. Marc Irving Lichbach and A. S. Zuckerman. Cambridge: Cambridge University Press. 142–71.

McChesney, Robert W. (1999). *Rich Media, Poor Democracy.* Urbana: University of Illinois Press.

—— (2013). *Digital Disconnect: How Capitalism is Turning the Internet Against Democracy.* New York: New Press.

McMillan, Tracie (2008). "Urban Farmers' Crops Go from Vacant Lot to Market." *New York Times,* May 7. Accessed March 27, 2014. http://www.nytimes.com/2008/05/07/dining/07urban.html?em&ex=1210392000&en=3f45ca39a536f8a7&ei=5087%0A.

Meikle, Graham (2002). *Future Active: Media Activism and the Internet.* New York: Routledge.

Melucci, Alberto (1996). *Challenging Codes: Collective Action in the Information Age.* Cambridge: Cambridge University Press.

———(1989). *Nomads of the Present.* Philadelphia: Temple University Press.

Mertes, Tom, and Walden F. Bello (2004). *A Movement of Movements: Is Another World Really Possible?* New York: Verso.

Milioni, Dmitra (2009). "Probing the Online Counterpublic Sphere: The Case of Indymedia Athens." *Media, Culture, and Society* 31.3: 409–31.

Mills, C Wright (1960). "Letter to the New Left." *New Left Review* 5 (September–October): 18–23.

Montes, Rodolfo (1995). "Chiapas Is a War of Ink and Internet." *Reforma,* April 26, 1995. Accessed April 19, 2014. http://www.hartford-hwp.com/archives/46/037.html.

Moore, J. T. S., dir. (2001). *Revolution OS.* Wonderview Productions.

Morris, Doug (2003). "Globalization and Media Democracy: The Case of Indymedia." In *Shaping the Network Society.* Ed. Douglas Schulyer and Peter Day. Boston: Massachusetts Institute of Technology Press. 325–52.

Moulier, Yves (1989). Introduction to *The Politics of Subversion: A Manifesto for the Twenty-First Century,* by Antonio Negri. Cambridge: Polity Press. 1–46.

Negri, Antonio (1989). *The Politics of Subversion: A Manifesto of the Twenty-First Century.* Cambridge: Polity Press.

Nogueira, Anna (2001). "The Indymedia Revolution: The History of the Globalocal Network in Three Movements." *Punk Planet* 43: 70–74.

Nugent, David (1995). "Northern Intellectuals and the EZLN." *Monthly Review* 47.3 (July–August): 124–38.

Offe, Claus (1985). "New Social Movements: Challenging the Boundaries of Institutional Politics." *Social Research* 52: 817–68.

Ohlemacher, Thomas (1996). "Bridging People and Protest: Social Relays of Protest Groups against Low-Flying Military Jets in West Germany." *Social Problems* 43.2 (May): 197–218.

Olesen, Thomas (2004). "The Transnational Zapatista Solidarity Network: An Infrastructure Analysis." *Global Networks: A Journal of Transnational Affairs* 4.1 (January): 89–107.

Ong, Aihwa (1999). *Flexible Citizenship: The Cultural Logics of Transnationality.* Durham, N.C.: Duke University Press.

Opel, Andy, and Rich Templin (2005). "Is Anybody Reading This? Indymedia and Internet Traffic Reports." *Transformations* 10 (February). Accessed April 19, 2014. http://www.transformationsjournal.org/journal/issue_10/article_08.shtml.

Ortner, Sherry (1984). "Theory in Anthropology since the Sixties." *Comparative. Studies in Society and History* 26: 126–66.

Panitch, Leo, and Sam Gindin (2012). *The Making of Global Capitalism: The Political Economy of American Empire.* New York: Verso Books.

Perine, Keith (2000). "IMC's Arresting Coverage: The Independent Media Center Is Using the Web to Cover the Many Protests and Arrests Taking Place outside the Republican Convention." *Industry Standard,* August 2. 335–338.

Perlstein, Jeff. (2001). "An Experiment in Media Democracy." In *The Battle of Seattle: The New Challenge to Capitalist Globalization.* Ed. Eddie Yuen, George Katsiaficas, and Daniel Burton Rose. New York: Soft Skull Press.

Petras, James (2001). "The Ford Foundation and the CIA: A Documented Case of Philanthropic Collaboration with the Secret Police." *Rebelión.* December 15. Accessed April 19, 2014. http://www.ratical.org/ratville/CAH/FordFandCIA.html.

Phillips, Susan (2000). "Puppet Makers Seized in Raid on Warehouse." *The Unconvention,* August 1.

Pickard, Victor (2006a). "Assessing the Radical Democracy of Indymedia: Discursive, Technical, and Institutional Constructions." *Critical Studies in Media Communication* 23.1: 19–38.

——— (2006b). "United yet Autonomous: Indymedia and the Struggle to Sustain a Radical Democratic Network." *Media, Culture, and Society* 28.3: 315–36.

——— (2014). *America's Battle for Media Democracy: The Triumph of Corporate Libertarianism and the Future of Media Reform.* New York: Cambridge University Press.

Poletta, Francesca (2001). *Freedom Is an Endless Meeting House.* Chicago: University of Chicago Press.

Proudhon, Pierre-Joseph (2011). *System of Economical Contradictions; or, The Philosophy of Poverty.* Calgary: Theophania Publishing.

Radford, Leslie, and Juan Santos (2006). "Seeds of Hope, Seeds of War." *CounterPunch,* July 13. Accessed March 27, 2014. http://www.counterpunch.org/radford07132006.html.

Radway, Janis (1991). *Reading the Romance: Women, Patriarchy, and Popular Literature.* Chapel Hill: University of North Carolina Press.

Raja, Samina, Changxing Ma, and Pavan Yadav (2008). "Beyond Food Deserts: Measuring and Mapping Racial Disparities in Neighborhood Food Environments." *Journal of Planning Education and Research* 27.4: 469–82.

Rajagopal, Arvind (2001). *Politics after Television: Hindu Nationalism and the Reshaping of the Public in India.* Cambridge: Cambridge University Press.

Rheingold, Howard (1993). *The Virtual Community: Homesteading on the Electronic Frontier.* Reading, Mass.: Addison-Wesley.

Riles, Annalise (2001). *The Network Inside Out.* Ann Arbor: University of Michigan Press.

Robinson, William, I (2004). *A Theory of Global Capitalism: Production, Class, and State in a Transnational World.* Baltimore: Johns Hopkins University Press.

Ronfeldt, David, and John Arquilla (1996). *Networks and Netwar: The Future of Terror, Crime, and Militancy.* Santa Monica, Calif.: Rand Corporation.

Rose, Nikolas S. (1996). *Foucault and Political Reason: Liberalism, Neo-Liberalism, and the Rationalities of Government.* Chicago: University of Chicago Press.

——— (1990). *Governing the Soul: The Shaping of the Private Self.* London: Routledge.

Roseberry, William, Lowell Gudmundson, and Mario Samper Kutschbach, eds. (1995). *Coffee, Society, and Power in Latin America.* Baltimore: Johns Hopkins University Press.

Ross, John (1995). *Rebellion from the Roots: Indian Uprising in Chiapas.* Monroe, Maine: Common Courage Press.

Rouse, Roger (1991). "Mexican Migration and the Social Space of Postmodernity." *Diaspora* 1.1 (Spring): 8–23.

Ruby, Jay (1991). "Speaking for, Speaking about, Speaking with, or Speaking alongside: An Anthropological and Documentary Dilemma." *Visual Anthropology Review* 7.2: 50–67.

Sahlins, Marshall (1981). *Historical Metaphors and Mythical Realities: Structure in the Early History of the Sandwich Islands Kingdom.* Ann Arbor: University of Michigan Press.

Sale, Kirpatrick (1995). *Rebels against the Future: The Luddites and Their War on the Industrial Revolution.* Reading, Mass.: Addison-Wesley Publishing Co.

Sargent, Lydia (2003). "Press the Press." *Z Magazine,* March. Accessed April 19, 2014. http://www.thirdworldtraveler.com/Media_Reform/Press_the_Press.html.

Sassen, Saskia (2001). *The Global City: New York, London, Tokyo.* Princeton, N.J.: Princeton University Press.

——— (1996). *Losing Control? Sovereignty in the Age of Globalization.* New York: Columbia University Press.

Sassen, Saskia, and Robert Latham (2005). *Digital Formations: IT and the New Architectures of the Global Realm.* Princeton, N.J.: Princeton University Press.

Schell, Jonathan (2003). "The Other Superpower." *The Nation,* April 14. Accessed April 19, 2014. http://www.thenation.com/article/other-superpower.

Schiller, Herbert (1976). *Communication and Cultural Domination.* White Plains, NY: International Arts and Sciences Press

Shirky, Clay (2008). *Here Comes Everybody: The Power of Organizing without Organizations.* New York: Penguin Books.

Short, Anne, Julie Guthman, and Samuel Raskin (2007). "Food Deserts, Oases, or Mirages?" *Journal of Planning Education and Research* 26.3: 352–64.

Shumway, Christopher A. (2003). "Democratizing Communication through Community-Based Participatory Media Networks: A Study of the Independent Media Center Movement." M.A. thesis, New School University. Accessed April 19, 2014. http://chris.shumway.tripod.com/papers/thesis.htm.

Sikkink, Kathryn (1993). "Human Rights, Principled Issue Networks, and Sovereignty in Latin America." *International Organization* 47.3: 411–41.

Spitulnik, Debra (1993). "Anthropology of Mass Media." *Annual Review of Anthropology* 22: 293–315.

Starn, Orin (2001). *Nightwatch: The Politics of Protest in the Andes.* Durham, N.C.: Duke University Press.

Stengrim, Laura (2005). "Negotiating Postmodern Democracy, Political Activism, and Knowledge Production: Indymedia's Grassroots and e-Savvy Answer to Media Oligopoly." *Communication and Critical/Cultural Studies* 2.4: 281–304.

Stoper, Emily (1983). "The Student Non-Violent Coordinating Committee: Rise and Fall of a Redemptive Organization." In *Social Movements of the Sixties and Seventies*. Ed. Jo Freeman. London: Longman Group.

"Subcommander Marcos Is More than Just Gay" (1994). *Monthly Review* 46.4 (September): 1.

Surowiecki, James (2005). *Wisdom of the Crowds*. New York: First Anchor Books.

Swyngedouw, Erik (1997). "Neither Global nor Local: 'Glocalization' and the Politics of Scale." In *Spaces of Globalization: Reasserting the Power of the Local*. Ed. Kevin R. Cox. New York: Guilford Press. 137–66.

Taber, Robert (2002). *War of the Flea: The Classic Study of Guerrilla Warfare*. Janesville, Wis.: Brasseys.

Tarrow, Sidney (2006). *The New Transnational Activism*. Cambridge: Cambridge University Press.

———(1998). *Power in Movement: Social Movements and Contentious Politics*. Cambridge: Cambridge University Press.

Teeple, Gary (2000). *Globalization and the Decline of Social Reform: Intro to the Twenty-First Century*. Amherst, N.Y.: Humanity Books.

Templin, Richard (2009). "Rage against the Machine: How Indymedia's Radical Project is Working to Create the New Public Sphere." Ph.D. dissertation, Florida State University.

Tilly, Charles (1986). *The Contentious French: Four Centuries of Popular Struggle*. Cambridge, Mass.: Harvard University Press.

———(2004). *Social Movements, 1776–2004*. Boulder, Colo.: Paradigm.

Tilly, Charles, and Lesley Wood (2009). *Social Movements, 1768–2008*. Boulder, Colo.: Paradigm.

Toffler, Alvin (1970). *Future Shock*. New York: Random House.

———(1980). *The Third Wave*. New York: Morrow.

Touraine, Alain (1971). *The Post-Industrial Society: Tomorrow's Social History: Classes, Conflicts, and Culture in the Programmed Society*. New York: Random House.

———(1981). *The Voice and the Eye: An Analysis of Social Movements*. Cambridge: Cambridge University Press.

Turner, Terrence (1992). "Defiant Images: The Kayapo Appropriation of Video." *Anthropology Today* 8.6: 5–16.

Tyler, Patrick E. (2003). "Threats and Responses: News Analysis; A New Power in the Streets." *New York Times*, February 17, section A.

Uzelman, Scott (2001). "Catalyzing Participatory Communication: Independent Media Centre and the Politics of Direct Action." M.A. thesis, Simon Fraser University.

Verhulst, Joris (2010). "The World Says No to War, Demonstrations Against the War on Iraq." In *The World Says No to War: Demonstrations Against the War on Iraq*.

Ed. Stefaan Walgrave and Dieter Rucht. Minneapolis: University of Minnesota Press. 1–20.

Vickers, George (1975). *The Formation of the New Left: The Early Years*. Lexington, Massachusetts: Lexington Books.

Virilio, Paul (1995). "Speed and Information: Cyberspace Alarm!" *CTheory*, August 27. Accessed April 19, 2014. http://www.ctheory.net/articles.aspx?id=72.

——— (2006). *Speed and Politics*. Trans. Mark Polizzotti. Los Angeles: Semiotext(e).

Vogel, Tom, Matt Moffett, and Jed Sandberg (1997). "Radical Groups Spread the Word Online—Tupac Amru's Web Page Is a Hot Spot." *Wall Street Journal*, January 6, 8A.

Walgrave, Stefaan, and Joris Verhulst (2006). "The February 15 Worldwide Protests Against the War in Iraq: An Empirical Test of Transnational Opportunities. Outline of a Research Program." Media Movements Politics. Accessed April 29, 2014, http://webho1.ua.ac.be/m2p/publications/1220283443.pdf.

Warren, Kay (1998). *Indigenous Movements and Their Critics: Pan-Mayan Activism in Guatemala*. Princeton, N.J.: Princeton University Press.

Weber, Max (1992). *The Protestant Ethic and the Spirit of Capitalism*. London: Routledge.

Williams, Raymond (1974). *Television, Technology, and Cultural Form*. London: Routledge.

Wolfson, Todd (2013). "Democracy or Autonomy: Indymedia and the Contradictions of Global Social Movement Networks." *Global Networks* 13.3: 410–24.

——— (2012). "From the Zapatistas to Indymedia: Dialectics and Orthodoxy in Contemporary Social Movements." *Communication Culture and Critique* 5: 149–70.

Wolfson, Todd, and Peter Funke (2014). "Communication, Class, and Concentric Media Practices: Developing a Contemporary Rubric." *New Media and Society* 16.3 (May): 363–80.

Wood, Ellen Meiksins (1986). *The Retreat From Class: A New True Socialism*. New York: Verso.

Wrigley, Neil, Daniel Warm, Barrie Margetts, and Amanda Whelan (2002). "Assessing the Impact of Improved Retail Access on Diet in a 'Food Desert': A Preliminary Report." *Urban Studies* 39.11: 2061–82.

Yuen, Eddie (2001). "Introduction." *The Battle of Seattle: The New Challenge to Capitalist Globalization*. Eds. Eddie Yuen, George Katsiaficas, and Daniel Burton. New York, Soft Skull Press. 3–22.

Yuen, Eddie, George Katsiaficas, and Daniel Burton Rose, eds. (2001). *The Battle of Seattle: The New Challenge to Capitalist Globalization*. New York: Soft Skull Press.

Zapatistas (1998). "Second Declaration of La Realidad: Closing Words of the EZLN at the Intercontinental Encuentro for Humanity and against Neoliberalism." In *Zapatista Encuentro: Documents from the First Intercontinental Encuentro for Humanity and Against Neoliberalism*. Ed. Greg Ruggiero. New York: Seven Stories Press. 31–58.

Zugman, Kara (2008). "The 'Other Campaign': The EZLN and New Forms of Politics in Mexico and the United States." *New Political Science* 30.3: 347–67.

Index

A trained socio-cultural anthropologist, **TODD WOLFSON** is currently an assistant professor of journalism and media studies at Rutgers University. He is also a community organizer and in 2006 cofounded the Media Mobilizing Project in Philadelphia.

THE HISTORY OF COMMUNICATION

Selling Free Enterprise: The Business Assault on Labor
and Liberalism, 1945–60   *Elizabeth A. Fones-Wolf*
Last Rights: Revisiting *Four Theories of the Press*   *Edited by John C. Nerone*
"We Called Each Other Comrade": Charles H. Kerr & Company,
Radical Publishers   *Allen Ruff*
WCFL, Chicago's Voice of Labor, 1926–78   *Nathan Godfried*
Taking the Risk Out of Democracy: Corporate Propaganda
versus Freedom and Liberty   *Alex Carey; edited by Andrew Lohrey*
Media, Market, and Democracy in China: Between the Party Line
and the Bottom Line   *Yuezhi Zhao*
Print Culture in a Diverse America   *Edited by James P. Danky and Wayne A. Wiegand*
The Newspaper Indian: Native American Identity
in the Press, 1820–90   *John M. Coward*
E. W. Scripps and the Business of Newspapers   *Gerald J. Baldasty*
Picturing the Past: Media, History, and Photography
Edited by Bonnie Brennen and Hanno Hardt
Rich Media, Poor Democracy: Communication Politics in Dubious Times
Robert W. McChesney
Silencing the Opposition: Antinuclear Movements and the Media
in the Cold War   *Andrew Rojecki*
Citizen Critics: Literary Public Spheres   *Rosa A. Eberly*
Communities of Journalism: A History of American Newspapers
and Their Readers   *David Paul Nord*
From Yahweh to Yahoo!: The Religious Roots of the Secular Press   *Doug Underwood*
The Struggle for Control of Global Communication: The Formative Century   *Jill Hills*
Fanatics and Fire-eaters: Newspapers and the Coming of the Civil War
Lorman A. Ratner and Dwight L. Teeter Jr.
Media Power in Central America   *Rick Rockwell and Noreene Janus*
The Consumer Trap: Big Business Marketing in American Life   *Michael Dawson*
How Free Can the Press Be?   *Randall P. Bezanson*
Cultural Politics and the Mass Media: Alaska Native Voices
Patrick J. Daley and Beverly A. James
Journalism in the Movies   *Matthew C. Ehrlich*
Democracy, Inc.: The Press and Law in the Corporate Rationalization
of the Public Sphere   *David S. Allen*
Investigated Reporting: Muckrakers, Regulators, and the Struggle
over Television Documentary   *Chad Raphael*
Women Making News: Gender and the Women's Periodical Press
in Britain   *Michelle Tusan*
Advertising on Trial: Consumer Activism and Corporate Public Relations
in the 1930s   *Inger L. Stole*

The University of Illinois Press
is a founding member of the
Association of American University Presses.

University of Illinois Press
1325 South Oak Street
Champaign, IL 61820-6903
www.press.uillinois.edu